CORPORATIONS
COMPASSION
CULTURE

CORPORATIONS COMPASSION CULTURE

Leading Your Business toward Diversity, Equity, and Inclusion

KEESA C. SCHREANE

WILEY

Published by John Wiley & Sons, Inc., Hoboken, New Jersey.
Published simultaneously in Canada.

For general information on our other products and services or for technical support, please contact our Customer Care Department within the United States at (800) 762-2974, outside the United States at (317) 572-3993, or fax (317) 572-4002.

Wiley publishes in a variety of print and electronic formats and by print-on-demand. Some material included with standard print versions of this book may not be included in e-books or in print-on-demand. If this book refers to media such as a CD or DVD that is not included in the version you purchased, you may download this material at http://booksupport.wiley.com. For more information about Wiley products, visit www.wiley.com.

Library of Congress Cataloging-in-Publication Data is Available:
ISBN 9781119780588 (hardback)
ISBN 9781119780601 (ePDF)
ISBN 9781119780595 (epub)

Cover Design: Wiley
Cover Image: ©gmast3r/Getty Images

SKY10024425_012521

To Mom: thank you for being an extraordinary woman, exemplifying curiosity, compassion, and kindness coexisting beautifully with self-respect, self-love, and power. I love you beyond words.

Contents

Preface ix

Acknowledgments xvii

About the Author xix

1 Inclusion, Equality, and Compassion in Business: An Overview 1

2 Uncomfortable, but Necessary: Connecting Racial History to Racial Injustice in Corporate Structures 31

3 Women's Corporate Leadership: Past Perceptions and Current Realities 61

4 Evolution of Companies Post-COVID-19 87

5 Inclusion and the Bottom Line: A Broken Structure 127

6 Gender Equity and Company Growth 165

7 Elements of a Compassionate Corporate Culture 203

8 Your Plan for Creating Inclusion through Compassion: What Works 235

9 Your Plan for Creating Gender Equity through Compassion: What Works 265

10 The Future: Compassionate Corporate Culture and Sustainable Business 299

Index 327

Preface

I'm a Black girl from Tennessee who secured the title of vice president before age 30. How'd I do it? I worked hard. I got my NYU master's degree and earned Series 7 and Series 63 banking certifications.

But make no mistake: even with all my accomplishments, I learned that for people like me, a VP title is still considered a privilege, not a right.

Here's my story.

The postrecession job market in 2008 was challenging for marketing professionals. But after acing three interview rounds, I landed a role at a global banking firm.

After several months, the firm asked me to serve on their Diversity and Inclusion (D&I) Roundtable. This was a responsibility on top of my day job, but it was worth it. It was an exclusive opportunity afforded to top talent leaders to influence the firm's D&I direction. We would be able to open doors for quality, prospective job candidates, as well as provide inclusion opportunities for existing professionals who had the desire and passion to become managing directors and C-suite members.

The prospect of this new role perked me up, especially considering the fact that I was seeing a lot of management turnover at my firm. In the short time I was with the company, I had four different immediate managers and two different managing directors. Still, I was being recognized. That made me feel valued as a person and secure in my prospects.

When I was about one year in, the person who hired me left. She had been a mentor and her departure left me with no one who knew my work well enough to advocate for me. A colleague ominously advised me that things would likely get tougher for our team.

What I didn't know at the time was that by "our team" she really meant "me."

I asked for a meeting with the managing director to get a better feel for her and her expectations. This woman recounted how much my previous managing director liked me. "The cat's meow" was how she described her perception of me. At the same time, she made equivocal comments, like how she was disappointed not to have been present in my initial interviews. What did it matter? I was here, wasn't I?

It all felt a little off, but I figured I'd be fine. My internal clients and my D&I Roundtable colleagues spoke well of me, and my work spoke for itself.

Then, a few weeks later, I had lunch with a colleague. She said she expected to be gone soon. We weren't particularly close, but she was the only other Black woman in our division. I think this is why she confided in me.

"I'm having a hard time getting required sign-offs, budget, and even information I need to do my job," she said. "I've been telling my old manager about this, just to gut check it with him. He agrees it sounds like something's going on, but he said his hands are tied."

I sympathized with her. I let her know I was having my own challenges with the new management. Honestly, though, I brushed off her reported experiences. A lot of turmoil always follows big management turnover. Maybe I was just in denial. Because every shred of my instinct screamed my own career was in trouble.

Things ground along for several more months in an uncomfortable status quo.

I was over two years into the job, when the managing director told me I'd be moving to a different manager and covering a different product. I had neither the background nor the education to market this product. However, she described the move as a better fit for me. I was advised there would be no training on the product, and I was discouraged from reaching out to the businesspeople who managed the product so I could learn from them.

Googling, asking ad hoc questions, browsing websites, and studying brochures was all I had to get up to speed.

I also had new teammates. With them, a palpable frostiness chilled the air. I sensed no enthusiasm for me or my work. But, ever determined to make a good impression, I decided to come in earlier, stay late, and speak up more, coming up with as many solutions as possible in meetings.

If I expected a thaw in the atmosphere, my efforts produced the opposite.

I always participated in non-work-related chats, happy hours, and office banter. But now, one colleague started making a big deal out of the fact that I didn't drink alcohol. Then ribbing got more persistent—at times continuing from happy hour until dinner and beyond. I heard declarations about my presumed lack of social life and lack of friends because I didn't drink.

I endured it, assuming it was only good-natured—if a bit misdirected—fun.

Then the incidents started to pile up.

Once, between meetings, four women from the team were discussing their struggles with weight loss right outside my office. When I got up and walked past them, they pointed out that, since I was thin, I shouldn't have a body complex. Except, of course, for my big butt.

More ribbing. A little indelicate. But nothing to get upset about.

It soon became clear my colleagues were making a proactive effort to avoid me. No one initiated a conversation with me unless it was absolutely necessary for a work-related purpose. To be included at all, I had to insert myself into other people's conversational circles or attempt to kick off a discussion on my own. Which was as arduous as kindling a fire with a flint and some dry leaves.

Then, I went to a holiday house party thrown by one of my team members. Here, the exclusion I'd been sensing, kicked into the highest gear yet. As usual, I walked over to a group, trying to find an opening. When I joined the circle, my colleagues stopped talking—dead cold. They regarded me for a bit and melted away.

By this time, no one was talking with me or engaging with me at work. No one addressed me in meetings or bantered with me outside of meetings. If I asked why I was being ignored, I got a pat answer. "I can't really understand your comments during meetings." Other times a colleague would act as if I needed an interpreter, turning to another with, "What I believe she is trying to say is . . ."

If you've ever had this kind of experience, you know it can be an elusive one to describe and pin down. Because how do you depict a lack? A something-that-is-not-there? The encouragement that's ABSENT. The nods of interest that DON'T EXIST. The inquiries about your comments and thoughts that NEVER HAPPEN. It's not until these things build up into unmistakable avoidance and silence that you understand SOMETHING is going on.

Like this incident:

A colleague and I bumped into each other when turning a sharp corner near the ladies' room.

"Excuse me," I said.

She gave me a good, slow look up and down. Then she walked off without a word.

This woman was a terrific conversationalist, always ready with a quip or a punch line. She was not the sort to be caught short by a stumble near the bathroom.

My colleagues seemed to be following some secret rule book with regard to me. And they were following it to the letter.

I decided I needed to do something. I would meet with my immediate manager. I had no job description, no training, and was excluded from the team. But, dwelling on that wasn't going to get me anywhere. I reasoned there must be a way I could support the success of the team and engage professionally (at least until I found another job). Maybe my manager could help.

I approached her with a simple question: What could I do to better serve the team?

"To be honest, Keesa, I really feel your brain synapses don't connect with each other."

Wow. I sucked in breath to steady myself. Lack of synapses? It was astonishing. I was ready for her denials. For the I-don't-know-what-you're-talking-about comeback. Even for severe criticism of my work. But this woman was saying the problem was with my actual *brain*.

Of course, I pressed for her to explain what this meant. She went on to clarify that, in her opinion, I didn't understand certain concepts intellectually. This rendered me incapable of producing outstanding, or even adequate, work products. My brain and my neural connections were simply not up to the task.

To my best knowledge, this woman, who held an entire conversation with me focusing on brains and synapses, held neither a neurosurgeon's nor a neuroscientist's degree. What she did hold was my future at that firm—in the palm of her hand. I left her office.

A short time later, it arrived: failure.

I was called into HR. The managing director was there as was the manager with the opinions on my gray matter. They told me my services were no longer needed, effective immediately. They wished me the best, then the managers embraced each other—as if they were the ones who'd gone through an ordeal—and left the room. I departed the building with my possessions.

Nothing had protected me. Not my NYU degree. Not my Series 7 and Series 63 certifications. Not my previous accomplishments at that very firm.

I thought about warnings that elders and friends gave for years that I just hadn't wanted to believe.

- "This is just how corporate America is when it comes to people of color."

- "They've been treating Black people like this for years."

- "Folks in charge could care less about people who work for them, especially when they're Black. They only care about making money and looking out for their own."

Maybe it was all true.

But maybe, I could do something different with the situation. Something different than accepting how things were and just give up.

I took a little while, but I was able to find a way.

I realized I could choose to have compassion for a manager who insulted my mind instead of inspiring my work. So I chose compassion for her. I came to understand that I could choose to forgive my misguided colleagues who had bullied me instead of supporting me. So I forgave them. It dawned on me that I could find a different path, one that would change such realities in the workplace. I could dedicate my future work to improving others' corporate experiences and demonstrate kindness and equality in leadership. So I chose all of that, too.

I made these choices because if I and people like me don't speak about the need for greater compassion and equality in business, those words may never get spoken. If we don't do something about it, those deeds will never get done.

This is why I've written this book.

Sure, there are cruel, cocky leaders who build and operate the world's largest institutions. But kind, committed, and compassionate leaders are also at the helm. Those voices need to be amplified. What those leaders are doing and how they are doing it needs to be documented and understood.

Why? Leaders who choose kindness, commitment, and compassion as their leadership style see improved corporate performance and greater financial return as the result.

Yes, you read that right. Increasing compassion and empathy in C-suites is not just good for workers—it is good for the bottom line.

How can we learn from and be the leaders who choose kindness, commitment, and compassion as their leadership style and who see greater corporate performance and return—as well as greater humanity in the workplace—as the result?

This book answers that question.

Because many of us have experienced a work environment like the one I have described:

- Being shut down or talked over on a conference call, repeatedly.

- Seeing internal job offers that went from a sure thing to being rescinded under dubious circumstances or after the interviewer sees your complexion

- Learning about the "meeting before the meeting," where a decision was made before you entered the room, rendering the meeting to a mere formality.

It's disappointing—even outrageous—these situations still happen especially knowing the generation after us will have their own similar stories. I hope that people like me sharing our stories, will, at a minimum, let them know they're not alone.

During COVID-19, cruelty to workers reached a new extreme. Employers previously overlooked mental and emotional workplace hazards, especially "micro"-level activities that are hard to legislate and impossible to prove. Now, employers have shifted to actions that are more brazen: inflexible paid sick leave policies for workers who engage the public (largely marginalized populations), deficient work-from-home procedures, and insufficient platforms embracing employee innovation that could bring companies out of difficult business environments.

Confronted with these realities, employees are refusing to give up basic dignities and professionalism in exchange for a paycheck. Employers' ethical breaches and responses to employee well-being risks point to the need to commit to one overarching goal: employers should build cultures that nurture employees' purpose and talents and inspire them to create solutions that enrich employees, serve customers, and increase revenue. This can only be done in environments where every employee feels just as important as the shareholder. Each of us at every level of leadership—managers, directors, associates, and assistants—arrive at work with a choice: choose actions and words that affirm productivity, inclusivity, creativity, and profitability.

And if you and your company don't know how to achieve inclusion, equality, productivity, compassion, and increased revenue in the workplace, you can learn.

Let's get started!

Acknowledgments

Gratitude. This best describes what I'd like to give to the generous people who supported me in creating this book.

To my outstanding Wiley family: executive editor Sheck Cho, your kindness and enthusiasm is just what I needed for my first book. You are so gracious. Managing editor Susan Cerra, our Friday afternoon jam sessions kept me on the right path. Jean-Karl Martin, your organization and ideal sharing helped me go to market in a way that was more efficient than I could have envisioned.

I'm thankful to be part of a community of authors and publishing professionals who embraced and encouraged my ideas. Anna Murray, thank you for seeing the vision. Your faith in my ability and my ideas were instrumental in each stage of this book. I'll do my best to pay it forward.

Seth Godin and Shawn Askinosie thanks for our Zooms, chats, emails, and sharing brilliant resources.

Sheila Levine, thanks for your dedication to this project and answering *all* my many questions.

Stacy Grossman, thanks for jumping in so quickly. Kelly Spors, your business insights were thoughtful and engaging. Tiffany Dufu, I appreciate your inspirational kindness.

Hilary Poole, you are fun, smart, and working with you is such a joy.

Conny S. Kazungu, PhD, your energy, and consistent readiness for the next adventure I rolled out, was invaluable.

Edna Varner, EdD, I am grateful for you being my first writing coach in eighth grade—and still the best decades later!

Erika Winston, JD, MPP, your brilliant clear-headedness is priceless and exactly what I needed.

Thanks to all my interviewees: Shawn Askinosie, Doug Bristol, Marcia Chatelain, Mark Cuban, Laura Freebairn-Smith, Shennette Garrett-Scott, Seth Godin, Rebecca Henderson, Trevon Logan, Juliette Menga, Anna Murray, Daniel Pink, Caitlin Rosenthal, Susanne Smith, and Debra Walton. Also thank you to my anonymous interviewees. I'm inspired by your generosity and business acumen. Thanks for sharing your vision that there is a better way of doing business.

A special round of thanks to my Refinitiv and Thomson Reuters management team, mentors, and sponsors—Karen Ashley, Brennan Carley, Tamara Dews, Emma Miller, Deirdre Stanley, and Debra Walton—and all my wonderful colleagues who supported this endeavor.

To my phenomenal family: I'm grateful that you're supportive while demanding I act with the highest intentions—Mom, Dad, Uncle Al, Aunt Bobbie, Uncle Phearthur, Aunt Ingrid, Aunt Henrietta, Aunt Anderine, Uncle Greg, Uncle Paul, Gram, Nanny, Bimp, Dominique Banks, Daryl Alexander, Reverend Grant Harris, my "parent friends" Wanda Starke and Ron Fisher, and Tiffany K. Schreane, my sister and best friend whose brilliance, candor, humor, and love helped me bring this book to life.

To the Spirit in which I live, move, and have my being.

About the Author

Keesa C. Schreane is an environmental, social, governance, and supply chain risk business leader and host of Refinitiv Sustainability Perspectives Podcast, engaging investors and business and sustainability communities on environmental, social, and governance (ESG) data and technology, regulations, corporate risk, global financial markets, as well as diversity, equity, and inclusion (DEI).

She's also a broadcast television and livestream contributor and writer with numerous outlets and publications:

- *Black Enterprise*
- *Essence*
- Facebook Live
- *Latina*
- NASDAQ
- Refinitiv Perspectives LIVE
- WDEF TV

Her expertise includes business development, sales and marketing, and employee resource group leadership, building successful strategies for operational enhancement and relationship management. She is a Certified Anti-Money Laundering Specialist (CAMS).

As founder of the You've Been Served Podcast™, she interviewed top industry leaders such as Seth Godin, Carla Harris, and Leena Nair, uncovering insights on increasing revenue, improving communities, and affecting lives through social impact, innovation, and service.

Keesa has served on numerous boards and committees aligning with her equity, inclusion, and compassion in business focus, including Business Resource and Investment Center, Girl Scout Council of Greater New York, Thomson Reuters Environmental, Social, and Governance (ESG) Ambassador, and Refinitiv Women's Business Resource Group.

Her work is recognized by the following industry groups and thought leaders:

- Featured guest on Reid Hoffman's Masters of Scale alongside LinkedIn CEO, Jeff Weiner
- HubSpot as "Top Female Marketing and Growth Expert"
- Masonry's 18 Content Marketing Bloggers to follow on Twitter

Connect with Keesa at https://www.keesaschreane.com/.

Inclusion, Equality, and Compassion in Business

An Overview

C hanging the course of a culture can be like changing the course of a ship. You turn the wheel slowly. The ship moves in two- or three-degree increments at a time. The degrees of movement are imperceptible, especially relative to the ship's size. Those onboard may not perceive a change from one minute to the next. But after a certain length of time they start seeing small changes in direction. Finally, those slow, steady, and careful minor turns yield a complete change in the direction of the ship. Ironically, it may feel to those onboard that the change happened all of a sudden, but in fact the ship had been turning for a long time.

This is a good analogy for what is happening with traditional corporate culture. Decades of lack of equity, lack of inclusion, and inequality are slowly shifting the course of business toward a culture of fairness and ethics in employee treatment. Changing the way we do business and how we interact with employees has been a slow process. Yet, it remains an imperative one.

As we enter the post-COVID-19 and Black Lives Matter (BLM) era, the move toward a new compassionate culture, with equality and inclusion as a foundation, is even more urgent. A compassionate culture empowers people to develop new ways to solve business problems and deliver solutions. For employees to tap into these higher levels of learning, creating, and working, they must feel valued, included, and treated ethically.

Compassion in business means creating a culture in which equality, inclusion, and kindness are foundational principles, integrated at every level. Through a compassionate culture, employees have the agency to bring creativity, innovation, intelligence, and imagination to their jobs.

A business can't be compassionate if it's not willing to practice equality and inclusion. Equality and inclusion are not the same as compassion, but they do go hand-in-hand. They complement each other. Practically speaking, companies that embrace decent pay, diverse hiring, inclusive language, and ethical behaviors likely have compassionate cultures.

Just how seriously have corporate leaders taken their responsibility to be compassionate, just, and equality-focused up until now? The data speaks for itself:

- **2014:** Facebook admits it has "more work to do" in recruiting after reporting 74% of their US senior workforce is White and 77% is male.

- **2019:** Five years later, Facebook has a US senior workforce that is 65% White, 25% Asian, and 67% male; all other ethnicities *still* report single digits.

- **2019:** Uber expects a near $90 billion initial public offering (IPO), even as their drivers strike over low pay.

- **2019:** Hundreds of McDonald's workers in US and UK cities staged walkouts over low wages, as well as made accusations that the fast-food giant had an unsafe work environment and allowed sexual harassment to take place.[1]

- **2020:** Black workers at Adidas protested outside the sportswear company's US headquarters in Portland, Oregon, saying they had experienced racial discrimination in the workplace—this despite the company brandishing a public image of being antidiscrimination.[2]

Organizations that represent the global corporate world (such as the World Economic Forum and Business Roundtable) have given us hope that the old ways of doing business are changing, based on statements they've made. For example, in 2019, the Business Roundtable's updated commitment noted the following:

> Investing in our employees. This starts with compensating them fairly and providing important benefits. It also includes supporting them through training and education that help develop new skills for a rapidly changing world. We foster diversity and inclusion, dignity and respect.[3]

Employees, suppliers, communities where businesses are located, and even organizations and governments are all invested in the business world. Whether they realize it or not, they all have a stake in corporate diversity, equity, inclusion, and commitments to dignified, respectful treatment of others.

Diversity is a term used to describe a workplace composed of employees with varying characteristics, such as sex, gender, race, ethnicity, sexual orientation, and disability.[4]

Inclusion refers to a workplace environment where the diverse backgrounds and perspectives of individual workers are embraced and respected, which promotes equivalent access

(*continues*)

(continued)

to opportunities and the full contribution of employees to the organization's success.

Workplace equality involves providing the same level of opportunity and assistance to all employees, regardless of gender, race, ethnicity, sexual orientation, disability, and so on. This includes pay equality when women and men are paid at the same rate for performing the same job.

Equity, involves providing people what they need to make things fair, and it naturally evolves from a workplace that promotes and maintains diversity, inclusion, and equality.[5]

Employees and suppliers are invested because they work at the companies. Communities are invested because they share natural resources with the companies. Organizations and governments depend on companies' partnerships to support societal change.

People invested in positive, forward-thinking movements in the business world hope that words like those just defined would be followed by deliberate action. But just when employees, suppliers, and communities thought companies would do better, many actually got worse.

Putting People First

In recent years, employees have become emboldened and louder about fighting infractions and inequities in the corporate world. Walkouts have become more orchestrated. Workers have protested unfair pay in an almost synchronistic style across regions. Demands for racial justice have grown more sophisticated. Brands have been persuaded to show solidarity as racial justice activists leveraged the power of advertising to hit the digital economy in a new way. Factory workers unapologetically raised their voices at feeling coerced to work in environments they felt were unsafe during the COVID-19 pandemic. Rather than fearing potential retaliation, these workers demonstrated their faith that the wider society would support their demands for greater protections.

For example, Shipt, a same-day delivery service owned by Target Corporation, came under fire for lowering its delivery drivers' pay amid the COVID-19 pandemic in 2020—a time when home delivery of groceries and consumer goods was surging. Workers protested the pay cuts with walkouts and work stoppages, arguing that it was wrong to reduce their pay when making deliveries posed a health risk. Earlier in the year, Shipt workers had also staged walkouts over the company not providing its drivers with the protective gear they needed to make deliveries safely.[6]

Walkouts and other strategic actions grew out of the need to implore corporations to change unethical behaviors, pay people fairly, and stop discriminatory practices. Put simply, these actions were laying the groundwork for compassionate activism in the workplace.

This activism was embraced and supported by some in the corporate world, but others refused to commit to the cause. At Tyson Foods, for instance, over 4,500 workers were diagnosed with COVID-19 and 18 died from the illness. Despite this, the company still refused to offer paid sick leave, instead opting to "relax attendance policies and update disability policy."[7] However, there were bright lights that penetrated the dark times.

Many corporations broadened health care access to include mental health and well-being services. In spring 2020, Starbucks started offering 222,000 of its US employees up to 20 free counseling sessions with a mental health therapist.[8] The insurance company AIA uses a digital screening program to check its employees for depression, stress, and anxiety and offers them a quarterly "recharge day." As Damien Mu, AIA's CEO for Australia and New Zealand, told *Financial Review,* "The unintended consequence of being high energy and working hard is the team thinks that is what is required to succeed. What they don't see is the down time we all need and that you are not always up."[9]

During the 2020 economic downturn, some firms made commitments to retain employees and did so with creativity. Instead of laying off employees during the pandemic, Verizon made the commitment to retrain 20,000 workers for different careers within the company.[10] During the Great Recession that started in 2008 and the 2020 pandemic, many companies furloughed employees rather than laying them off—a strategy that assists with a company's short-term cash crunch, while still providing employees with benefits.

These positive, compassionate examples are a start. But unless corporations and their leaders change how they do business and how they treat their most valuable resource—people—they will fail fast. They will not survive among the next generation of business leaders, who have an inherent leaning toward creativity that only happens when employees feel comfortable and supported. Creativity—instead of old-school, destructive competition—delivers innovation that not only leads to revenue generation but also supports a firm's longevity.

The first step toward building a compassionate culture, with equality and inclusion at its core, is making a commitment to putting people first. Here is what a people-first focus looks like:

- Communicating how employees' jobs make a difference in society
- Embracing diverse talent while exploring new markets
- Creating a work culture in which employees exude enthusiasm, excite customers to patronize their firms, and advocate for their brands in their communities

- Committing to doing their best to protect employees day-to-day and also in the event of a catastrophe

- Offering employee incentives that drive company loyalty and real payoffs

What Is Compassion and Why Does It Matter?

Compassion in business means inspiring people to aim as high as they can in their conduct and their innovation each day. That can include basic kindness and cordial daily interaction between colleagues, but it goes a lot further than that. Compassion empowers people to be open—to replace fear of failure with faith in their abilities, learn from challenges, and construct creative approaches to business problems. A compassionate culture supports the mental, physical, and economic well-being of employees, as well as their professional growth, by governing with integrity and care that comes with positions of power.

Believe it or not, compassionate leadership is practical. When there is compassion in business, a culture of equality, inclusion, and kindness follows. People feel better about the work they do, leading to higher levels of productivity. They increase their sales and are more committed to their work.

Research finds compassion triggers brain activity associated with learning and reward in decision-making, as well as creating positivity and "kinder and more eager to help" attitudes.[11] Additionally, compassion is seeing a problem (or suffering) and responding to that problem in a way that includes "courage, tolerance, equanimity."[12]

This is exactly the type of activity successful businesses want to govern relationships with customers. They express a desire to help customers and serve them by solving customers' problems through products and services. They become obsessed with fulfilling the customer's specific need, while engaging with kindness to support customer retention.

This is also how successful corporations seek to engage with shareholders. They exhibit strong, thoughtful decision-making skills with the aim of serving (helping) their interests by providing solutions to increase profitability in business.

Seeing compassion through the lens of serving others and solving problems clarifies how compassion relates to a company's relationships with customers and shareholders.

Seeing compassion through this same lens can also offer insight into how corporate leaders should aspire to serve their employees. This aspiration to serve employees should exist for all management levels, from frontline supervisors to CEOs. Learning, decision-making, equanimity, and tolerance are all ways companies can express their focus on people through compassion toward their employees.

Inclusiveness and equality reflect a leader's courage to think differently from society or even from the old business culture that has conditioned that person. Inclusiveness and equality require less focus on self and more focus on understanding others; less emphasis on the type of competition that has destructive qualities and more emphasis on cooperation that creates a legitimate partnership with everyone in the business ecosystem, including employees.

This may sound theoretical, but there are practical ways this plays out in real, day-to-day corporate leadership. Each employee and stakeholder, regardless of their title, has agency to choose how to act toward colleagues. Compassionate business leaders know that decisions they make in the boardroom, including decisions they make on behalf of the organization, can significantly affect not only individual employees and customers but also families and wider communities. Leaders who understand compassion will support their employees' mental and physical well-being with fair pay, equal treatment, and ensuring that the company's behaviors and language foster innovation to support the enterprise and each employee in it.

Compassionate business leadership includes making thoughtful, courageous decisions in especially challenging environments. This is done by looking for creative solutions, seeking counsel and expertise from others, and seeing beyond traditional answers. When corporate heads lead with compassion, their employees, suppliers, and communities willingly support that leadership. Employees and others bring higher degrees of creativity to support business growth. This perspective also gives insight into why some businesses don't see this type of commitment from employees. It is because in inequitable environments, where behaviors such as microaggression and destructive competition flourish, the culture isn't conducive to employee comfort and the creativity needed to innovate. Resisting the courageous, compassionate form of leadership is why the old corporate culture is steadily self-destructing.

Old corporate culture has presented an especially difficult situation for many members of historically underrepresented—not to mention underestimated—demographics. Alleged "pipeline" issues—claims that it is not possible to find enough qualified people of color and women for certain positions—perpetuate underrepresentation in the workplace. Abysmal underrepresentation in C-suite positions, especially for Black women, shows corporate leadership continues to underestimate the leadership abilities of this demographic. As of the second quarter of 2020, only two Black women have ever led Fortune 500 companies, Ursula Burns of Xerox and Mary Winston of Bed, Bath & Beyond.

The demands for racial justice, employee equality, and improvements to the post-COVID-19 workplace are driving change in how business is done and whom business is done with. Yet, too many executives are still clinging to outdated ways to govern and lead. This is demonstrated by the numbers of unhappy employees and purpose-starved corporate cultures.

How Did We Get Here?

Business has always been the driver of innovation and economy in the world. So what happened? Looking at the big picture, most working adults with a bit of historical perspective agree things are better than they were a hundred years ago. Working conditions are safer and better regulated on the whole. Violence and discrimination toward people of color in places of work and exclusionary practices based on gender and ethnicity are no longer *legal* (albeit at times *acceptable*).

Given all that progress, how did we get to a place where strikes, walkouts, inequality, low wages, discriminatory practices, debilitating stress, and lack of pay parity became all too familiar? Part of it has to do with the nature of the actions against employees. Some would say that microaggressions have now replaced deliberate discriminatory and violent behaviors. And all microaggressions are *not illegal*, so they have not been regulated out of business. (More about this specific behavior in Chapter 2.)

The best firms continually expend resources, intelligence, and time listening to others to understand how to create a fairer, more just culture. The best leaders root out potential threats to employee well-being. These leaders recognize threatening behaviors, including exclusion, inappropriate language, and unequal treatment, may sometimes be *legal* but are still *unacceptable*. These leaders have a choice between adjusting the existing culture and building a new foundation from the ground up. This choice is daunting.

For some, this situation all started in the early 1970s. Milton Friedman, the Nobel Prize–winning American economist, famously asserted his view in a 1970 *New York Times Magazine* piece called "The Social Responsibility of Business Is to Increase Its Profits." This excerpt speaks directly to his thoughts about corporations' role in creating a just, fair culture:

> The businessmen believe that they are defending free enterprise when they declaim that business is not concerned "merely" with profit but also with promoting desirable "social" ends; that business has a "social conscience" and takes seriously its responsibilities for providing employment, eliminating discrimination, avoiding pollution and whatever else may be the catchwords of the contemporary crop of reformers. In fact they are—or would be if they or anyone else took them seriously—preaching pure and unadulterated socialism. Businessmen who talk this way are unwitting puppets of the intellectual forces that have been undermining the basis of a free society these past decades.[13]

Friedman's essay helped fuel a mindset, influencing how many corporate leaders across the United States and around the world viewed their role for the next 40 years. Instead of balancing the needs of shareholders with other stakeholders—including their commitment to caring for employees' well-being—this so-called Friedman Doctrine spurred many leaders to see their sole objective as maximizing shareholder value.

In 2017, former World Bank director Steve Denning wrote this:

> Friedman's article was a godsend. Executives no longer had to worry about balancing the claims of employees, customers, the firm, and society. They could concentrate on making money for the shareholders. Adam Smith's "invisible hand" would make everything else come out right.[14]

Of course, Friedman's article wasn't the only reason for this shift toward putting profits before people. Other trends in the 1970s, such as slow economic growth, corporate leaders' friction with labor unions, and increased foreign competition, certainly contributed to this emerging mentality. But Friedman's article was used by many leaders to justify their brash pursuit of profitability and share price gains. It helped propel the shareholder value movement that took off in the 1980s and 1990s with eponymous cutthroat CEOs such as Sunbeam's Al Dunlap (nicknamed "Chainsaw" and "Rambo in Pinstripes") and General Electric's "Neutron" Jack Welch.[15]

This movement led to a spate of corporate mergers and takeovers with profit-driven leaders viewing employees as dispensable, using mass layoffs and overall downsizing as a way to slash expenses and, in turn, rev up stock prices. GE, for example, laid off more than 100,000 workers during Welch's time as CEO. He promoted management practices such as ranking employees by performance and brazenly firing those deemed as underperformers. He unabashedly championed a non-equality philosophy when it came to managing employees—even decades after he left the helm. In 2017, Welch told the site Freakanomics:

> Look, differentiation is part of my whole belief in management. And treating everybody the same is ludicrous. And I don't buy it. I don't buy what people write about it. It's not cruel and Darwinian and things like that, that people like to call it. A baseball team publishes every day the batting averages. And you don't see the .180 hitter getting all the money, or all the raises.

Welch's tough management style paid off handsomely for GE shareholders at the time, as GE's stock price grew 4,000% during his tenure.[16]

But the shareholder-first practices of Welch and many other like-minded corporate leaders had the ultimate effect of eroding employee trust. In the 1980s and 1990s, the "corporate social contract" was officially broken. For instance, many companies during this period suspended their employee retirement pensions—replacing them with a stock market–dependent plan called the 401(k). Many also slashed health benefits. Labor union membership plummeted from 25% to 15% between 1978 and 1988, in part because unionized jobs were often the target of layoffs.[17]

This fraying of the corporation-employee relationship created other problems. The purchasing power of most US workers' wages has stagnated since the 1970s and hasn't been buoyed even in times of historically low unemployment.[18] This has widened the rift between top executives and typical workers. And because executives usually receive stock as a big part of their compensation, they are strongly motivated to drive up their company's share prices, often at the expense of the people working for them.

Here's the irony: for many companies, all this emphasis on maximizing shareholder value didn't even produce the sought-after outcome. Several studies have shown that mergers and layoffs in the 1980s and 1990s actually had minimal or even detrimental effects on the share prices of many of the companies that engaged in them. One just needs to crunch the long-term returns on the S&P 500 to see that the era of shareholder primacy did not create outsized returns for regular investors. In fact, it seems to have had little effect at all. The markets returned an average of 9.63% between 1956 and 1986 and 9.99% between 1986 and 2016. Both those periods lagged the 10.77% return seen between 1926 and 1956.[19] What's more, the overall longevity of corporations seems to be on the decline. The life expectancy of companies in the S&P 500 declined from 61 years in 1958 to less than 18 years today.

The shift toward focusing on shareholder value wasn't just a US phenomenon. Similar to Friedman, many other economists and business leaders across the globe defended and championed similar "free-market" capitalist ideals over the past century—encouraging companies to focus on profits above all else. Austrian economist Friedrich von Hayek, another Nobel Prize winner, concluded that seeking social justice was a waste of time and that no outcome to market activity could be considered just or unjust.[20]

The 1980s and 1990s is considered a heyday in modern times for profit-only-driven cultures. Yet, this philosophy of putting profits ahead of people has been deeply ingrained in corporate culture since the early industrial days. Corporate language itself has always been brutal, leaving room for neither equality nor compassion. It's standard to talk about "annihilating" another company, "running competition out of business," "dominating" a market, or "beating" individuals, and so on.

There is also a lingering notion that some people are divinely chosen to be leaders instead of others. This corresponds quite conveniently with the belief that some have been ordained by higher powers as more capable, intelligent, and privileged, just because of their sex or race. (These notions lay foundations for racial and gender inequities that will be discussed in later chapters.)

Difference between Externally Facing Philanthropy and Internally Facing Compassion

Clearly, corporate leadership is a complex construct. This is amplified when values and beliefs don't seem to align with bottom-line growth. The notion of "compassion" in business often gets reduced to the simple concept of corporate philanthropy. In the 21st century, progress in corporate philanthropy and benevolence kicked into high gear. Philanthropy benefits a firm's reputation and enhances sales prospects who appreciate the charitable work. But, although philanthropy may be lauded externally, inside corporations it's often perceived as a drain on profits and an unnecessary operating expense, especially in market downturns. Further, just because a company is philanthropic doesn't mean it treats employees well.

Philanthropy communicated through corporate websites and annual reports tout externally focused "corporate social responsibility" programs. There is nothing wrong with this: doling out resources and funding to communities and causes should continue to be highly regarded. But charity alone will not help corporate culture survive the coming decades. Valuing people, not just valuing profits, is the long-term solution. Investing in the people inside our enterprises—in their education, growth, and well-being—strengthens the communities and marketplaces where businesses operate. It's also the way to strengthen the employee-employer relationships needed to innovate and drive businesses forward.

True corporate compassion can't be a separate subsidiary or a spin-off of the primary enterprise. It's not something that can be tacked on as an afterthought. Compassion begins with leadership that integrates the values of courage, inclusion, purpose, and equality into business practices as foundational to the internal business culture.

Compassion: What's in It for Me?

A business culture with compassionate characteristics as the foundation is linked directly to improved employee performance, according to 2013 research by UC Berkeley's Greater Good Science Center:

> Happy employees also make for a more congenial workplace and improved customer service. Employees in positive moods are more willing to help peers and to provide customer service on their own accord. What's

more, compassionate, friendly, and supportive co-workers tend to build higher-quality relationships with others at work. In doing so, they boost coworkers' productivity levels and increase coworkers' feeling of social connection, as well as their commitment to the workplace and their levels of engagement with their job.[21]

Some researchers chide organizations for measuring empathy in a corporation (which many people equate to compassion on a broad level). They believe measuring it "takes the heart out of it." Rather, they say, compassion should simply be a key value at the corporate level, not treated as a quantifiable metric.[22]

The point of agreement is when employees feel engaged at their company, the company sees a quantifiable difference in employee performance. For example, according to a Gallup Survey:

- Engaged employees and teams experience 17% greater productivity.

- Engaged employees experience a 20% increase in sales.[23]

Feeling appreciated opens the door to feeling comfortable and becoming more creative at work. Employees who feel valued will share more ideas and, as a result, offer more value. In the end, this cultivates innovation, which improves both the culture and the corporation's bottom line.

Making Tough Decisions Compassionately

But what happens when business pressures increase and, in the heat of the moment, a company's needs outweigh employee well-being and creativity? For example, there may be business expansion opportunities calling for employees to work for a period of time in a hazardous environment, with no health protection. Or a market downturn may occur when management foresees the need for employees to work longer hours to get a product to the market, but the company won't have the income to pay them right away.

Look at it this way: when business is booming, the economy is solid, and customers are buying in large numbers, it's easy to put employees first. Managers may even seek to share power, giving employees a say on how the organization's culture is governed. However, when revenue is on the line, the economy is tanking, and customers are unable or unwilling to buy products, typical corporate culture reverts to a hard-line approach. Managers are inflexible to the needs of employees and exclude them from decision-making.

In tough times, corporate culture can get even tougher on employees. What happens when an action that might inconvenience employees could nonetheless improve the company's long-term growth? Even for the most fair-minded business leader, profits will likely weigh more than compassionate treatment of employees in those examples. The scary thing is, in our super-competitive market environment, these scenarios have become more commonplace. C-suite leaders are making decisions about the health, well-being, and personal economies of thousands of people. These leaders see before them a limited number of alternatives to business problems. Each alternative has "casualties." Consequences for those casualties can be debilitating.

Even in these situations, leaders should be tethered to their guiding principles dictating the type of leaders they are and the type of culture they uphold. Compassionate leaders are creative, engage a variety of stakeholders for feedback, and use their intelligence and imagination to deliver the best results. They see people as their most valuable resource. Their guiding principles include cultivating people.

The root of the problem is that business leaders resort to thinking of employees as expendable, instead of viewing them as the lifeblood

17

Inclusion, Equality, and Compassion in Business

of the business and should be treated with compassion and dignity, even in arduous circumstances when there are no "good" options to choose from. Commoditizing people in the workforce, and not adhering to a people-first business mentality, has steadily eroded corporate culture. Today, corporate culture is slowly shifting toward more of a people orientation. But, to return to our ship-turning analogy: this change won't happen overnight. There are still plenty of corporate leaders who instinctively view shareholders as the primary (if not sole) concern in decision-making.

There is always room for grace here. Making poor decisions does not equate to intentionally desiring to harm employees. In fact, it's possible the majority of leaders feel they have no choice when making decisions that negatively affect employees. They may not have the resources and information needed to expand their view of business solutions in challenging environments.

The Old Days: Carnegie and the Homestead Strike

Andrew Carnegie is a great example of philanthropy and the ideal of leading with compassion and integrity. Leadership is complex, with many variables. Looking critically at key decisions Carnegie made that affected employees provides a teachable moment as well. Giving grace to leaders and moments where they falter is important. Learning lessons from poor decisions to prevent repeating them is critical in turning toward a new corporate culture built on compassion, equality, and inclusion.

Carnegie is arguably the most celebrated philanthropist of his ilk from the 20th century, and for good reason. His philanthropic contributions remain unmatched. He gave away over $350 million during his lifetime—by one estimate, that would be about $65 billion today.

I first became familiar with Andrew Carnegie through Napoleon Hill's book *Think and Grow Rich* and Dennis Kimbro's *Think and Grow Rich: A Black Choice*. Millions of readers like me saw Carnegie as a generous teacher sharing universal keys to success and giving new generations an understanding of how faith, determination, and belief in one's self outweighs obstacles. He did well financially, he made many investors wealthy, and he accomplished even more after his lifetime by directing his wealth to be used for good globally.

In his 1889 article, "The Gospel of Wealth," Carnegie discussed the chasm between wealthy and working classes and how inequality can quickly become the norm in large corporations:

> We assemble thousands of operatives in the factory, in the mine, and in the counting-house, of whom the employer can know little or nothing, and to whom the employer is little better than a myth. All intercourse between them is at an end. Rigid castes are formed, and, as usual, mutual igno-rance breeds mutual distrust. Each caste is without sympa-thy for the other, and ready to credit anything disparaging in regard to it. Under the law of competition, the employer of thousands is forced into the strictest economies, among which the rates paid to labor figure prominently, and often there is friction between the employer and the employed, between capital and labor, between rich and poor. Human society loses homogeneity.[24]

Carnegie's historical writings on the relationships between owners and workers provide an important lens to view labor relations of the present day. That said, his theoretical ideas contrast starkly with the company's actions during a critical business negotiation just a few years later.

19

Inclusion, Equality, and Compassion in Business

As Carnegie Steel Company ascended, Carnegie chose Henry Clay Frick as his business partner. Frick was known as a man who got things done and saw the benefits of authoritarian-style management. Carnegie largely favored unions and believed in partnering with workers to avoid breaking strikes and bloodshed, although he felt in some cases they interfered with efficiency and were "elitist" in their membership. Despite their differences in style, neither could have expected the deadly outcome at Homestead Steel Works in Homestead, Pennsylvania, in 1892.[25]

In this era, factory work was grueling and poorly paid, spaces were crowded, and tasks were repetitive. Working 12-hour shifts in physically dangerous environments was very common. From faulty equipment to the lack of alertness after the end of long shifts, the loss of a finger or even a life was a real concern. Workers organized to demand a wage that was fair for the extended hours and heightened risk of breadwinners whose families depended on them to put food on the table.

At the time of the Homestead Strike, Carnegie had traveled back to his native Scotland, leaving his company chairman, Frick, in charge. In his written correspondence, Carnegie assured Frick he had his confidence in resolving the situation.

But during negotiations for pay increases, Frick's proposal of a 22% wage *decrease* escalated into a full-blown strike. Frick brought in a group known as Pinkerton Detectives, a private, armed security force, to disrupt the strike. The armed Pinkertons faced off with striking employees and violent conflict ensued, resulting in the deaths of nine workers and seven Pinkertons. Dozens more were injured, and state militia ultimately intervened to end the standoff.

There are lessons to be learned about actions and reactions during crisis mode. In hindsight, it's easy to talk about de-escalation strategies, pay discussions, and seeing workers as partners. But, when you're in the midst of a heated exchange, and both parties have relevant points and arguments, the way forward may not seem so clear. It is in these seemingly impossible, no-way-out situations that compassionate leaders can aim higher and create solutions that may have a short-term business impact, but a longer-term benefit—a benefit that brings greater commitment from employees and shows how the company seeks to serve employees.

Today's World

The business world has changed in a thousand ways since Carnegie's day. To take just one example, Carnegie and Frick never had to deal with the 24-hour news cycle, Twitter, or the accelerated rate of social change that we have today. Old-school corporate culture likewise needs to do better in keeping up with the swift pace of the social media dominated landscape. Too many leaders are failing to prepare for how much more swiftly movements progress today than they did in past generations.

Social media pervasiveness; a global consciousness of equality, fairness, and inclusion; and greater financial power enable today's movements to be stronger and last longer. These issues affect the company's reputation and bottom line.

The 2019 Uber wage strikes provided a clear example of these forces in action. In addition to concerns about wages, Uber drivers were also concerned about gender bias, sexual harassment, and allegations of a toxic corporate culture.[26] The May 2019 strikes had a massive impact on Uber's share prices; the company's $45 IPO price had dropped to $25.58 by November. This compounded other investor concerns, such as the viability of its UberEats venture.[27] Then the COVID-19 pandemic hit, and share prices tumbled further, down to $14.82 on March 18, 2020. Uber's stock price held steady in the following weeks of spring and early summer in the $20 to $30 plus range, but they have yet to return to that original IPO high.

Inclusion, Equality, and Compassion in Business

In the banking sector, Wells Fargo's leadership appeared to be similarly caught off guard when their corporate culture came under fire in the early 2000s. Employees claimed that nearly impossible sales goals of sometimes up to 20 products a day resulted in a toxic and stressful environment. From 2006 to 2015, the bank's stock rose 67%. But, it turned out that the rise in stock price had been partly due to a number of unethical sales practices, such as the creation of 2 million fake accounts. Ultimately, Wells Fargo eliminated sales goals from its retail side, and the company was faced with a $185 million settlement.[28]

During 2016, Wells Fargo stock hit a $45 low, but just as bad was the impact on the bank's reputation—this was especially damaging given the era—post-2008 financial crisis, when big banks were vilified and viewed with skepticism.[29] Their share price continued to struggle over the four-year period after 2016, peaking over $60, but never getting much higher.[30] These examples are cautionary tales. The old corporate culture of putting revenue generation above all else does not always work. This culture is steadily changing. Leaders need to quickly understand how they can balance running a profitable business, while treating employees inclusively, equitably, and compassionately.

Achieving Balance: High-Performing Business and Outstanding Treatment of Employees

Corporations can still build sprawling societies, deliver innovation, empower capital markets, and generate revenues without sacrificing the well-being of employees. Making inclusion and equality foundational components of compassionate business enables us to create, innovate, and increase profits while improving the lives of people inside and outside our corporations.

When leaders are passionate about improving the well-being of their workers, it shows. They deliver pay parity, and commit to an inclusive environment, even during challenging moments.

Leaders are humans and they have their own lenses through which they see the world. The goal in redefining business and leadership is not to make everyone cookie cutter. The goal is not to stifle business growth. The goal is to ensure leaders continue to act decisively and move deliberately with confidence while remaining conscious of the ways in which their cultures, actions, and policies affect everyone in the business landscape, from employees to partners to communities to shareholders.

Carnegie and Frick are considered "mainstream" corporate leaders because they were White men of great economic wealth. They had influence in business circles. Their names were synonymous with success and philanthropy. Their stories of industry are the stories known to the masses, but mainstream stories reflecting successes born from fair treatment of employees exist in a more modern context, too.

Howard Schultz's work to build and evolve Starbucks is considered one of the greatest modern stories of a company that made compassion part of its business model. During his time at the helm, Schultz valued creating a culture of trust and partnership with employees. As he wrote in his 1997 book, *Pour Your Heart into It*, "There is no more precious commodity than the relationship of trust and confidence a company has with its employees."[31]

In particular, Starbucks is a brand known for taking action on racial injustice in communities. Some may criticize the effectiveness, swiftness, or strategy, but even most critics do credit Starbucks with action. One specific case was an incident in 2018 at a Starbucks in Philadelphia when a manager called police officers on two Black men because they didn't order anything while seated for a few moments waiting on a business partner's arrival.[32]

The CEO at the time, Kevin Johnson, was quick to offer an official apology to the men.[33] More broadly, Starbucks made the decision to close 8,000 locations for a one-day racial bias training for employees, which ultimately had 175,000 staff participants.[34] This

23

was a fairly remarkable move for such a large company, even though some employees questioned the ultimate effectiveness of the training. But the fact that Starbucks surrendered roughly $12 million in potential profit as a result of closing down the stores for the training speaks to how strongly they feel about educating employees and improving community relationships.[35]

Whole Foods Market cofounder John Mackey is another example of a leader who values a high degree of compassion. In his 2013 book *Conscious Capitalism,* he talks about the prevalent environment most employees contend with daily. In one example, he references the frequency of heart attacks occurring on Monday, which some experts attribute to the dread of returning to work. Mackey contends that work doesn't have to equal drudgery. When Mackey led Whole Foods Market (before Amazon acquired it in 2017), one element he focused on was improving health insurance for employees.

Underrepresented and Underestimated Leaders Are Compassionate Leaders Too

Mainstream corporate leaders, their business savvy, and brilliance at generating profits are on full display all around us as historical figures. No research required. They are important stories. But they are not the only important stories.

Historically, society has done a poor job highlighting non-mainstream corporate narratives that may serve as either cautionary tales or as celebratory stories about the power of leading and governing with equality, inclusion, and compassion. This is especially the case with underestimated and underrepresented groups such as women and Blacks, Indigenous, and people of color (BIPOC).

Things are changing. Business narratives are becoming more diverse and inclusive. During movements such as #MeToo and #BlackLivesMatter, social media, storytellers, and academics shared stories featured in media more prominently and consumed by the public more voraciously. They shared stories of business titans who included equality, inclusion, and compassion in their enterprises. These stories were of people of color, women, and other groups who were left out of the mainstream narrative previously. The momentum in which these narratives are now being consumed is another example of the slow, but steady, moving ship. These narratives are way overdue in being recognized.

Workers of color and women have had to navigate hurdles ranging from violence to modern microaggression to harassment, even when in leadership positions. Historically, these underestimated and underrepresented leaders prioritized social purpose, profit, and compassion just as the early industry titans who are more widely celebrated in historical texts and oral histories. Underrepresented leaders and their stories of brilliant business savvy, ethical treatment of workers, and compassion are just as worthy to be told, and repeated, as any mainstream business story.

Chapter 2 examines ways in which underrepresented people were treated in business historically, as well as how underrepresented people emerged as business leaders, managing compassionate leadership toward people who make up those corporations. Generations of poor treatment in and by the mainstream culture make the case that businesses need to root out systematic racism before they can expect further social license to operate. This rooting-out process starts with bringing inclusion, equality, equity, and compassion into corporate cultures.

Chapter 1 Takeaways

- Compassion in business means inspiring employees and others in the business ecosystem to bring their best work, their highest intelligence, and their greatest level of creativity and enthusiasm.

- Compassion needs to accompany inclusion and equality for workers to feel comfortable enough in their environments to think and act creatively and confidently, driving revenue generation.

- Compassion complements inclusion and equality. All three are needed for business to evolve, continue its role as a driver of innovation in society, and generate revenues.

- Inclusion, equality, and compassion have not traditionally been at the heart of business (nor of society in general). But times have changed, and a lack of compassionate culture can be the downfall of 21st-century businesses.

- Workers and others in the business ecosystem have begun slowly course-correcting this flaw in old school business culture. This is an essential evolution, particularly after social changes resulting from COVID-19 and BLM.

- Innovation and growth do not need to come at the expense of compassionate treatment of employees.

- One way leaders and corporations falter is refusing to allow equality, inclusion, and compassion into their enterprises. This usually happens when they desire greater wealth than the nearest competitor by any means, lower employee pay, and neglect accountability. Milton Friedman's 1970s declaration solidified this construct into gospel.

- Compassion, unlike philanthropy, is neither a separate subsidiary nor a spin-off. It is a behavior that must be a part of the business culture.

- Andrew Carnegie is an iconic business titan of American history (that is, a powerful, wealthy, philanthropic enterprising White male). And yet, he is a great example of what can happen when a successful, well-known business leader makes a poor decision. Even if a corporate culture progresses and profits from unethical tactics, those tactics and activities result in mistrust that neither the employee nor the marketplace (that is, the customer) forgets.

- When the corporation suffers, the shareholder ultimately suffers.

- Historically, society has done a poor job recognizing accomplishments of individuals from underrepresented and underestimated groups who lead and govern with equality, inclusion, and compassion. This is changing. Highlighting these narratives is way overdue.

References

1. https://www.wsj.com/articles/mcdonalds-workers-strike-to-protest-pay-and-harassment-complaints-11558627417; https://www.cnn.com/2019/11/12/business/mcdonalds-protest-uk-gbr-scli-intl/index.html
2. https://www.nytimes.com/2020/06/10/business/adidas-black-employees-discrimination.html
3. https://www.businessroundtable.org/business-roundtable-redefines-the-purpose-of-a-corporation-to-promote-an-economy-that-serves-all-americans
4. https://www.talentlyft.com/en/resources/what-is-workplace-diversity
5. https://social-change.co.uk/blog/2019-03-29-equality-and-equity

6. https://www.npr.org/2020/04/27/843849435/hometown-heroes-or-whatever-low-wage-workers-want-more-than-praise; https://www.bizjournals.com/twin cities/news/2020/07/14/target-shipt-walkout-threat-pay-changes.html

7. https://www.businessinsider.com/tyson-4500-covid-19-cases-as-meat-industry-blames-workers-2020-5

8. https://stories.starbucks.com/press/2020/starbucks-transforms-mental-health-benefit-for-us-employees/#:~:text=Beginning%20April%206%2C%20Starbucks%20will,no%20cost%20to%20the%20user.

9. https://www.afr.com/work-and-careers/leaders/how-corporate-australia-is-tackling-the-mental-health-crisis-20191212-p53jgw

10. https://www.cnn.com/2020/07/14/business/verizon-jobs-ceo-hans-vestberg/index.html

11. https://www.psychologytoday.com/us/blog/the-clarity/201703/compassion-is-better-empathy

12. http://ccare.stanford.edu/research/wiki/compassion-definitions/compassion/

13. https://www.nytimes.com/1970/09/13/archives/article-15-no-title.html

14. https://www.forbes.com/sites/stevedenning/2017/07/17/making-sense-of-shareholder-value-the-worlds-dumbest-idea/#f42dc252a7ed

15. https://www.newsweek.com/business-roundtable-corporation-purpose-friedman-doctrine-1455975

16. https://www.businessinsider.com/jack-welch-the-former-ceo-of-general-electric-has-died-2020-3

17. http://www.irle.berkeley.edu/files/2005/Shareholder-Value-and-Changes-in-American-Industries-1984-2000.pdf

18. https://insight.kellogg.northwestern.edu/article/wage-stagnation-in-america

19. https://www.businessinsider.com/30-year-sp-500-returns-impressive-2016-5

20. https://www.independent.org/publications/tir/article.asp?id=1404

21. https://greatergood.berkeley.edu/article/item/why_compassion_in_business_makes_sense

22. https://qz.com/627435/corporate-attempts-to-quantify-empathy-show-just-how-little-companies-value-it/

23. https://www.gallup.com/workplace/236366/right-culture-not-employee-satisfaction.aspx

24. https://www.carnegie.org/about/our-history/gospelofwealth/

25. https://www.history.com/shows/men-who-built-america

26. https://www.vox.com/the-goods/2019/9/5/20849632/uber-public-relations-crisis-qanda

27. https://www.cnn.com/2019/11/06/tech/uber-stock-lockup/index.html

28. https://www.npr.org/2016/10/04/496508361/former-wells-fargo-employees-describe-toxic-sales-culture-even-at-hq

29. https://money.cnn.com/2016/09/26/investing/wells-fargo-stock-fake-account-scandal/index.html

30. https://www.google.com/search?q=wells+fargo+stock+price&rlz=1C1LENN
_enUS539US542&oq=wells+fargo+stock+price&aqs=chrome..69i57j69i59j0l6.719
8j0j9&sourceid=chrome&ie=UTF-8
31. Schultz, Howard. *Pour Your Heart into It* (New York: Hachette, 1997).
32. https://www.nydailynews.com/news/national/starbucks-manager-called-cops-
minutes-black-men-arrive-article-1.3942931
33. https://www.businessinsider.com/starbucks-ceo-apology-black-men-arrested-
viral-video-2018-4
34. https://time.com/5294343/starbucks-employees-racial-bias-training/
35. https://www.usatoday.com/story/money/2018/05/26/starbucks-racial-bias-
training-costly/642844002/

Uncomfortable, but Necessary

Connecting Racial History to Racial Injustice in Corporate Structures

When people on management teams plan and strategize to provide a good or service, they discuss expectations for the future while also examining the lessons of the past. They want to understand what led up to the present moment in the marketplace or how they built a certain reputation in a specific region or within the industry. They talk about what the marketplace expects of the brand and how they can improve marketplace engagement.

Unfortunately, when examining the relationships among groups of people who make up their organizations, they often don't take that same analytical approach. They don't, for example, probe past injustices to learn what went wrong and how they might create more equitable outcomes today. They don't explore what led to the massive levels of distrust within certain demographics toward corporate culture. In particular, an honest investigation into the history of "working-while-Black" makes corporate America deeply uncomfortable. That discomfort has stalled awareness of the perspectives of people of color in general—and Black people in particular—when it comes to their histories in the workplace. It has also stalled progress toward equality.

The discomfort is understandable but unproductive, because these explorations are valuable to understanding our perceptions of each other in the workplace, as well as how we choose to validate our experiences and contributions, especially those of people of color. Clear and honest views into the past are needed to solve the present tensions between people of color and the corporations they work for. Truth is, Black people have a lot of reason to be skeptical of corporate culture.

I recall a point earlier in my career when I thought I was being "managed," when in fact I was being managed out of the firm. A manager who'd been with the company for decades, but who just took over as my manager, shared with me that he had gone to other stakeholders to collect information on me *specifically* to get their thoughts on where I was not delivering. There was no context. There were no examples to back up stakeholder comments. There was no opportunity for me to be part of those meetings. There was the fact that I was the only Black on the team. There was the fact that I experienced continuous isolation. There was the fact that the scenario boiled down to the word of one White male senior manager to another White male senior manager, who shared a long, positive relationship with each other. His ambition was to hand me a pink slip, and longevity of tenure was on his side. His efforts were thwarted when he was only able to find one stakeholder out of a dozen willing to support his efforts. That was still one too many as far as I was concerned, and it created a chasm between my manager and me. I was on my guard during each interaction with him, balancing self-preservation while trying to build a network of people I could trust within the business group.

What's the point of this story, you ask? Consider the amount of time he spent attempting to recruit people to damage my professional reputation. That time could have been spent on other efforts: developing new customer retention strategies, researching the marketplace for emerging opportunities, or analyzing revenue. Instead, this manager chose to spend his time contacting several leaders to inquire about my individual performance. In turn, I spent hours on the defensive. Hours I could have invested into training myself on a new skill or prospecting new customers. Instead, I reread each of my emails with microscopic precision. I reviewed every word I might utter ahead of any encounter with him to avoid his public analysis of whether *I* had chosen the right phrase. Once, in front of a group of about half a dozen customers, I introduced him as head of the group. He immediately corrected me saying "No. No. I *manage* Keesa and the whole team." Again, his public analysis was reserved for me alone.

This environment did not invite me to speak up with new ideas. He wasn't challenging my ideas, scrutinizing them, or asking for a clearer hypothesis. These were blatant, repeated attempts to shut me down before I even reached the idea share stage. It was nearly impossible for either of us to focus on peak productivity under these circumstances, creating a lose-lose situation.

Of course, that's just one anecdote. But I can say with a high degree of confidence that every person of color in the corporate workforce has not just one but multiple anecdotes that are similar and, oftentimes, worse. Ultimately it's not a question of any single person's subjective experience. The problem is much larger, and runs deeper, than the experiences of one.

This chapter examines the historical basis for the distrust that people of color, and particularly Black employees, often feel toward business and business leaders, including examples and concepts related to these issues:

- The Black American working experience
- Entrepreneurship
- People of color in leadership today
- Colorism infiltrates global corporate environments
- Corporate America's workplace racism, rooted in slavery

The Black American Working Experience

The entire history of working-while-Black offers example after example of why Black people continue to feel unwelcome in the workplace and/or skeptical of White management. From the beginning, the working world has been treacherous waters for Blacks specifically, who could experience oppression, violence, or even death for just trying to do their jobs. It can be tempting to wave away this history, declaring that the working world has changed—that, in particular, working-while-Black has changed. But the history of injustice in working-while-Black hasn't gone away. The reality is that distrust, abuse, and violence in the workplace is a part of a larger legacy. To deal with the present lack of compassion, equality, and inclusion at work, we must understand its origins. Knowledge of the past will help us steer toward a better future for business culture.

The first Americans to work-while-Black were of course the enslaved people kidnapped from their homes in Africa and brought to our shores under some of the most horrific conditions imaginable. But the end of slavery did not mean the end of the exploitation of Black labor. As noted by W.E.B. DuBois, "the slave went free; stood a brief moment in the sun; then moved back again toward slavery." Violence toward and exploitation of the Black labor force dates back to the 19th century. It began as soon as the slaves were set free and benefited the overall national economy. When the 13th Amendment to the US Constitution was ratified, it said there should be no slavery and involuntary servitude, *except as a punishment for those convicted of a crime*. In the South, an economy devastated by civil war, some White citizens responded by adopting forced labor as punishment for petty crimes or crimes that were vague and subjective. This was an early example of how some in power redefined the law to benefit themselves, demonstrating egregious ethical conduct. Further, some states and entities subjugated Blacks

34

through intimidation and the use of disposable labor: as many as 200,000 Black Americans were forced into back-breaking work in factories and mines, living in subhuman conditions, starved, beaten, flogged, and sexually violated. They died by the thousands.[1]

The Black Codes, established during the Reconstruction era, involved granting Blacks certain freedoms such as buying and owning property, marrying, and making contracts and court testimonies (involving other Blacks only). But the central aim was to restrict Black labor. Penalties for breaking labor contracts included arrest, beatings, and forced labor. All-White police and state militia forces throughout the South doled out these harsh punishments.

The Black Codes exemplify the dangers of working-while-Black, or even attempting to do so, dating back to the late 19th century. In essence, these systems were created to reinstitutionalize freed people and the newly established Black workforce under the auspices of incarceration. The Black Codes give context into just how difficult it was for Blacks to enter the official paid workforce, even after emancipation from slavery. In Chapter 1, we talked about how White workers in the steel industry faced dangerous workplace conditions. But Black workers in the South dealt with an even more sinister reality.

Even after slavery Black workers had to figure out how to best advocate for themselves, because it wasn't clear that their work and their labor power would be respected or valued. Even the most basic idea of getting the wages that you earned at the end of the day was something that Black workers always had to worry about. All of those concerns have created a

(continues)

Uncomfortable, but Necessary

legacy about anecdotes about unfair wage practices and racism. All these have required Black people to be really vigilant in the workplace.

—*Dr. Marcia Chatelain, associate professor, Department of History, American Studies Program at Georgetown University, and author of* Franchise: The Golden Arches in Black America[2]

Suspicion Well-Earned: The Freedman's Savings and Trust

These examples help explain the distrust people of color often feel toward their employers. But we can also look through the lens of consumers and investors—and, here again, people of color often feel suspicious of White corporate systems. That mistrust is well-earned, rooted in devastating events. Freedman's Savings and Trust Company provides a perfect example.

After slavery ended, the US government determined that former slaves needed to participate fully in workforce activities. They wanted this to go beyond basic food and shelter to include access to financial services as well.

On March 3, 1865, Congress established Freedman's Savings and Trust Company with the purpose of helping Blacks understand and leverage the financial services system. The company also focused on hiring and training Blacks to work there. The rationale for the bank was clear: large numbers of Black men had been on the payroll of the Union Army, and paid labor needs a means to see returns and access capital.

Over the years, Freedman's grew. Deposit amounts were small, generally from $5 to $50, but added up to millions as deposits poured in from thousands of Blacks eager to establish financial services access. During its existence, Freedman's Savings and Trust Company had 37 branches and more than 70,000 depositors and $57 million in deposits (adjusted for inflation).[3]

Along with a beautiful headquarters in Lafayette Square in Washington, DC, dozens of branches began popping up around the country. Then the problems began. Some were unforeseen, such as the Panic of 1873, which caused yields on government securities to sharply decrease, thus reducing the return. The panic affected the entire economy and can't be laid at the feet of Freedman's.

But the same can't be said for the bank's poor management. Freedman's didn't operate with the same rigorous oversight and risk controls that exist in banking systems today. Questions about the prudence of sinking $200,000 into a building on Lafayette Street went unasked. Then, there was the revelation that a Freedman's board member, a White man named Henry Cooke, was siphoning funds from the bank to his own enterprise. The US Government saw the bank was headed downhill, with all this hard-earned money from former slaves riding shotgun.

Efforts to bring in Frederick Douglass to oversee the bank were too late. A post-reconstruction political environment and poor oversight took its toll. The bank remained operational until 1874. More than 61,000 depositors lost over $3 million. Little was recouped.[4]

The creation of the Freedman's Savings and Trust Company in 1865 shows Blacks leveraging their wages to participate in the capital-building structure, as well as their trust in that financial corporate structure. Both their finances and their trust were exploited.

(continues)

(continued)

Caitlin Rosenthal is an assistant professor of history at UC Berkeley and the author of *Accounting for Slavery: Masters and Management,* which is a history of slaveholders' business practices. Using Freedman's as an example, she talks about the impact of distrust in the workplace between underrepresented people and mainstream cultures:

> For Black capitalism to make a difference the capital actually has to be held by Black Americans. They have to be the owners and to be in these positions of power. If you can create a structure where the ownership of the capital and the control over the capital is in the community then I think that that's really powerful.[5]

Unions and Black Workers: Friend or Foe?

Given the importance of labor unions to employee-employer relationships—including expectations about productivity, protection, and pay—unions have long been a part of the Black employees' path to higher levels of inclusion, equality, and decent pay. But the path to equality has been a rocky one. To consider just one example, White employees of the Georgia Railroad went on strike in 1909, demanding that Black employees, who were paid less, be replaced with White workers who would, solely based on race, be paid more. When the strike eventually ended up in federal arbitration, the White union lost. Why? Because it was decided that paying Blacks equal to Whites would undermine the entire purpose of hiring Black workers in the first place. It's worth noting that the union in this case, the Brotherhood of Locomotive Firemen and Enginemen, was not only a White-only union but also acted consciously to the detriment of Black workers.

This is far from the only time that "diversity" in the workplace has been used to set one group of workers against another. Caitlin Rosenthal, assistant professor at University of California at Berkeley and author of *Accounting for Slavery: Masters and Management,* put it in stark terms:

> Railroad managers and owners made [the case] for diversity [in hiring], but the business case they made was that having a diverse workforce would allow them to divide workers against each other and have more control over them. They said, "oh, we need to hire people with different racial backgrounds, but we're going to use that as a strategic advantage to prevent them from unionizing." So there are people who've made business cases for diversity before, and they aren't always ones that we would feel good about now.[6]

Time and again, workers of color have discovered that diversity efforts are not always what they seem on the surface. History offers countless examples of this phenomenon. A 1907 report indicated that Black workers faced prejudice in trade unions and were permitted to work only where Blacks were highly concentrated so not to threaten White workers.[7] The point is, the unions that helped protect the mental, physical, and financial well-being of workers didn't cover Blacks.

The Black Experience in Agriculture

The union-dominated industrial jobs were not the only ones available to Blacks. As a matter of fact, national farm statistics show that the opportunities for economic mobility among Blacks were actually to be found in agriculture, a trend that peaked in the 1920s. At the time, there were almost 1 million Black farmers. (Today that number is down to only 1.3% or about 45,000 of the 3.4 million total farmers, of which 95% are White.[8]) As the financial obstacles of the Great Depression took their toll on the farming industry, the New Deal legislation passed to assist White agricultural workers was not extended to Black ones. As James Gilbert Cassedy notes:

> Protective labor legislation of the 1930s, such as the Social Security Act, the National Labor Relations Act, and the Fair Labor Standards Act, did not extend to agricultural workers, although 31.8 percent of the African American population in 1940 was employed in agriculture (40.4 percent in the South).[9]

In addition, working in agriculture had its own set of challenges. Blacks who were able to save enough money to buy land had to first find a White landowner willing to sell to them.[10] Once they purchased or settled, White merchants sold them tools and goods needed to tend to the land and produce crops. Business fairness and ethics weren't legislated in this environment, so merchants were able to vary the prices and premiums they charged. Some agriculture unions weren't as prevalent or well organized as other unions but, even with the agriculture unions, Black farm workers who stood up against unfair commerce practices by White merchants often paid with their lives.

Moreover, from the New Deal through the early 1960s, federal subsidies allocated for farmers sometimes didn't make it to Black agricultural workers because of "local politics." The inequities of not receiving the same subsidies as their White counterparts reduced their ability to keep their farming profitable and put them at an economic and professional disadvantage to their peers.[11]

In September 30, 1919, Black sharecropper families gathered near Elaine, Arkansas, to discuss membership in the Progressive Farmers and Household Union, a union of African American tenant farmers and sharecroppers, for the purpose of getting a fair price for their cotton and helping them buy land. Late in the evening White men shot into the church where the meeting was taking place. Days later, Whites who opposed Black farmers' efforts invaded Elaine, resulting in the slaughter of many Black men, women, and children.[12]

Not being afforded the same rights, pay, and protections as White colleagues was a reality whether you were on the railroad, in the factory, or tilling fields. When people say "systemic racism," these examples show what they mean. For generations, in all economic sectors, people of color have experienced unethical treatment, unfair pay, and harassment. This costs not only workers but also their employers. Society at large suffers when Black workers are denied full participation in the economy-strengthening gross domestic product (GDP) and participation in capital markets.

Violence and Terror as a Barrier to Entry into the Marketplace

Black business leaders were savvy when wielding power in the capital structure. Throughout the late 19th and early 20th centuries, several Black business leaders and their employees enjoyed equitable work environments and the ability to achieve greater social purpose, too. This didn't work out as well for others. Some business leaders, who sought to have their own enterprise and share the marketplace with White, established business, did so while paying the price in terms of brutality, violence, destruction of their business, and even death.

In 1892, a mixed-race neighborhood in Memphis was the home of two grocery stores. People's Grocery was a Black-owned store that enjoyed significant success. The other grocery was owned by William Barrett, a White store owner.[13] What happened between

41

these two establishments offers a perfect example of what happens when racism exists in a marketplace where violence is an acceptable solution.

Allegedly, a quarrel between White and Black children playing a game near People's Grocery escalated into a quarrel between adults, including workers from the People's Grocery. After the dispute, the White men involved allegedly threated to return to the store later on Saturday. Sensing *return* was code for confrontation, People's Grocery shopkeepers went to the store Saturday night and armed themselves in preparation for a confrontation. After the men came into the grocery store, People's Grocery shopkeepers shot and wounded them.

After the confrontation and subsequent shooting, the three Black storekeepers, Thomas Moss, Calvin McDowell, and Will Stewart and several Black men were "dragged from their home and jailed." A mob broke into the jail and zeroed in on Moss, McDowell, and Stewart. Each of the three People's Grocery store owners were then shot and killed.[14]

Research by Ida B. Wells highlights the assumption that when White-run businesses felt threatened by Black-run businesses, they resorted to violence to eliminate the competition.[15]

Another example is the case of the Tulsa Massacre of 1921, home to Tulsa, Oklahoma's Black Wall Street. Violence ensued, after what was later determined to be a false accusation against a Black youth, and White members of the community destroyed the Black Wall Street section of town. More than 1,200 homes were burned and hundreds more were looted. The community lost stores, churches, a school, a library, the hospital, two newspapers, and much more.

Healthy markets expand and grow. Racism in business in all its vile forms, from violence and brutality to intimidation and passive aggressive behaviors, is unhealthy, uncivil, and unethical. These examples demonstrate how racist attitudes and actions may start in public spaces, but they slither their way into business environments. Racist behavior that is tolerated by social culture, eventually diffuses into business culture. Although some of these behaviors and actions may be illegal and unethical, business leaders can still create and maintain discriminatory and violent cultures while operating completely within the parameters of what is acceptable. This is the origin of the systemic racism, or racism that is ingrained in the culture, that people of color experience in corporate culture today.

There are historical moments of positivity that we can look to for inspiration for compassion and inclusion and the bottom-line benefits that follow. Many center on Black entrepreneurship.

Entrepreneurship

One way people of color have maneuvered out of uncompassionate, biased workplaces to create inclusive and equal corporate experiences is through entrepreneurship. Even during some of the most brutal years in the history of Blacks in business there were success stories. Many people are familiar with the story of Madame C. J. Walker, recorded as the first woman self-made millionaire, but there are other examples of Black titans of industry operating to contribute to the community, while also opening up new markets and generating revenues for their firms.

In 1898, North Carolina Mutual Insurance Company began with a response to a pressing market need. As mentioned, when people of color acted in their capacity as consumers (not just employees) they were historically met with exclusion and many times didn't receive the same level of service Whites received. When Blacks needed to bury their dead or provide for survivors, they counted on private organizations, societies, and churches.[16]

Providing life insurance for the Black community was a case of compassion combined with service to an underserved market. Compassion plus capitalizing on high levels of quality service to underserved communities was a clear way to dominate the market that mainstream organizations left wide open. This is a good lesson for today. When corporations see veiled discriminatory practices, refusal to serve, or giving poor, lackluster service to a community or demographic, savvy leaders must analyze it as a potential market opportunity instead of falling in line with what's acceptable by the majority.

This is what North Carolina Mutual did. One of its founders, John Merrick, leveraged what we in the 21st century describe as "soft skills" such as compassion and relationship building to create several successful businesses and workplaces.[17]

John Merrick began his career as a barber and brick mason. Parlaying his technical skills and his ability to befriend his clientele, Merrick moved from a partnership in a barbershop to ownership of several barbershops to founding one of the largest Black businesses of its time. But ultimately Merrick's fortune was not made with bricks or haircuts but with insurance. Professor Douglas Bristol of the University of Southern Mississippi explains:

> John Merrick's mutual life insurance company started out of his compassion, because there were people who had some misfortune happen. Members of the Black community would come in and ask for donations. And so he thought of a more dignified way to do that. At first, he started a mutual aid society, where people pay dues to get benefits. And then when there was a movement to regulate these mutual aid companies he started the North Carolina Mutual Life company, and took a big risk with his money. At that point, he had to just front the money so there

had to be a minimum bond posted at the state insurance commissioner. At that point, they weren't making money. But he did it anyway.[18]

By 1920 Merrick's firm grew to be the largest Black-owned company in the world. It had more than 1,000 employees, was earning nearly $2 million, and held about $30 million in assets, which translates to about $350 million in modern dollars.[19] The company was located in the Parrish Street area of Durham, North Carolina. Durham was one of several thriving communities of color in the United States—which were also sometimes known as Black Wall Streets—where Black owners, employees, and consumers enjoyed fair and equitable services, wages, treatment, and prices.

Compassionate leaders of the time were also able to ensure their suppliers practiced diversity (back before the phrase *supply chain diversity* was even in the lexicon). One example was A. G. Gaston, who had enterprises ranging from Birmingham's first Black-owned financial institution, an insurance firm, as well as the A. G. Gaston Motel.[20]

Gaston's brand of compassion included a fearlessness and focus on making sure there was equality within the full business structure, including vendors, not just consumers, employees, and owners. Suzanne Smith, associate professor of history and art history at George Mason University, offers some thoughts on the significance of Gaston:

> A. G. Gaston: he's really a corporate kind of guy, and the way in which he navigates his power as a businessman and the rising civil rights movement is utterly fascinating to me. He's able to both appease the White business community in Birmingham while also letting Martin Luther King Jr. stay at his motel; he just really is sophisticated in how he uses his power. And he uses this economic power to kind of fight

45

Uncomfortable, but Necessary

in the movement in all of these fascinating ways. He got criticized by White people who thought he was being too supportive of the Black movement and then Black Power people thought he wasn't doing enough.

He was so ahead of his time, and he had such a vision. He was able early on, I think, to figure out how to use that economic power. He put pressure on car dealerships in Alabama. He's buying all his hearses from these car dealerships, but then they're not hiring Black people to work in it to sell cars. So he goes to the White car dealership and he says, "I'm not going to keep buying my hearses from you unless you hire Black people as salespeople," and he pushes integration into this car dealership because they needed his money. He bought a lot of cars every year. He bought a lot of hearses and he knew he could do that.[21]

Despite multiple tiers of complexities in being Black-owned businesses, compassionate service to and knowledge of their markets led to successful and profitable enterprises. This focus on genuinely serving consumers, employees, and suppliers is now in vogue. Business leaders need to be on notice. We're moving away from—as Michelle Obama told the 2020 Democratic National Convention—a "greed is good and winning is everything because as long as you come out on top nothing else matters," mentality into a culture of prioritizing the good of the whole business, including those inside the business. We're moving, slowly yet vehemently, toward a business culture in which prioritizing people inside the company and ensuring inclusivity across all levels of the business *is* winning.

Black workers remain skeptical when businesses don't readily adopt this culture. We have proof positive that skepticism is well-founded when looking at the numbers of Blacks and other people of color making up leadership positions at firms.

Corporations Compassion Culture

Scholar Doug Bristol of the University of Southern Mississippi explains how competition between Black entrepreneurs was carried out in a healthy way:

> In the 19th century Black barbers had what were called first-class shops. John Merrick [Durham] and Alonzo Herndon had a shop on Peachtree Street where they employed 20 barbers. I mean, there were only two other barbers operating on that scale. They beat their competition just by offering services and a number of employees that nobody could meet because these were palatial accommodations. They had bathhouses, you'd get a massage, people shaving your face while you're sitting in the chair; they competed with services.[22]

People of Color in Leadership Today

The 2018 Board Diversity Census of Women and Minorities on Fortune 500 Boards, issued by Harvard Law School in February 2019, noted a critical need for inclusivity in C-suite leadership and company boardrooms. People of color in corporate America are still largely invisible. According to the report, only 16.1% of board seats in the Fortune 500 are held by people of color.[23] See Table 2.1.

Furthermore, the wage gap between White senior-level executives and other groups is significant. On average, Black men earned 87 cents to every dollar earned by a White man in 2019; Black, Latinx, and Native American women earned 75 cents for every dollar; and Asian women earned 93 cents.[24] Hispanic men earned 91 cents for every dollar earned by White men and White women earn 81 cents for the White man's dollar. Interestingly, Asian men earned $1.15 for every dollar earned by a White male in 2019.[25]

Table 2.1 Breakdown of Fortune 500 Total Board Seats by Race/Ethnicity: 2018

Race/Ethnicity	Percentage of Fortune	500 Board Seats
Caucasian/ White	83.9	83.9
Black	8.6	16.1
Latinx	3.8	
Asian/ Pacific Islander	3.7	
Other	0.1	

Source: Data from DeHaas, D. (2019) Missing Pieces Report: The 2018 Board Diversity Census of Women and Minorities on Fortune 500 Boards, The President and Fellows of Harvard College (February 5, 2019).

The lack of diversity at the senior level creates an environment in which people of color must deal with mental gymnastics not required of their White peers at work. They are not represented, they are paid substantially less than their colleagues, and they often feel that managers don't even put forth an effort to understand their points of view. If you think about what it's like to deal with these inequities, combined with such psychological mistreatment as being isolated by colleagues or having your insights and contributions to meetings ignored, it's obvious how an employee's sales and production numbers can be negatively affected.

Looking at the data makes it clear that a compassionate culture where leadership and employees actively promote inclusion is necessary for a firm to keep pace and lead in the new evolving global corporate era. Compassionate culture today is a necessity, not a luxury.

Colorism Infiltrates Global Corporate Environments

In the United States, we're dealing with the remnants of centuries of slavery, resulting in systems designed to oppress people of color socially and economically. Fruits of that system continue to thrive today. For starters, let's take the stratification of races based on a color hierarchy and differential treatment based on skin color. Known as *colorism,* this prejudicial or preferential treatment of people occurs solely based on their skin color. And although the Black Codes and Jim Crow laws may be unique to the United States, colorism definitely is not. In Westernized societies well beyond the United States, color and colorism is intricately related to race and racism.[26] If there is a hierarchy, then darker-hued people fare worse than lighter-skinned people, regardless of their ethnicity. Where a person lands on the "Blackness" scale could determine social and economic standing. This is our backdrop for disproportionate bias, microaggressions, and racism filtering down to current corporate culture.

Taking this a step further, Blacks have often been set against other minority groups. Most notably, the *model minority* myth used to wedge a divide between Asian Americans and Blacks. The perceived high level of success among Asian Americans is used as a weapon to downplay racism and the struggles of other minority groups, especially Black Americans.[27] In other words, if "they" (who may be defined Asian or some other ethnic group) can be successful within a certain system, then the problem doesn't lie with a racist system but rather with the groups who are not as successful.

In her famous book, *The Color of Success,* historian Ellen Wu explores the model minority stereotype.[28] The stereotype is used to cherry-pick the prosperity of some professionally successful historic ethnic minorities. More nefariously, it is used to avoid taking responsibility and making changes toward racial progress in the United States. This continual racism increases the exclusion, lack of compassion, and immobility of Black Americans in the workplace.

Although all historically marginalized groups have unquestionably experienced discrimination and oppression, these experiences

49

Uncomfortable, but Necessary

can be completely different and unique. We can't have a view of corporate and business success that negates centuries of slavery and the economic loss experienced by Blacks in America.

What is the result of this lack of historical awareness? One impact has been the fact that people of color are tremendously underrepresented in senior roles. There is a sinister scale that weighs who may have it "worse" and why. A study by economist Nathaniel Hilger of Brown University indicates that upward mobility among Asian Americans from the 1970s was due less to the stereotype that Asians "take education more seriously" and more to the simple fact that their fellow Americans became less racist toward them.[29] This shift in public perception and image as nonthreatening, industrious, and law-abiding citizens who seldom complain provided a pathway up the professional ladder.

You can see the same phenomenon at work when the spectacular success of individual members of a minority group is, essentially, weaponized against the group as a whole. Most obviously: "Clearly the United States is not racist because Barack Obama was president for eight years." This laser-like focus on the individual—*so-and-so did it, so why can't you?*—is sometimes used as a smokescreen to disguise the many structural obstacles that stand in the way of Black Americans as a group. The idea that Black failure and grievance are *not* due to racism and structural inequities allows for a segment of White America, including sectors of the corporate world, to avoid the responsibility of addressing racism both inside and outside the workplace.[30]

Corporate America's Workplace Racism, Rooted in Slavery

Corporations hoping to understand parallels and patterns between historical dynamics for people of color at work then and now must take a critical look at conduct that may be legal but is still unacceptable. Although some of these behaviors are legal, none of them are *ethical*. This is where compassion comes into play. Just because something is legal, or even acceptable at one point in time, doesn't mean it's the right thing to do. When corporations and their employees create cultures that accept despicable and pedestrian conduct, despite its legality, it breeds mistrust in the organization specifically and in the institution of business in general.

Large numbers of Blacks and other people of color would likely agree that the words *compassion, equality,* and *inclusion* do not accurately reflect their historical or present working experiences. There are too many stories of being systemically shut out of C-suite corporate structures or having to master processes, knowledge, and people management with a humbleness and adroitness not required of their peers. Frustration kicks in when White managers and colleagues are oblivious, or claim to be oblivious, to the ways in which the corporate world is different for Black people.

And let's not forget, these cultural inequities have real-world economic consequences. Marcia Chatelain discusses the concept of *racial capitalism*. It can be summarized as a level of respect and value afforded people in business based on their race:

Racial capitalism shows ways that we think about how people are racialized. How their racial identities determine their possibilities in the world and determine the ways that they're treated.

So, when we're talking about racial capitalism, we're talking about ways that value or devalue is placed on specific people and their personhood. Racial capitalism has been a healthy way for people to understand the history of slavery and the continued abuse of African Americans even after the end of slavery.

51

Uncomfortable, but Necessary

It's also important in racial capitalism to understand how people are treated in other kinds of labor forces in which certain racial and ethnic groups tend to dominate and can also explain other types of exploitation. This includes when we look at Latinx people in agriculture even with certain types of women in domestic work. It helps us understand how value is assigned.[31]

Historically, Blacks laid the foundation for the wealth that successful business owners were able to enjoy in the early industrial days up until now, yet they were devalued at every turn. There were approximately 3 million enslaved people in the United States by the time slavery was abolished. These were not paid employees, and they were not willing volunteer workers. They were, what we call in modern days, forced labor.

These humans survived an ongoing intercontinental trafficking scheme that continued for centuries. Herded up and chained, they endured abhorrent overcrowding in the trafficking process, experienced humiliating physical and sanitary conditions, and suffered complete displacement from their culture and kin. They were not lavishly transported by patrons who sought to support their art or craft. They were not "immigrants" looking for "a land of dreams and opportunity," as was controversially claimed by Dr. Ben Carson in his first speech as Housing and Urban Development Secretary.[32] They were brutalized, maimed, and killed at owners' and supervisors' whims. There was no labor union to help them. There was no regulatory agency to protect them. Aside from emerging and established abolitionists, there were neither international relief organizations nor nongovernmental organizations (NGOs) pouring in massive amounts of money and volunteers to save them.

Although that may sound like ancient history to Whites, it's important to understand that many Black people don't view it that way at all. When I took my first job at a Wall Street firm, elder mentors from church and extended family cautioned me to be mindful that industry "doesn't care a thing about us." That observation sprang from a number of experiences that are all too common among people of color in the workplace. For example, the experience of training a series of (White) managers who were less qualified and yet, somehow, climbed the ladder significantly faster. The experience of seeing their ideas adopted by and credited to others. False assumptions about their intellect and education when they walked through the door. My elders wanted me to successfully avoid these pitfalls—or at least successfully navigate around them—while keeping my composure and compassion no matter the circumstance.

Unfair, unleveled business playing fields are a primary aspect of the old corporate culture that leaders must address. It is not enough to talk about them—what's needed is concrete action. If businesses want to benefit from top talent, these practices have got to go.

Right now you may be thinking, "Okay, sure. But how?" One step is to educate ourselves as corporate leaders about the history of how businesspeople have created heinous work conditions, exploited inequality, and ultimately benefitted long term from our lopsided system. Consider these observations author Ta-Nehisi Coates made in *The Atlantic:*

> By 1860, there were more millionaires (slaveholders all) living in the lower Mississippi Valley than anywhere else in the United States. In the same year, the nearly 4 million American slaves were worth some $3.5 billion, making them the largest single financial asset in the entire U.S. economy, worth more than all manufacturing and railroads combined.[33]

Those benefits still pay business dividends today. Although no monetary value can adequately compensate for historical abuses,

Blacks have yet to see any sort of reparations, be they social, economic, or professional. What's more, lack of pay parity, psychologically abusive discrimination, and large-scale exclusion from higher levels of the economic system are still taking place.

We are dealing with a different type of playing field in modern times; for instance, there is an entire body of law related to the physical protection to workers. However, it's difficult to legislate unethical, uncompassionate workplace behaviors, especially ones that don't yield physical damage. Today's behaviors attack employee psyche and often challenge their ability to work effectively and bring their most innovative selves due to equivocal tones and language used.

The common term for these subtler types of workplace abuses is *microaggressions*. Kevin Nadal, professor of psychology at John Jay College of Criminal Justice, describes the term this way: "Microaggressions are defined as the everyday, subtle, intentional—and oftentimes unintentional—interactions or behaviors that communicate some sort of bias toward historically marginalized groups. The difference between microaggressions and overt discrimination—or macroaggressions—is that people who commit microaggressions might not even be aware of them."[34]

A prevalent example is when underrepresented people are left out of relevant meetings or electronic communications or they aren't included on inside knowledge that other colleagues share at virtual watercoolers. These are all tactics that keep them ill-informed for key decision-making, resulting in poor positioning when it's time to discuss succession planning and promotion.

Following are other examples that destroy trust between colleagues and stoke hostility and distrust, all of which affect performance:

- Isolating a colleague or having unspoken agreements to not address and acknowledge that person inside and outside of meetings

- Ignoring her comments in meetings

- Talking over her in meetings

- Refusing to share critical information

- Refusing to include him in meetings critical to job functions

- Discrediting her feedback and performance, including doing so in front of peers and management

- Participating in misplaced conversation about physical attributes

- Making condescending remarks about origin or pronunciation of his name

Selfish, thoughtless behavior isn't solely the experience of people of color, of course. But these behaviors are used successfully and pervasively to create an uncomfortable, sometimes toxic environment for people of color. Further, when microaggressions go unchecked, they are an opportunity to circumvent protections against workplace racism.

When aggressors are called on the carpet for their behavior, a common response is to say, "It was just a little joke." Or that the person of color is being "too sensitive." If people of color challenge low performance ratings with clear evidence of outperforming consistently, an intimidating response meant to shut the employee down is "I can get someone very senior (translation = old friend) to back me up."

The phrase "bring your whole self to work" was a recent, popular statement encouraging people of different backgrounds to not wear "the mask" that Paul Lawrence Dunbar wrote about in the poem *We Wear the Mask*.[35] Workers were asked to be open, vulnerable, and completely untethered to past unspoken rules concerning assimilating within mostly White corporate environments.

55

Uncomfortable, but Necessary

The "bring your whole self to work" era brought neither decreased microaggressions nor increased numbers of people of color to the C-suite and pay parity with White colleagues. Undercutting Blacks' ability to thrive professionally, and using microaggression and intimidation, has been a part of our corporate business culture for decades. This has continued, whether we wear the mask or not. And, as I discussed at the beginning of the chapter, every microaggression—every false allegation about performance, every moment of isolation in a meeting, every condescending comment—comes at the cost of worker confidence, productivity, and even the bottom line.

A 2020 report by McKinsey on 17 leading companies demonstrated a significant correlation between a diverse leadership team and financial performance.[36] Leadership representation matters. Increased revenue is generated in these spaces that are diverse at the executive level. In particular, companies that were in the top tier for cultural and ethnic diversity on their executive teams were 33% more likely to have industry-leading profitability. We can add compassion to that metric to ensure that diverse candidates who are recruited are also retained, in part because of a welcoming culture, in the corporate workplace.

Interestingly, many times people of color who experience workplace injustices tend to either overlook them or work through a mental assumption that their race or ethnicity has nothing to do with what may just be a personality difference.

Idris lives in the United Kingdom and describes himself as Afro-Caribbean. His career as a marketing executive for banking firms has spanned nearly two decades. "I'm the first person who really wouldn't use my color in this way. Just speaking to some of my Black friends who are outside the industry, who've looked at my career who have looked at my skill set. My friends keep telling me, you know, if you were this [race], trust me, you would not have these situations. In this case, I believe them."

The grave mistrust Blacks have pertaining to workplace treatment and corporate establishment may have begun with how their ancestors were treated as forced laborers, but it didn't end there. Throughout the 19th and 20th centuries, we can find examples of White-led terror and violence against Black workers and their entrepreneurial endeavors. Today, dealing with the mental impact of workplace microaggression, while simultaneously processing ongoing physical violence against Black and Latinx people in public spaces, continues to take a toll. This sets a backdrop for current racial justice demands in the workplace and beyond. In other words, the pursuit of racial justice is not separate from the compassionate workplace—it is a vital component.

Perhaps most disturbing is the fact that unethical behavior, exclusion, and inequality at work have a long and sordid history—a history that employers don't acknowledge and make no attempt to correct. The fact that we're still fighting for racial justice well into the 21st century confirms those behaviors are still alive and well. To see the link between historic injustices and today's injustices, simply replace discriminatory treatment, lack of pay, and workplace abuse from the past with today's discriminatory treatment, pay inequity, and unchecked microaggressions, and we find a connection. Racial discrimination just takes a different form in the 21st century than it did in the 19th or even 20th centuries.

This is not comfortable work, but it is necessary work. We must acknowledge and learn from history to rectify the present, and then we can build a new workplace culture in which people of color drive innovation, achieve C-suite positions, receive fair pay, and drive revenues without being encumbered by systemic racism.

Chapter 2 Takeaways

- Historical events have sown seeds of distrust. Business communities in partnership with employees, vendors, and consumers should educate themselves on this history as a step toward solving present-day issues in the workplace.

- For corporations and their leaders to successfully solve issues of racial inequities at work, understanding the history of people of color and work is critical. One way to do this is through a lens of how people of color were treated, valued, and devalued historically.

- Distrust by Blacks and other people of color toward old business culture is justifiable, given experiences as employees, vendors, owners, and consumers.

- Microaggressions in the workplace are real, even if they are sometimes unintentional. They are not conducive to high productivity, because they have a potential impact to hinder someone's focus, decrease their productivity, and lay seeds of a hostile work environment.

- Just because conduct is legal or acceptable doesn't mean it's the right thing to do. This is where a clear dedication to compassionate leadership was missing in the broader culture. Clarity on compassion resolves confusion about tolerating behaviors that are acceptable by society but are unethical, unequal, and hurtful physically or economically. Lead with compassion and the right thing to do is clear.

References

1. https://www.usnews.com/news/national-news/articles/2017-02-07/exploiting-Black-labor-after-the-abolition-of-slavery

2. Interview with the author. Chatelain Marcia, Racial capitalism, July 13, 2020.
3. http://freedmansbank.org/
4. Ibid.; https://www.occ.treas.gov/about/who-we-are/history/1863-1865/1863-1865-freedmans-savings-bank.html
5. Interview with the author. Rosenthal Caitlin, Accounting for Slavery: Masters and Management, Department of History; July 16, 2020.
6. Ibid.
7. https://www.archives.gov/publications/prologue/1997/summer/american-labor-movement.html
8. https://www.nass.usda.gov/Publications/Highlights/2019/2017Census_Farm_Producers.pdf; https://www.theguardian.com/environment/2019/apr/29/why-have-americas-Black-farmers-disappeared
9. https://www.archives.gov/publications/prologue/1997/summer/american-labor-movement.html
10. Ibid.
11. https://www.theatlantic.com/magazine/archive/2019/09/this-land-was-our-land/594742/
12. https://www.nytimes.com/2019/09/30/opinion/elaine-massacre-1919-arkansas.html
13. https://lynchingsitesmem.org/lynching/peoples-grocery-lynchings-thomas-moss-will-stewart-calvin-mcdowell
14. http://historic-memphis.com/biographies/peoples-grocery/peoples-grocery.html
15. https://www.history.com/news/ida-b-wells-lynching-memphis-chicago
16. https://www.scalawagmagazine.org/2019/07/Black-wall-street/
17. https://www.investors.com/news/management/leaders-and-success/john-merrick-went-from-slavery-to-riches/
18. Interview with the author. Bristol Douglas, John Merrick's mutual life insurance company started out of his compassion, because there were people who had some misfortune happen, July 6, 2020.
19. https://www.investors.com/news/management/leaders-and-success/john-merrick-went-from-slavery-to-riches/
20. https://savingplaces.org/places/a-g-gaston-motel#.Xz1kEm5KjIU
21. Interview with the author. Smith Suzanne, Thoughts on the significance of Gaston, July 6, 2020.
22. Interview with the author. Bristol Douglas, How competition between Black entrepreneurs can be carried out in a healthy way, July 6, 2020.
23. https://corpgov.law.harvard.edu/2019/02/05/missing-pieces-report-the-2018-board-diversity-census-of-women-and-minorities-on-fortune-500-boards/
24. https://www.payscale.com/data/gender-pay-gap
25. https://www.payscale.com/career-news/2019/04/the-gender-pay-gap-has-closed-5-cents-since-2015-but-dont-celebrate-yet; https://www.payscale.com/

data/racial-wage-gap-for-men; https://www.nationalpartnership.org/our-work/resources/economic-justice/fair-pay/quantifying-americas-gender-wage-gap.pdf; https://www.payscale.com/data/gender-pay-gap

26. https://www.annualreviews.org/doi/abs/10.1146/annurev-soc-060116-053315
27. https://www.npr.org/sections/codeswitch/2017/04/19/524571669/model-minority-myth-again-used-as-a-racial-wedge-between-asians-and-Blacks
28. https://www.oregonlive.com/opinion/2016/12/the_real_reasons_the_us_became.html
29. Ibid.
30. https://www.npr.org/sections/codeswitch/2017/04/19/524571669/model-minority-myth-again-used-as-a-racial-wedge-between-asians-and-Blacks
31. Interview with the author. Chatelain Marcia, Racial capitalism, May 13, 2020.
32. https://apnews.com/60ee1b62df4f41a4a1af0a3749e90370/Ben-Carson-compares-slavery-to-immigration-to-America
33. https://www.theatlantic.com/business/archive/2014/06/slavery-made-america/373288/
34. https://www.npr.org/2020/06/08/872371063/microaggressions-are-a-big-deal-how-to-talk-them-out-and-when-to-walk-away
35. https://www.poetryfoundation.org/poems/44203/we-wear-the-mask
36. https://www.mckinsey.com/~/media/mckinsey/business%20functions/organization/our%20insights/delivering%20through%20diversity/delivering-through-diversity_full-report.ashx

Women's Corporate Leadership
Past Perceptions and Current Realities

I was in middle school in Chattanooga, Tennessee, when I first read that Oprah Winfrey had attended Tennessee State University. As soon as I saw this, I lost it! In my sixth-grade mind, I saw Oprah riding along the same streets I did when my family and I would travel from Chattanooga to Nashville. She walked the same sidewalks, maybe even ate at the same Nashville restaurants as I did! This had real meaning for me. At the time, I wanted to be a journalist. I had just started doing public service announcement commercials, but Oprah-esque status was the ultimate goal. Each commercial I worked on brought me one step closer. Back then, I had no idea the number of obstacles that faced her or that would face me in my career. All I knew was that every day at 4 pm EST, I could see Oprah. And in her, I saw my own possibilities. She was Black, like me. She was female, like me. She had lived in Tennessee, like me. Seeing her career was like seeing my own future projected and playing out right in front of me.

As it turned out, I did not become an Oprah-esque journalist. Instead, I became an executive in financial data leading million-dollar campaigns, strategizing successful customer engagement programs, analyzing data to mitigate risks, communicating capital markets' shifts, and empowering brands to connect with their communities. In taking on these tasks, I still spend a lot of time thinking about role models and the significance of representation—not just representation in the form of numbers and charts, but representation that can truly be *seen*. Data and analysis tell us that the visual representation of female role models helps support gender parity in corporate sectors. There's a theory called the role model effect, which states that the more we see women in senior roles in corporations, the more girls and women will aspire to those roles and take action needed in attaining them.[1] The fact is, the role model effect is an influencing factor with many people who are underrepresented. My own story, of seeing Oprah in all her intersectionality succeed in journalism, represents this. So, too, does the tale of young Jacob Philadelphia, who wanted to see if he really shared the same hairstyle as President Obama, and had his wish to touch President Obama's hair granted in a viral moment.[2] There was Tulane law student Ariel Campos, who went to law school because of seeing Supreme Court Justice Sonia Sotomayor, and then had the opportunity to introduce Justice Sotomayor during Tulane's Presidential Speaker Series.[3] Today, girls and women who witnessed Kamala Harris become the first woman vice president of the United States bask in the possibilities for their own careers.

Seeing examples of those who've accomplished goals before you provides a critical step toward acquiring the confidence we all need to lead. When you can see it, you can become it. But even with the role models we currently see, there are still too few women in leadership roles.

Contributing to this lack of progress is women's slow entry into important emerging sectors, such as technology, in larger numbers. These newer sectors tend to be higher paid, with greater demand for young workers, than some traditional jobs. A World Economic Forum 2020 survey lays out the sobering workplace trend.

Positively, the so-called role model effect may be reaping dividends in terms of leadership and wages. Improving political empowerment for women has, as a general rule, corresponded with increased numbers of women in senior roles in the labor market.

In contrast to this positive progress in the lofty world of leadership, women's participation in the wider labor market has stalled and financial disparities are increasing. Globally, the trend is towards a deteriorating picture in emerging and developing economies, which is offsetting the gains made in OECD countries.[4]

The report highlights three primary reasons for this: women have greater representation in jobs that are being automated, not enough women are entering professions where wage growth is the most pronounced (most obviously, but not exclusively, technology), and women face the perennial problem of lack of support, because little value is placed on caring for children, elderly, and the domestic sphere, as well as having very little access to financial capital.[5]

This demonstrates what those of us in business already know: societal norms cascade down into business cultures that impede and disrupt women's success in business. We can't blame pipeline issues. We can't blame lack of talent. We can't even blame lack of mentorship. Goodness knows many women have been prepped, prodded, and mentored ad nauseum for the purpose of getting them ready for a promotion that, sadly, never arrives. Business culture, which includes outdated definitions of what leadership looks and acts like, is squarely to blame. Businesses can't fix this until they understand how a history of bias toward male leadership pervaded our corporate culture and still influences who becomes a leader and who is not considered leadership material.

This chapter considers the historical basis behind the lack of female advancement and equity within the corporate working environment. It will discuss examples relating to these issues:

- Women, work, and value
- The lessons of history: Maggie Lena Walker and St. Luke Penny Savings Bank
- World War II and the Transformation of Work Culture for Women
- Housewife as businesswoman: The 1950s and 1960s
- Women and wages: Growing disparities
- Racial and gender discrimination in the workplace
- Intersectionality: The experience of women of color in the corporate workplace
- Compassion and empathy: Improving the workplace for women

Women, Work, and Value

To be considered as a leader, your skills must first be considered valuable. *You* must be considered valuable. Historically, we have not seen myriad types of work that women perform—not to mention the skills that women acquire to perform it—as being particularly valuable. This is partly because domestic labor has not been thought about as true "work" until fairly recently. Another reason has to do with the way our history is narrated: there is so much focus on men in workplaces during the industrial period that it's easy to assume women weren't there, too. But the truth is, women and men worked side-by-side in agricultural work that predates the shift to factories and mills that occurred in the 19th and 20th centuries. At this point in history, women's work domain was largely within the home. Homes weren't considered workplaces, so the work performed there wasn't considered real labor. But whether women continued working in agriculture and farming at their homes for no pay, or performing domestic work outside their own homes for very little pay, it was hard work and the rewards were few.

European women were also just as active as men in agriculture up until industrialization. Only the wealthiest of women didn't work in the fields. Women simultaneously cared for elders and children and tended the house, as well as sometimes holding outside domestic jobs, part-time jobs with inconsistent hours, or even off-the-books work that wasn't recorded. In effect, women faced the "double burden" of having two workloads, without any of the financial rewards.[6] Put all of these tasks on a scale opposite the men's daily grind, and the women's work just never measured up in the eyes of society.

In order for the work at the factories and mills to run smoothly, workers' home lives needed operational order and optimization. It is highly unlikely a man could carry out the physically intensive labor required at his outside job if women were not creating and maintaining domestic order at home. Nevertheless, lack of wages and even lack of respect for women's contributions during this period demonstrate how values did not align with seeing domestic work as equal to the labor performed by men.

The experiences of women of color in the early 20th century reflect an even more intense reality of devaluing their skills and demeaning their personhood. Black women's labor market participation outpaced women of other races because they had always been seen as workers first (before being wives and mothers) as an aftereffect of forced positions during slavery. Also, since Black men's work situations were so unpredictable due to discriminatory practices, Black women's income has historically been mandatory to keep Black families afloat.[7]

Shennette Garrett-Scott is associate professor of history and African American studies at University of Mississippi. Here she discusses the plight of women of color in the late 19th-century workplace.

Women, especially African American women, Latinx women, and immigrant women, were confined largely to low-paying domestic work. They were given the most dangerous work in factories and in industry and then, of course, low pay, backbreaking agricultural work. These women were susceptible to this kind of work, and people used this as an excuse not to treat them as women or to give them the same rights as other women because the work they did was not considered feminine. It wasn't considered the kind of work that a genteel kind of woman would do because they got dirty, etc. So, they were laboring under that kind of discrimination, but they also were really subject to racial sexual violence.

Women who were working in the homes were subjected to harassment, rape, also brutality of [the] men and women [they were working for]: being beaten, verbally abused, and also economic exploitation. These people could withhold your salary saying that you were sick or that they didn't like your work, so not only were you not paid very well, but they found ways even to squeeze these kinds of workers for even more, to extract more value from them.[8]

Low pay, low value, and employers' sometimes brutal behaviors toward the women they employed created a clear caste distinction between working women and the people who employed them. Working women were considered second-class citizens in the workplace.

The Lessons of History: Maggie Lena Walker and St. Luke Penny Savings Bank

Pay inequality, sexual exploitation, and harassment were all too common, but they weren't the only narratives that existed for women at work. There did exist, even in the early 1900s, strong, ethical business cultures that recognized a woman's worth, even in sectors dominated by men. One important example is Maggie Lena Walker, one of the earliest female bank founders, and the first Black woman bank founder. She opened St. Luke Penny Savings Bank in 1903 with $9,000; three years later, the bank held deposits of about $170,000.[9]

Walker's brand of compassion in business played out in a number of ways—first by hiring predominantly female staff and training them to support their ascension in banking and beyond. Maggie Lena's staff repaid her for creating this culture by helping her grow the business and the bank's deposits exponentially.

Shennette Garrett-Scott is the author of *Banking on Freedom: Black Women in U.S. Finance Before the New Deal*. Here, she explains the groundbreaking story of Maggie Lena Walker, who was the first Black woman to charter a bank.

Maggie Lena Walker helped to organize the St. Luke Penny Savings Bank, but she also ran the St. Luke

(continues)

(continued)

Insurance Association, this huge insurance corporation worth millions of dollars. She was keenly aware that in the early 20th century, African American women did not have even the same limited opportunities that White women enjoyed in white collar, clerical kinds of positions. So, as White women were fighting in their own ways to be taken seriously as businesswomen, Black women were stuck or pigeonholed in domestic service work and unskilled, low-paid agricultural work. The idea of a well-dressed office worker as a Black woman was something that most people didn't get to see, but for Walker that was really important. And so, the St. Luke Penny Savings Bank and the Independent Order of St. Luke Insurance Company was the largest employer of white collar, Black women workers in Richmond and I would argue in the country.

Walker understood the benefits of a mostly female workforce; that was one of the reasons why she encouraged education. St. Luke set up an educational fund, providing loans to women to continue their education, either a professional education—going to a business school to learn more about bookkeeping or accounting, for example—so that they could rise up in the ranks within the business. She also encouraged her women workers to invest, and to give charitably to schools and colleges.

The other thing she encouraged them to do was to save. She would encourage women workers to save their money so that they could buy homes and buy property. We think that she perhaps may have had them set aside a part of their earnings, and they had bank accounts at the bank, so when they saved a certain amount, that they had these easy loan terms that they could use to purchase their own homes. So, in that way, this kind of compassionate, very woman-centered thinking about Black women as workers contributed to the growth of women in the company, but also into the community.

And I would argue that what Walker teaches us today is that when you make that kind of investment in your employees, you realize greater productivity, a greater commitment, and longevity. Also I think that it does improve your bottom line overall, because in thinking about St. Luke, these women were instrumental in spreading the organization to more than 20 states, to revenues in excess of millions of dollars a year in 1920 dollars, which, of course, equals hundreds of millions of dollars in revenue and sales today.

Women-owned companies, such as Walker's St. Luke Penny Savings Bank, were known as places where women were treated equally in terms of hiring practices, pay, and training. These work environments provided a fairer playing field where women were appreciated for their expertise.

Women thrive on purposeful work, just like men do—and especially so in turbulent times when industry and country need their skills and strengths. World War II is a prime example of women quickly and dutifully giving their best in challenging circumstances. It also demonstrates how some corporations repaid their loyalty after the war was over.

World War II and the Transformation of Work Culture for Women

World War II transformed the United States for women as hundreds of thousands not only joined the war effort but entered the civilian workforce as well. But although the war sparked a major advance for women in the workplace, it's important to note that the war did not *create* working women. A great many women—as already noted, especially immigrants and women of color—were already in the workforce before the war began. The percentage of women in the US workforce increased from 27% to nearly 37%; by 1945, about one out of every four married women worked outside the home.[10]

The economic opportunities presented to women at this time were much better than they'd been before the war, but even in the Rosie the Riveter era, the wage gap still existed. In 1944, female workers were making an average of $31.21 per week compared to their male counterparts, who made $54.65 weekly. Meanwhile, many narratives we hear and images we see of women assisting war efforts are those of White women; Black women were excluded from advertisements for positions and faced racism in the workplace. One exception, interestingly enough, was in the government sector. The group of Black women who made up the 6888 Central Postal Directory Battalion ensured mail that had a two-year backlog made it to troops in Europe. From 1945 to 1946, they distributed mail from England to France, uplifting the sprit and morale of troops who longed to hear from families. They did their job while demonstrating a professionalism and comportment that contradicted stereotypes of both race and gender.[11]

Unfortunately, when the war ended, the Women's Bureau of the US Department of Labor did not have a plan for these women workers. As much as many women wanted to keep their jobs, most companies and factories at the time let their female workers go, only to replace them with (sometimes far less qualified) men.[12] Thanks to the war effort, these women had the necessary skills and experience to work in industries such as automotive and manufacturing plants. Yet they were treated with the same pre-1940s mentality that they faced before the war. Many women assumed the experience and seniority that they had gained during war time would be taken into account when the men returned, but in general this was not the case. After the war, many manufacturers opted to return to peacetime production and only men were called back. Unfair gender discrimination nationwide meant women who had years of seniority in car plants, as riveters and welders holding high-paying jobs, found themselves ineligible for similar positions.[13]

Consider the example of the Ford Motor Company, which laid off thousands of women to make room for the (largely inexperienced) men coming back from war.[14] During wartime, the company had employed women as one-fourth of its wartime labor force, mostly producing defense machinery including military vehicles. By 1946, only 4% of the company's employees, including those performing traditional "gender" roles such as clerks, were women.[15] Shortly after the war ended, so did the employment of a large percentage of these women. And lest you think that women went quietly and happily back to the kitchen, think again. At Ford's Highland Park plant, for example, female members of the United Auto Workers Local 400 labor union protested against the loss of jobs.[16]

For Black women, the situation was worse. The war period had been a key economic opportunity for Blacks, who benefitted from an expanding labor force and the Second Great Migration from the Deep South into cities where the jobs were. Despite this, Black women still

71

found fewer job opportunities than White women, and they faced more workplace discrimination. For example, a 1943 survey by the United Auto Workers (UAW) found that only 74 of 280 establishments that hired women were willing to hire Black women. Another study by the National Metal Trades Association found that only 29 of 62 plants that hired women employed Black women, and Wagner Electric Corporation in St. Louis, Missouri, had 64% White women employed but refused to hire Black women through the war.[17]

It's clear that employers nudged women of all races out of the workforce in order to make room for the men. This was considered entirely acceptable—even expected—at the time, but with hindsight we can see that although it might have been legal and socially acceptable, it was not ethical. This is an important lesson for us in contemporary times, as we strive to create more compassionate workplaces: sometimes the compassionate decision may not be what "conventional wisdom" dictates.

Housewife as Businesswoman: The 1950s and 1960s

Although some women continued to work outside the home, many who returned to the home founded their own business culture, one that opened income-generating doors for women even as they were denied jobs outside the home.

An early example of this is Avon, founded by David McConnell, a door-to-door salesman. He discovered that his free fragrance gift to housewives who listened to his sales pitch was more popular than the actual product being sold, so he started focusing on the fragrances. He even came up with the then-groundbreaking ideal that women selling to other women would have tremendous success.[18] This direct sales model, which allowed women to work from home at their own pace while generating substantial incomes, has succeeded for generations and continues to reap benefits for contemporary firms such as Pampered Chef (housewares) and Traveling Vineyard (wines).

Today, we call this a side hustle. Another company that led the way in this movement was Tupperware. Today, Tupperware is a multibillion-dollar firm with operations all over the world.[19] But the word *Tupperware* is practically synonymous with the 1950s.

This name recognition has withstood generations largely due to the work of Brownie Wise, a savvy sales and marketing businesswoman who knew how to generate excitement among other saleswomen. Inventor and founder Earl Tupper had the foresight to bring in Brownie Wise as vice president. Wise, a single mother with department store and other sales experience, demonstrated ingenuity in her "party" marketing strategy, taking sales pitches to homes with hosts, food, and friends. Tupper saw her success with this strategy and brought her into the fold.

As part of Tupper's organization, Wise's Tupperware Patio Parties generated better sales than the Tupperware sold in stores. Once recruited into the VP role, Wise transformed marketing by recruiting women to sell the products among their networks of women friends as their customers. The bowl initially hadn't sold well—it was perceived as too hard to open and close compared to the glass jars people were used to. Consumers had to learn to close the seal, using what was called the "burping technique," and this is where Wise's use of the personal demonstration really shone. The more friends demonstrated using the bowls, the easier they seemed to open and close. Sales increased exponentially: by 1954 the company earned $25 million, which is approaching a quarter billion dollars in today's money.

Wise was a trailblazer in many ways. Her party approach to sales would be a precursor to many other companies and a whole home sales and multilevel marketing movement. Her ingenuity was quickly recognized. In 1954, she was the first woman on the cover of *Business Week.*

Wise's genius was in knowing how much purposeful work meant to women and being able to deliver opportunities where women felt they were making contributions while improving their own personal economies. The lesson here is that compassionate leaders understand the roles appreciation and agency have in developing employee innovation and increasing sales. Equality and inclusivity are only the base line here. Combine that with giving employees opportunities, solving the problem of lack of income mobility, and helping them fulfill their purpose by doing work they enjoy. Accomplishing these—all while delivering a marketplace need—creates the compassion component that gives businesses an edge. From travel opportunities to trophies, Wise brought out loyalty and enthusiasm in employees. They, in turn, brought their highest intelligence and innovation to their sales abilities, making Tupperware a global powerhouse.[20]

Although we can appreciate Wise's ingenuity and success, her story also offers a cautionary tale about the importance of a woman protecting herself as an employee and advocating for the value she brings, no matter what kind of business culture she finds herself in. By 1958, Wise was seen as personifying the Tupperware brand, and she was given public credit for much of the company's success. But Wise didn't own the company and held no equity in it. She and her boss, Earl Tupper, got into conflicts off and on for a variety of reasons, and her tremendous celebrity certainly didn't help. Ultimately, in 1958, he fired her. She ended up with a severance package equivalent to a year's salary—about $30,000, or over $300,000 in today's dollars—but only after taking Tupperware to court.[21]

In Wise's case, her good work in driving millions of dollars in sales *didn't* speak for itself. She never had a stake in the empire she built. She didn't have equity, so she walked away with relatively little of what she had created. We can dispute whether Tupper owed her anything other than the severance package (which she had to fight for in court!). We can pontificate about the purpose of contracts, getting legal insights before launching into a new venture (there weren't a lot of women corporate vice presidents at the time), or whether even an employer's compassion should extend beyond a mutual parting of ways. But all that's left is a woman, whose innovation and sales savvy helped a company reach levels they had never before neared, departing with no equity in what she built. She was treated like any other employee because that's how Earl Tupper thought of her.

Women and Wages: Growing Disparities

Whether we're talking salary or severance, Wise's example shows that women must act to ensure their own personal economy. But to do this, they need the legal and regulatory support that market forces don't always provide. One recent legislative victory showing women's progress (as well as lack of progress) in ensuring personal financial well-being is the Lilly Ledbetter Fair Pay Act of 2009. The law opened the way for worker protection against discrimination, while calling out and challenging a corporate culture that accepts pay disparities. The law's namesake, Lilly Ledbetter, was a manager at Goodyear Tire & Rubber Co. plant in Alabama. She discovered her male peers earned significantly more than she did. After filing a complaint with the Equal Employment Opportunity Commission (EEOC), she was awarded back pay of about $3.3 million in compensatory and punitive damages, but she was unable to collect due to the Supreme Court upholding a lower court ruling that her claim should have been filed within 180 days of the employer's decision to pay a worker less. This is pretty ridiculous considering most workers, such as Ledbetter, wouldn't know about a pay disparity until long after the employer "decides" to pay them less.[22]

The Lilly Ledbetter Act shows that rectifying unfair pay practices isn't limited to one organization but needs to be tackled broadly. It needs to be rooted out globally. One reason for this is that gender and worker wage discrimination is a bad practice not just for workers but for the larger economy, as well as for individual corporations.

Janet Yellen, former Federal Reserve Board Chair, argues in a Brookings Institute essay that women's limited participation in the workforce, as well as lower wages, strikes a blow to overall economic growth, especially when combined with aging populations and lower production capacities.[23] If this is so—if wage disparities are not only bad for women but also for men, companies, and the entire economy—how do they even exist?

A 2007 article in the *Harvard Business Review* by Alice Eagly and Linda L. Carli pointed to employment patterns of men versus those of women as one explanation for the wage gap. Men's greater number of paid labor hours, factoring in women taking time off for child-rearing as well as domestic work, which is neither valued nor recognized, results in men earning more. And let's not forget the advantage that comes with starting a career at a higher salary. HBR cites a 1980–1992 study showing that White men started out ahead of other races and genders when entering the workforce, and this advantage followed them throughout their managerial careers.[24]

Suggesting that the disruption, disappointment, and discrimination women encounter makes office culture somewhat maze-like, Eagly and Carli argue that women's experiences in the corporate world are more aptly portrayed as a labyrinth rather than a glass ceiling. I see the reasoning for this. For starters, the metaphor of the glass ceiling presumes that women climb to a certain level atop the corporate level and are then stopped from climbing higher. But women don't only experience professional damages at the most senior levels of their careers. In fact, women experience various injustices along the way; in some cases, these injustices even ensure that women exit the workforce before they are even on track for managing director, SVP, or the C-suite. A labyrinth is more representative of the actual journey of a woman's career. It's not a one-time encounter with a ceiling—it's an ongoing experience.

Interestingly, the labyrinth metaphor (unlike the glass ceiling!) is not entirely negative. After all, a labyrinth offers several paths to the end goal—one person's journey may not look exactly like another's. There may be lateral moves, combined with vertical moves, combined with periods of pursuing depth of knowledge in an existing role. There is wisdom in knowing that the road does not always need to be linear, and this emerges as a theme throughout most women's careers. As Eagly and Carli write, "Passage through a labyrinth is not simple or direct, but requires persistence, awareness of one's progress, and a careful analysis of the puzzles that lie ahead."[25]

The self-awareness and clarity of career focus that come with each move made in the maze are key benefits of the labyrinth. Another benefit may be the support you get from others during your journey. However, not every person in your journey intends to aid or support. One of the most sinister parts of the labyrinth is the harassment some women experience at the hands of workplace predators, male and female.

Racial and Gender Discrimination in the Workplace

In the fall of 1996, Texaco settled a discrimination lawsuit brought by Bari-Ellen Roberts, a former Black woman staffer, for $176 million. It later emerged that senior-level executives participated in discriminatory practices, as well as using offensive language against their Black employees.[26]

During the trial, Roberts described applying for a position after her supervisor left and "receiving a high enough grade during

77

her evaluation to warrant her promotion." And yet, after senior management reviewed the evaluation, the grade was reduced, making her ineligible for the promotion; a White male with less experience was placed in the position. She was also described by supervisors as "uppity." What is also concerning is the perception that minorities and women were competent enough to support but not actually be executives.[27]

In another significant case from the same year, Chevron was sued over workplace discrimination of women and Black workers. Chevron agreed to pay $8.5 million in a class-action lawsuit on allegations on discrimination against approximately 777 female employees in promotion, pay, and assignments within the company. The lawsuit claims that Chevron often bypassed qualified women for promotions giving male counterparts up to $80,000 and higher in salaries. The resulting settlement also included a fund from which women would be compensated for emotional distress.[28]

A more recent lawsuit was brought against McDonald's. In 2018, 50 McDonald's female employees held a protest against sexual harassment at the workplace.[29] The lawsuit that sought $5 million in damages for workers was accompanied by a list of complaints including a culture of sexual harassment, a history of handling sexual harassment complaints poorly, and rampant abuse of female employees while at work. This pervasive culture of sexual harassment in the workplace and complaints being ignored by higher levels of management highlight the importance of having a work culture based not only on trust and respect but compassion as well.

In 2005, Laura Zubulake—a former high-level employee of the Union Bank of Switzerland (UBS)—sued the bank after a male executive told her she was "too old and ugly and cannot do the job."[30] She also claimed belittlement, exclusion from company events, and was left shocked after being invited to a strip club in Boston by a male superior. She was fired after two years but was eventually awarded $15 million by the court.

Workplace discrimination based on gender is not unique to the United States. In 2001, Schroders, an investment bank and part of Citigroup, was found to have committed sex discrimination in its London office against Julie Bower, an equities analyst. Bower not only received lower bonuses compared to her male colleagues and was paid less but also she claimed unfair dismissal.[31] What is particularly unfortunate is Bowers had ovarian cancer during the process. Although she was able to settle with the company, she experienced considerable emotional distress during this time.

Intersectionality: The Experience of Women of Color in the Corporate Workplace

Since the 1970s, women have progressively gained a firmer footing in the corporate world, seeing increases in pay along the way. But this change has not affected all women to the same degree. Women of color continue facing the complex realities of intersectionality in the workplaces.

In fact, systemic *gender-based racism* in the corporate workplace is rampant. One way this is demonstrated is by the pay gap that exists for women of color. As demonstrated in Table 3.1, Black, Latinx, and Native American women are not only paid 38%–45% less than White men but also less than White women. Further, women of color face worse treatment compared to White women at the workplace, including getting worse results when they ask for pay raises and promotions.[32] A report from LeanIn.org and McKinsey also found that a mere 4% of C-suite executives are women of color compared to 18% of executive level roles occupied by White women.[33]

Table 3.1 Gender Pay Gap by Race Relative to White Men: 2019

White men	$1.00
White women	$0.79
Asian men	$1.15
Asian women	$0.90
Black men	$0.87
Black women	$0.62
Native American men	$0.91
Native American women	$0.57
Latinx men	$0.91
Latinx women	$0.55

Source: The Gender Pay Gap Has Closed 5 Cents Since 2015—But Don't Celebrate Yet, PayScale, (April 26, 2019). Available at https://www.payscale.com/career-news/2019/04/the-gender-pay-gap-has-closed-5-cents-since-2015-but-dont-celebrate-yet; Racial Wage Gap for Men, PayScale, (May 7, 2019). Available at https://www.payscale.com/data/racial-wage-gap-for-men

Further, on average, women in the United States make 18% less than men but for women of color the pay disparity is even more outrageous.[34] See Table 3.2.

Table 3.2 Percentage of Inclusion by Race in Executive Positions

Race/Ethnicity	Percentage of Workforce	Percentage of Executive Positions
White	78	85.2
Latinx	17	4.3
Blacks	13	3.2
Asian Americans	6	5.9

Source: Modified from This is where there are the most Hispanic executives (and it's not where you think), Fast Company, (January 28, 2020).

In terms of treatment in the workplace, women of color have it worse and continue to face venomous work environments.

Corporations Compassion Culture

A study looking at the conditions of working in corporate America demonstrated the tough and uncompassionate conditions employees faced, especially women of color. The callout included responses from executives, middle managers, and entry-level staffers about their experiences within such industries as tech, finance, media, health, and more. Several Black women reported about the lack of diversity as they climbed up the corporate ladder watching as women and Blacks were systematically forced out of leadership.[35] Other employees expressed that within the private sector most workers in leadership positions were mainly White males, and women of color were absent in decision-making processes. Another employee stated how uncomfortable it felt to be the only woman of color at all events including networking, happy hours, and meetings. Other Black women complained of microaggressions and microinequities.[36]

The exclusion women of color face at work is a stark contrast to White women, and one such example is hair. For decades, Black women have adapted to work climates that have disrespected them culturally and excluded them. Hairstyles such as braids, locs, and afro-hair among women of color have been termed as unprofessional and used to exclude them in corporate workplaces. This resulted in the introduction of the CROWN Act (Create a Respectful and Open World for Natural Hair Act) in 2019, which protects women of color from discrimination based on hair. However as of this writing, only 22 states have passed this law nationwide.[37] Chapter 9 contains a broader discussion of these intersectionality issues.

Compassion and Empathy: Improving the Workplace for Women

Focusing on women's skill sets, competencies, and unique contributions are the best way to drive a successful agenda for women's engagement in the workplace. Transformational approaches to leadership, as opposed to transactional ones, are more efficient ways to conduct business. Additionally, transformational leadership is the type that is most associated with female leadership. Transformational approaches include laying out future objectives, empowering team members, and moving toward innovation, whereas transactional approaches are more aligned with rewarding good work and penalizing bad work.

Additionally, empathy (another stereotypically feminine characteristic), especially as it relates to sensing the needs of other underrepresented people, is a compassionate behavior that will lead businesses into the future. During her 2010 TED Talk, Sheryl Sandberg told a story about speaking in front of an audience where she mentioned she'd take only two more questions before leaving. After the two questions were asked, the women in the audience lowered their raised hands, whereas several men kept their hands raised. Sandberg decided to stay a bit longer and answer more questions. It was only afterwards, after a woman brought it to her attention, that she realized the need to be aware of the dynamic at play and acknowledge the women in the room who had lowered their hands.[38]

Flexibility is also another way that compassion can be leveraged along with greater gender equality. When it comes to female employees, flexibility most obviously relates to child- and elder-care needs (to be discussed more in Chapter 9), but it can go beyond that.

One discrimination lawsuit against Walmart revealed that "manager meetings," which, it is fair to presume anyone hoping to advance in the corporation would need to attend, included trips to strip clubs, a sales meeting that had a predominant football theme throughout, and a team-building exercise where quail hunting was the activity.[39] Clearly the strip club is an inappropriate setting for a business meeting and can safely be labeled a baseline bad practice, but leaders should recognize more subtle distinctions with the other examples. Not everyone has aptitude and interest in certain sports. This doesn't mean that sports themes should never be a part of team building. It only means a degree of flexibility should be allowed when seeking to be inclusive. We don't need to play into inaccurate stereotypes (for example, switch up from football themes to kitchen-related themes). Instead, we should allow room for everyone to learn something new; teams shouldn't always talk in sports speak. It's compassionate and professional to be flexible and switch up themes and activity types used for company engagements.

Progressive business leaders recognize when their environments are shifting, their demographics are changing, and their audience's tastes are evolving. They are forward thinking. This is the reason their businesses will be prepared for the evolution of corporate culture to a more compassionate culture.

Chapter 3 Takeaways

- Understanding the history of women in the workplace can help corporations and senior leaders effectively handle today's gender inequities at work.

- For years, women worked alongside men at home. Some worked beside them at factories and plants, but these numbers of women in these workplaces grew exponentially during the war. Women can perform and have the right to perform any and all work at equal wages.

- Historically women have been sidelined and passed over in favor of men. An example of this is the way in which women were shut out of workplaces when men returned home from war. Remnants of this type of exclusion continue today.

- Women of color as a whole have had additional struggles and burdens in the workplace that White women have not.

(continued)

(continued)

This was the case in domestic work environments, too, where they were subjected to ongoing harassment, low wages, and abuse.

- Intersectionality must be a key part of discussions and genuine efforts to advance and promote women in corporate environments.

- It is imperative that change occurs for *all* women in the workplace. Women of color do face similar issues as White women in corporate settings, only theirs are heightened (pay gap is wider, microaggressions are pervasive, etc.).

- Trust in a company and its leadership is critical to a business's success. Women's distrust in business culture is higher than men's and with good reason and factual evidence. Employers who earn their trust will be rewarded by innovation, loyalty to the firm, and bottom-line benefits.

- Understand that effective leadership is not gender-specific; rather, it requires cultivating a culture of compassion for everyone in the workplace, not just members of minority groups.

References

1. https://www.ncbi.nlm.nih.gov/pmc/articles/PMC3394179/
2. https://time.com/4640222/president-obama-jacob-philadelphia-photo/
3. https://law.tulane.edu/news/student-meets-justice-sotomayor-role-model-who-inspired-her-law-studies
4. https://www.weforum.org/reports/gender-gap-2020-report-100-years-pay-equality
5. https://www.weforum.org/reports/gender-gap-2020-report-100-years-pay-equality

6. https://blog.europeana.eu/2019/09/a-womans-work-is-never-done-womens-working-history-in-europe/

7. https://www.epi.org/blog/black-womens-labor-market-history-reveals-deep-seated-race-and-gender-discrimination/

8. Interview with the author. Scott-Garrett Shennette, The plight of women of color in the late 19th century workplace, July 13, 2020.

9. Scott-Garrett Shennette, Banking on Freedom Black Women in U.S. Finance Before the New Deal, Columbia University Press (7 May 2019). 2019 Columbia University Press.

10. https://www.history.com/topics/world-war-ii/american-women-in-world-war-ii-1 https://oxfordre.com/americanhistory/view/10.1093/acrefore/9780199329175.001.0001/acrefore-9780199329175-e-55

11. https://www.history.com/news/black-woman-army-unit-mail-world-war-ii

12. https://oxfordre.com/americanhistory/view/10.1093/acrefore/9780199329175.001.0001/acrefore-9780199329175-e-55

13. Schweitzer, Mary M. "World War II and Female Labor Force Participation Rates." *The Journal of Economic History* 40, no. 1 (1980): 89–95. www.jstor.org/stable/2120427

14. Schweitzer, "World War II and Female Labor Force Participation Rates"; https://oxfordre.com/americanhistory/view/10.1093/acrefore/9780199329175.001.0001/acrefore-9780199329175-e-55

15. Schweitzer, "World War II and Female Labor Force Participation Rates."

16. Milkman, Ruth. *Gender at Work: The Dynamics of Job Segregation by Sex during World War II* (Champaign: University of Illinois Press, 1987), 136.

17. Anderson, Karen Tucker. "Last Hired, First Fired: Black Women Workers during World War II." *The Journal of American History* 69, no. 1 (1982): 82–97. doi:10.2307/1887753

18. https://www.beautylish.com/a/vxquv/the-history-of-avon

19. https://www.bbc.com/news/magazine-13331830

20. https://www.pbs.org/wgbh/americanexperience/features/tupperware-wise/

21. https://www.smithsonianmag.com/smithsonian-institution/story-brownie-wise-ingenious-marketer-behind-tupperware-party-180968658/

22. https://www.investopedia.com/terms/l/lilly-ledbetter-fair-pay-act.asp#:~:text=The%20Lilly%20Ledbetter%20Fair%20Pay%20Act%20of%202009%20is%20a,rectification%20under%20federal%20antidiscrimination%20laws

23. https://www.brookings.edu/essay/the-history-of-womens-work-and-wages-and-how-it-has-created-success-for-us-all/

24. https://hbr.org/2007/09/women-and-the-labyrinth-of-leadership

25. Ibid.

26. Bari-Ellen, Roberts. *Roberts vs. Texaco: A True Story of Race and Corporate America* (New York: Avon Books, 1998), 1–2.

85

27. "Roberts' Journal of the Discrimination Case." *Woman and Leadership Archives.* Loyola University Chicago.
28. https://www.spokesman.com/stories/1996/nov/08/chevron-strikes-deal-to-settle-sex-bias-lawsuit/
29. https://www.aclu.org/legal-document/ries-v-mcdonalds-michigan-state-court-complaint
30. https://www.standard.co.uk/news/banker-wins-15m-for-ugly-dismissal-7237680.html
31. https://www.theguardian.com/business/2001/apr/10/14
32. https://fortune.com/longform/working-while-black-in-corporate-america-racism-microaggressions-stories/
33. https://leanin.org/women-in-the-workplace-2019?gclid=CjwKCAjw1ej5BRBhEi wAfHyh1APT0LQurLLllOE1GrMjY28Yn4bVFdKwPtCcXotgocwylPaP9oTAPRoCf e8QAvD_BwE; https://www.businessinsider.com/how-work-is-failing-women-of-color-2019-10
34. https://leanin.org/equal-pay-data-about-the-gender-pay-gap; https://iwpr.org/publications/annual-gender-wage-gap-2018/
35. https://fortune.com/longform/working-while-black-in-corporate-america-racism-microaggressions-stories/
36. Ibid.
37. https://www.businessinsider.com/diversity-and-inclusion-change-company-culture-for-black-women-2020-2
38. https://www.ted.com/talks/sheryl_sandberg_why_we_have_too_few_women_leaders/transcript?language=en
39. https://hbr.org/2007/09/women-and-the-labyrinth-of-leadership

Evolution of Companies Post-COVID-19

Business environments constantly evolve in response to changes in customer demands, supply availability, and various other market forces. But the COVID-19 pandemic was more than just a minor adjustment; it shook and changed the global business culture in ways that no one anticipated. Without warning, business environments were forced to evolve swiftly simply to remain operational.

Late March 2020 looked like a whole new world. Those of us working in offices had abandoned our daily commutes. Symbols and images of traditional, structured organizations disappeared—for example, there were no more massive executive offices separated from rows of employee cubicles. Hallway sounds of rolling luggage bags carrying suits for jet-setting salespeople ended abruptly. Lunch and coffee break cliques disbanded.

Among white collar workers, working from home became the norm. With fewer in-person communications, "meeting before the meeting" networking, and watercooler talks, a different dynamic emerged between leaders and employees. Hierarchies flattened. Information was less siloed, and differences between leading and managing became more defined.

For blue collar workers, employment insecurity became a glaring reality as millions of people lost their jobs within a matter of weeks during the spring of 2020. Our definition of "frontline workers" changed almost overnight, as grocery clerks, Amazon warehouse workers, and food delivery people, along with health care workers, were called on to put their lives at risk to provide essential services. The pandemic also revealed the gig work environment to be more exploitative than many had realized.

Small and big companies alike faltered. But in the midst of a global pandemic, volatile markets, and scary unemployment numbers, employee well-being and mental health took center stage. Building higher levels of trust, responding to mental health needs, and experimenting with new communication and bonding tools opened the door to a new way of doing business.

Businesses that successfully navigated the post-COVID-19 environment found ways to balance virtual teams, remote client engagement, and more prevalent digital experiences, while also dealing with the realities of ongoing restructuring. Maintaining this type of business environment required genuine concern and care for the needs of the people who make up the business. A new paradigm for corporate culture has evolved, post-pandemic—one that prioritizes employees' mental well-being and purpose, while establishing bilateral trust between workers and management.

This chapter will examine the workplace disruptions and changes brought on by the pandemic, as well as the importance of corporate compassion in a post-COVID-19 environment. It will specifically explore these issues:

- Keeping employees physically safe and healthy
- Insensitive corporate and government policies
- Financial fears of business leaders and employees
- Prioritizing employee mental health
- Redefining employee communication and collaboration
- Management at a distance: Trust versus micromanagement
- Connecting compassion with profitability

Keeping Employees Physically Safe and Healthy

No one anticipated the velocity of change to the global business culture brought on by COVID-19. For office workers, the physical work environment of the traditional corporate structure became a health and safety risk seemingly overnight. As social distancing guidelines emerged, it became clear that packed conference rooms, breakroom socializing, and shared workspaces placed everyone at risk of exposure to coronavirus. The pandemic forced business leaders who had consistently resisted teleworking within their organizations to quickly embrace remote work arrangements. Working from home provided a higher degree of safety for these employees, but it also showcased a glaring distinction between white collar workers and everyone else.

Many corporations with white collar workers rolled out remote work initiatives. But other types of laborers weren't so lucky. According to several global studies, those most likely to be affected and die from COVID-19 worked low-paid, low-skilled, manual, or factory jobs. For example, data from the United Kingdom indicated that those in low-skilled jobs were four times more likely to die from the virus than those in professional or white collar jobs. In fact, 21.4 deaths per 100,000 were reported among that group, compared to 5.6% among white collar male workers.[1]

United Food and Commercial Workers International (UFCW) represents 1.3 million grocery, meatpacking, retail, and health care workers in the United States and Canada. In June 2020, the union announced that almost 29,000 of its members had been infected by COVID-19 during the first 100 days of the pandemic, with 238 deaths. During the month of April alone, 46 of the union's grocery members died. In the month of May, 5,901 new grocery store workers were infected.[2]

A study by the Office for National Statistics on COVID-19 Fatalities in England and Wales indicated that women working in health care are two times more likely to die from COVID-19 than women in professional jobs, while those working as construction laborers, security guards, taxi drivers, retail workers, and factory workers have the highest rates of death involving COVID-19.[3]

With little precedent for how to go about keeping workers safe, corporate response to worker-related infections varied widely. Some companies did a great deal to address their workers' fears; others did comparatively little.

At Whole Foods Supermarket, workers were only allowed to take unpaid leave during the pandemic, which represents a stark change from the generous leave and health insurance policies that Whole Foods offered prior to being purchased by Amazon. The limited offering of unpaid leave resulted in employees coming to work although they were sick.

Occupational Safety and Health Administration (OSHA) received 35 complaints related to Amazon worksites, including their Whole Foods Shoppers locations. As a result of the complaints, Amazon eventually implemented a variety of measures, including 150 process changes such as enhanced cleaning, social distancing, and sufficient protective gear for workers.[4] They introduced new technology including wearable devices that alert workers when they get too close to one another while working.[5]

Amazon also implemented safety measures such as enhanced sanitization, extended pay, and benefits options, testing, and temperature checks.[6] They offered two weeks of paid leave for workers diagnosed with COVID-19 and provided financial support to Amazon partners and contractors.[7] Since making these changes, Amazon's stock has increased significantly. After bottoming out about $1,600 in mid-March, share prices rose to $3,000 on July 6.[8]

In the United States, the Center for Economic and Policy Research (CEPR) has pushed for more occupational information on COVID-19 deaths. The National Center for Health Statistics (NCHS), which falls under the umbrella of the Centers for Disease Control and Prevention (CDC), releases provisional death counts broken down by race, sex, and age.[9] However, unlike countries such as the United Kingdom, occupational information is not included—unfortunately, this means we can only rely on individual news reports and theorize about how blue collar occupations have been hardest hit and disproportionately affected by the pandemic.[10]

As news of rising death tolls among blue collar professions permeated the airwaves, fear gripped these workers across the globe. Although working from home seemed to be the safest route against infection, it simply was not an option for bus drivers, janitorial professionals, plant workers, and the countless other blue collar professions that keep the global economy moving. During the beginning stages of the COVID-19 outbreak, 90% of the 2.9 million jobs lost between February and March were from positions such as hairdressing and bartending, where teleworking was not an option.[11]

For blue collar workers who could remain in their jobs, concerns quickly turned to their safety within the work environment. In the absence of a federal plan, it was up to state and local health officials to implement and enforce safety protocols for the most vulnerable workers, which meant a wide variety of policies and compliance levels. The CDC provided high-risk workers with guidelines for lowering their chances of contracting and dying from COVID-19, including staying home when sick, cleaning and disinfecting work areas, and wearing cloth face coverings.[12] Yet, not every employee was afforded the opportunity to follow these guidelines with rigor.

Throughout the spring of 2020, news reports featured many insider critiques of inadequate work conditions and safety measures. Amazon workers staged small demonstrations nationwide, inspired by allegations that the corporation's warehouses were ill-equipped to protect employees from the spread of the virus. New York's attorney general agreed with this assessment, stating that "Amazon's health and safety measures taken in response to the COVID-19 pandemic are so inadequate that they may violate several provisions of the Occupational Safety and Health Act."[13]

On May 1, International Worker's Day, workers from such companies as Amazon, Instacart, Shipt, FedEx, and Walmart staged a "sickout" in protest of unsafe work conditions.[14] Inadequate personal protection equipment, the inability to social distance, and insufficient sick leave policies were among the numerous complaints.

These inadequacies have been particularly prevalent within the meatpacking industry. Since the outbreak of COVID-19, state and federal regulators have received complaints from meatpacking plants about the safety of workers on the job. For example, a worker at Pilgrim's Pride poultry processing plant in North Carolina complained that the plant was not notifying employees when coworkers tested positive for the virus. Workers at both Smithfield Foods and Tyson packing plants have complained about the lack of protective gear while at work, as well as a point system that penalized workers for absences even in the event of illness.[15]

Thousands of meatpacking employees were infected within the first few months of the pandemic, resulting in the closing of numerous processing plants.[16] In response to concerns about a potential meat shortage, the Trump administration pushed for reopening of the plants. The United Food and Commercial Workers (UFCW) International Union, which represents more than 250,000 meatpacking and food processing workers across the country, opposed the reopenings of 14 meatpacking plants due to employee risks.[17]

Months into the pandemic, meat packing plants were still feeling the effects. In August, California health officials ordered the closing of a Foster Farms poultry plant after more than 350 employees tested positive for COVID-19 and eight workers died. Despite safety guidelines provided by the Merced County Health Department, health officials reported that the plant failed to conduct adequate testing and reconfigure break rooms to allow for social distancing.[18]

Health Care Workers

COVID-19 has also significantly affected health care workers, physically, mentally, and emotionally. The nature of their profession and their close proximity to infected patients makes social distancing impossible to achieve. OSHA recommendations for medical worker safety involve a combination of precautions, including contact protections, airborne precautions, and eye protections such as goggles and face shields.[19] But limited access to gloves, masks, goggles, face shields, and gowns left thousands of health care workers ill-equipped to protect themselves while caring for COVID-19 patients. The situation was particularly dire in the early weeks of the pandemic, but even as late as the fall of 2020, some health care workers were still having trouble accessing sufficient protective equipment.

"Without secure supply chains, the risk to health care workers around the world is real," said WHO Director-General Dr. Tedros Adhanom Ghebreyesus. "Industry and governments must act quickly to boost supply, ease export restrictions and put measures in place to stop speculation and hoarding. We can't stop COVID-19 without protecting health workers first."[20] As of September, more than 1,700 health care workers had died from coronavirus in the United States.[21] These tragic numbers included physicians, nurses, and paramedics, along with such health care support staff as hospital janitors and nursing home workers.

Facing an increased risk of contraction, many health care workers dealt with the challenges of mental and emotional burnout. Susan R. Bailey, MD, and president of the American Medical Association (AMA) stated, "I think that we have to be extra aware of the special, psychological as well as physical needs of our health care workforce to help get them through this."[22]

In a study published in the *Journal of the American Medical Association Network Open*, researchers in China found that nurses, particularly female nurses, suffered pandemic-related psychological burdens. Surveying more than 1,800 nurses and doctors who treated COVID-19 patients, researchers found that 71% reported "distress," 50% described depression, 44% suffered anxiety, and 34% had insomnia. Another study by University of Rome researchers found that nearly half of 1,300 surveyed health care providers reported post-traumatic stress disorder (PTSD) symptoms.[23]

Teachers and Students

Questions of whether to close schools and when (and how) to reopen them safely weighed heavily on large segments of workers. Not only do schools serve as workplaces, but they also provide de facto child care. Parents count on schools to provide regular daily, safe, reliable learning environments for their children. Safety issues affected adult school workers, students, and students' working family members. At the outbreak of COVID-19, teachers and school administrators found themselves facing the physical and emotional dangers of COVID-19. "Without protections in place, staff and students—and the families they go home to at night—will not be safe from the virus," stated Michael Mulgrew, president of the United Federation of Teachers.[24]

In early 2020, close to a billion young people worldwide remained home following the closure of schools in response to the pandemic.[25] Teachers work in close proximity to the populations they serve, sharing closed classrooms with other instructors and students of all ages. But in most schools, spacing and overcrowded classrooms made social distancing virtually impossible.

As the months progressed, American school districts grappled with the possibility of reopening schools for instruction. While the federal government pushed for schools to resume in-person, many teachers and teachers' unions resisted these changes, citing fears of community spread. Educators in school districts across the country protested and fought to keep schools closed in the fall. The United Federation of Teachers, the trade union of teachers in New York City, includes about 75,000 of the city's teachers and school staff. President Michael Mulgrew stated that he didn't think it possible for schools to open on time. He warned that "it might be one of the biggest debacles in the history of the city."[26]

In jurisdictions where school boards decided to reopen, teachers' unions pushed for stronger safety precautions, such as masks and adequate ventilation in the classrooms.[27] With 1.1 million students, New York City represents the largest school district in the country. After vacillating between various reopening plans, NYC schools had a delayed, controversial opening in the fall that brought the grade levels back in waves.[28] Hybrid systems of alternating between in-person schooling and virtual schooling became a way to reduce physical interaction, while ensuring students' education continued.

Concerns over reopening extended to the faculty and administrators of colleges and universities. Just as many of these institutions finalized their reopening plans, infection numbers surged nationwide. Many colleges reversed their decisions to bring back students, instead opting for online instruction.[29] Although some colleges and universities did open, lack of social distancing and unauthorized social gatherings resulted in spikes of positive cases, which put students, staff, and faculty at significant risk of infection. Some schools changed course, choosing to send students home and switching to an online learning environment.

"We understand the concern and frustrations these changes will raise with many students and parents," explained University of North Carolina–Chapel Hill chancellor Kevin Guskiewicz. "As much as we believe we have worked diligently to help create a healthy and safe campus living and learning environment, the current data presents an untenable situation. As we have always said, the health and safety of our campus community are paramount, and we will continue to modify and adapt our plan when necessary."[30]

Gig Workers

Just as COVID-19 highlighted risks to blue collar workers, health care professionals, and educators and staff, it also revealed deficiencies with the gig economy. Discussions and accusations about gig worker exploitation and tip theft have been occurring for years. In fact, estimates claim that gig workers are paid less than $10 an hour after expenses.[31] It became abundantly clear to American consumers that gig economy companies extended a promise of economic freedom that they didn't live up to. Although many gig economy workers were providing essential services, they were not treated fairly or afforded standard protections such as pay, health care, and job security.[32] The pandemic forced these companies to change their approach to pay equality in order to save their reputations and maintain viability in the market.

At the start of the pandemic, many gig industry businesses faced mounting pressure to treat their workers as valued employees by providing benefits such as paid leave and health insurance. One such example is the food delivery industry, which is populated by gig workers through companies such as Instacart. Valued at approximately $14 billion, Instacart is one of the many companies that has faced criticism for cutting worker pay.[33] In cities such as San Francisco, the company cut worker's pay by 30% to 45%, without advance notice. These cuts came in addition to claims that the company was eating into their workers' tip money and using those funds to then pay their workers. On social media, several workers shared screenshots of pay decreases ranging from 11% to 19%.[34]

DoorDash also faced accusations of poor worker pay and mishandling workers' tips.[35] In early 2020, the company faced an injunction in California to treat its workers as employees. The lawsuit was filed amid claims that DoorDash failed to help its workers navigate the economic fallout of COVID-19, denying them benefits and better pay.[36]

California was one of several states that sought to protect gig workers with stricter classification guidelines. Lawmakers sought to codify a court ruling that gig economy companies must reclassify their workers as employees, which would guarantee a baseline minimum wage for these workers. However, in November 2020, California voters approved Proposition 22, which exempts many gig companies from offering workers benefits such as paid sick time and unemployment insurance.[37] Companies such as Uber, Lyft, Instacart, DoorDash, and Postmates strongly lobbied against the legislation, asserting that it would "decimate businesses."[38]

However, there has been some positive response to criticisms regarding treatment of gig workers. In the case of Instacart, for example, changes included an overhaul of their pay system to one in which a service fee is used to pay workers along with a tip structure that goes straight to the worker.[39] Other companies, such as DoorDash, have altered their policies to include 14 days paid sick leave to anyone diagnosed with COVID-19.[40]

Adequate sick leave policies directly link to the creation of a compassionate business culture. They benefit employees by allowing them to take time for self-care and healing or to seek necessary medical assistance. Paid sick leave also enables workers to care for loved ones when needed. With these policies in place, employees do not have to make the impossible choice of prioritizing their health or prioritizing their job.

Paid sick leave also benefits employers. When employees feel compelled to come to work while feeling sick, they put everyone in the workplace at risk of potential exposure. It can also be dangerous and risky for employees under the influence of medication to handle important job duties.

Insensitive Corporate and Government Policies

Fears of physical health and safety, the future of their employment, personal finances, childcare, and schooling combined to take a toll on the mental well-being of employees across the spectrum of professions. With schools and daycare facilities shutting down, working parents—especially single parents and working women—faced another incredible challenge. For those forced to work out of the home, finding appropriate childcare while working became a problem.[41] For those working remotely from home, juggling home schooling and childcare with work responsibilities proved extremely difficult.

Parental burnout was a very real phenomena during COVID-19. A survey on "Stress in Times of COVID-19" by the American Psychological Association done in April and early May 2020 found that 46% of parents with children under the ages of 18 reported higher stress levels in comparison to 28% of adults who had no children.[42]

Parents have assumed several practices at home to deal with parenting during the pandemic including juggling schedules and split-shifting, which allows for a range of time when one parent looks after the children and the other works, and then they switch, taking turns through the day.[43] Companies faced mounting pressure to support parents and their childcare needs. In fact, even companies that had not previously offered family-friendly benefits implemented policies such as paid parental leave, flexible work schedules, and access to affordable childcare options.[44]

The president of a Florida property management company explained that the childcare needs of his employees became a major obstacle during the pandemic. "The main challenge we are facing with our employees is the added childcare needs with summer camps and schools being shut down. Especially the employees with children under the age of 12, the switch to online learning has been a huge burden. A way we have tried to combat this challenge is to let anyone who needs help work from home and/or reduce their hours in order to give them more time to watch their children."

Concerns over the lack of testing and insufficient childcare for families made the gradual return to work unpredictable and messy. Yet, even with widespread fear and uncertainty among the nation's workforce, many corporate leaders pushed to reopen the economy.

The nation's auto industry employs more than 150,000 factory workers across the country. Most of these companies reopened their facilities near the beginning of May, even as infection numbers continued to rise. Gerald Johnson, vice president of global manufacturing at General Motors, stated, "We're confident, we're ready to go with the proper safety protocols in place. We surveyed our supply base. They are as committed as we are. They're as ready to start as we are." This narrative was particularly concerning considering the fact that two dozen Ford, GM, and Fiat Chrysler workers had already died from COVID-19 complications.[45]

Tesla CEO Elon Musk was criticized as being tone-deaf when his company announced the presumption of production without any

99

mention of precautions or safety measures for workers, including testing.[46] Despite lawsuits against the company, a reopening was scheduled. Tesla employees were told they would be ineligible for benefits and unable to apply for unemployment if they did not go back to work.[47]

These sentiments gave the perception that business leaders were more concerned with profits than the well-being of their employees. Even in the midst of growing infection numbers, many companies and governments forced workers back to work with inadequate concern for their fears and worries.

Partially fueling these actions were state concerns over their abilities to meet rising unemployment claims. The US Department of Labor reported that 1.9 million Americans filed for state unemployment as of June 2020. Many state governments made the assertion that workers could and should return to their employment if their business reopened despite safety or childcare concerns.[48] State officials in Iowa publicly called for companies to report if an "employee refuses to return to work."[49] Oklahoma established a "Return to Work" e-mail for businesses to report employees who refuse jobs. Under the program, hundreds of businesses reported employees for refusing to return to work.[50]

Ohio's Department of Job and Family Services also requested that employers "report employees who quit or refuse work when it is available due to COVID-19."[51] Using a "COVID-19 Employee Fraud" form, officials evaluate unemployment benefits claims from people who are refusing "suitable work" so that they could be found ineligible.[52] Missouri received more than 1,000 reports of workers who refused to return to their jobs.[53] South Carolina and Alabama also told employees that they could not collect unemployment benefits if they refused a job offer.[54]

This lack of compassion was not conducive to creating a productive post-COVID-19 business culture. Workers have felt increasingly overlooked and alone, as the government and private sector forced them back into unsafe and uncertain work environments.

Financial Fears of Business Leaders and Employees

The financial fears brought about by the pandemic were pervasive and understandable in light of what employees saw going on around them. Widespread business closures seemed to run counter to the reaction of Wall Street, which, after the initial shock had passed, steadily made gains in the second and third quarters of 2020. For workers who were not benefitting from stock market gains, but saw their hours reduced or experienced furloughs, their personal economies seemed unstable and financial markets appeared nonsensical, evoking even more anxiety.

Several large national and global corporations undertook a painful downsizing or went out of business entirely. Oil and gas driller company Whiting Petroleum and Diamond Offshore filed for bankruptcy in late April 2020. J. Crew was one of the first major US retailers to file bankruptcy amidst the pandemic, while 24-Hour Fitness, which had almost 400 gyms across the country, closed more than 100 of its locations citing "the disproportionate impact the coronavirus pandemic has caused on the fitness industry."[55]

Dean & Deluca a luxury grocery store chain with 42 locations also started to downsize. High-end retailer Brooks Brothers, which was established over two centuries ago and was frequented by celebrities and US presidents, closed roughly 51 of its 250 stores.[56]

Internationally, David's Tea in Montreal, Canada, filed for bankruptcy and planned to close 124 of its 220 stores across Canada and the United States. Debenhams in the United Kingdom, which employs more than 20,000 people, struggled to stay afloat and liquidated its business in Ireland. McDermott International, a construction and engineering company, filed Chapter 11 bankruptcy to eliminate approximately $4.6 billion in debt.[57]

The impact of these corporate bankruptcies reaches beyond CEOs and shareholders. When filing a Chapter 7 bankruptcy, the company ceases to exist; it liquidates its assets to pay creditors, which often includes employee retirement and health plans. Employees feel the financial and emotional effects of these changes, particularly in a climate where they are already experiencing the triple threat of an international health crisis, racial injustices, and employment instability. Workers saw reports of job loss and rising unemployment rates, along with contrasting reports of stock market increases that followed the initial downturn. Although these market gains suggested a thriving economy, employees found their livelihoods at risk, along with their much-needed retirement benefits.

There is a clear link between employment and consumption. When people aren't working, they consume less. When they consume less, businesses shut down and add to the unemployment numbers. For many decades, US consumers have been considered an economic engine for growth. As of 2012, consumers were responsible for a little below 71% of US gross domestic product (GDP) and just over 15% of the world's GDP.[58] In 2019, consumption accounted for 70% of the GDP.[59]

According to the US Bureau of Labor Statistics, more US jobs, such as retail, service, and hospitality, depend on consumer spending than any other economic sector.[60] So it is not surprising that the negative impact of COVID-19 on consumer spending has also negatively affected employment. Consumer demand significantly and quickly dropped with the pandemic, causing long-term ramifications for businesses.

Businesses faced a new economic reality in which consumer spending has shifted. Consumer credit is less available, and a large segment of the population may default on debt further affecting purchasing power.[61] A report by the US Chamber of Commerce found that 43% of small businesses will not survive the tense economic times of the pandemic.[62] This is not surprising when even large luxury companies such a Neiman Marcus faltered under the harsh economic conditions created by the coronavirus. The retailer has closed most of its locations and almost 14,000 of its employees were furloughed.[63]

Prioritizing Employee Mental Health

The impact of the coronavirus pandemic shed much-needed light on mental health as a broader social issue. At a basic level, the pandemic has transformed the daily lives of workers in virtually every profession, and these changes have significantly heightened anxiety levels among workers.[64] A survey of 80,000 people provided by Survey Monkey found that 86% of Americans were worried about the outbreak.[65]

A Kaiser Family Foundation survey found that nearly half of the people in the United States felt the coronavirus pandemic was harmful to their mental health and well-being.[66] The survey also showed that 19% of respondents said the pandemic had a major impact on their mental well-being, 88% said they experienced extreme stress, and 69% stated it has been the most stressful time of their career.[67]

As a group, workers are facing unheard of levels of anxiety. According to the on-demand mental health care provider Ginger, nearly 7 in 10 workers stated that the pandemic has been the most stressful time of their professional career, creating even more worry than major events such as 9/11 and the 2008 Great Recession.[68] A study by Mental Health Index found that the risk for depression among US workers rose by more than 100% since February 2020.[69]

From a manager's perspective, it's important to realize that high-stress levels result in reduced productivity within the work environment. In an April 2020 survey of US full-time workers, 62% of respondents reported losing at least one hour of productivity a day due to COVID-19-related stress, with 32% reporting a loss of more than two hours per day.[70] During the pandemic, 4 in 10 employees reported feeling less productive as a result of poor mental and emotional well-being.[71]

Unfortunately, many employees suffer with their mental health struggles in silence. Too many employers lack not only empathy but also an understanding of the fact that the mental well-being of employees is a productivity issue. According to a 2006 survey, employees fear judgment and retaliation from bosses and peers because of mental health concerns.[72] This should not be the case.

Compassionate businesses focus on strengthening their employees. Firms that took the fears and the mental well-being of employees seriously prioritized mental health and wellness initiatives in the workplace by either enacting new or strengthening existing mental health programs. There has never been a better time for a new corporate culture focused on compassion and normalizing the mental well-being of employees. Furthermore, enacting such policies will contribute to improved performance and a more resilient post-COVID-19 workforce.

Good news is found in a survey of US workers during the pandemic in that 57% of employees were receiving mental and emotional support, 28% reported having access to flexible scheduling and working hours, and 24% reported taking regular breaks throughout the day.[73]

Ally Financial is an example of a company that responded quickly to the mental and emotional challenges of their employees. Its leaders provided their workforce of 8,700 with free access to mental health professionals, well-being modules to promote physical and mental health while working from home, and 100% coverage for virtual doctor visits.[74]

This pandemic has shown how critical it is to embrace our humanity, be understanding and caring—and that holds true for companies, too," said Kathie Patterson, chief human resources officer. "At Ally, we've been driven by what's right—just like our mantra to 'Do It Right'—and we will do whatever we can to support the well-being of customers and employees . . . Everything we do is through the lens of care and support. That's the culture of Ally. When you get culture right everything else falls into place and there is no better time to let that shine than right now."

Pacific Gas and Electric Company (PG&E) established a website dedicated to mental health and access to information. It also provides virtual counseling through its employee assistance program (EAP).[75]

Phoenix-based HR Company Store held training classes to help educate managers on how to identify and support employees facing mental health issues.[76] "Supervisors want to help, but because of all the laws surrounding HIPAA and privacy, they are not sure what they can and cannot say to an employee. By hosting this training, we provided them with the tools they need to help their team member appropriately," explained CEO Laurie Brednich.

The CEO of EaseCentral focuses the company's mental wellness efforts on employee anxiety. The company offers and

(continues)

(continued)

promotes teletherapy options so that employees can feel more comfortable getting help without feeling compelled to provide managers with explanations.[77] "Mental health doesn't have a schedule, and it's often hard to find time in one's schedule to see a therapist," said David Reid, CEO of EaseCentral. "Offering the option to set up text or even FaceTime sessions entices everyone to keep their mental health in check."

Colonial Life pushes an employee wellness strategy that includes emotional, social, and physical health. The company has developed a more holistic approach to well-being in the workplace.[78] "Employers need to expand the definition of well-being to include mental, emotional, social, financial, and physical health. We need to adopt a more holistic approach that recognizes these connections as well as those between employees and the workplace," explained Bill Deehan, senior VP of sales for Colonial Life.

COVID-19 has thrown the need for mental health support into sharp focus, but the benefits of these initiatives are not limited to the current environment. Businesses that prioritize employee mental health generally enjoy stronger loyalty and improved performance by their teams—and not just in times of crisis. As members of Generation Z enter the workforce and Millennials seek to further their professional goals, they will seek out employers that promote healthy lifestyles. According to the Society for Human Resource Management (SHRM), 48% of the best-performing companies offer holistic wellness programs to their employees.[79]

Across the globe, large and small companies are responding to the mental health challenges brought by COVID-19. A survey by the

National Alliance of Healthcare Purchaser Coalitions reported that 53% of 256 employers are now providing both emotional and mental health programs for their employees.[80]

Starbucks announced a program in early April 2020, entitling employees working at least 20 hours per week to mental health benefits provided through their EAP. This includes 20 annual sessions with a therapist or mental health coach. The empathy demonstrated by Starbucks with this initiative has far-reaching effects, affecting more than 220,000 workers and family members across the world.[81]

In the wake of the pandemic, studies have demonstrated the positive economic effects of providing mental health support for employees. Prior to the pandemic, studies showed that mental health among workers accounted for about 40% of short-term disability and 30% of long-term disability.[82] Furthermore, a report by the World Health Organization (WHO) on mental health found that the cost of depression and anxiety accounted for an estimate of $1 trillion per year in lost productivity. However, the report also found that for every $1 put in for treatment for common mental disorders, there is a return of $4 in productivity and overall health.[83]

A study of 10 Canadian companies also showed a positive return on investment (ROI) for workplace mental health programs. The study found that the median annual ROI on mental health programs was CA$1.62 at 7 of the 10 companies. The companies that had workplace mental health programs for three years or more reported a median annual ROI of $2.18.[84] These statistics emphasize the importance of investing in proactive programs to promote mental health and emotional well-being in the workplace. These employer initiatives prevent, reduce, and manage diseases that can negatively affect employee productivity. According to the CDC, physical, mental, and emotional health enhancements promote stamina, focus, and work output.[85]

Dr. Roger Sahoury, author of *Gladiator's Guide to Corporate Health & Wealth* stated, "When a team understands how much a company cares about each individual person, the people will work harder, be more dedicated and can more easily operate as one unit. If the overall wellness of an organization is evaluated and treated holistically, a company can minimize mechanical and structural problems while maximizing culture and profitability."[86]

The CDC estimates $3 of every $4 an employer spends on health costs go to treat preventable conditions such as hypertension, diabetes, obesity, and depression.[87] When caught early, these conditions can be treated at a much lower cost. Among 22 different studies about the correlation between wellness programs and health care costs, the average return on investment was $3.27—meaning that for every dollar that was spent on a wellness program, the company saved $3.27 in reduced health care costs.[88] These cost savings are further amplified when measured against employee absenteeism due to illness or injury, the costs of training replacement employees, and the overtime costs associated with covering absent employees.

Redefining Employee Communication and Collaboration

The overwhelming need for remote work environments has also created a need for compassionate business models. Although communication technologies such as Microsoft Teams and Zoom became preferred platforms, they cannot replace the social capital gained from interacting with managers and coworkers in person. Crafting a workplace environment where digital engagement meets or exceeds in-person engagement requires deliberate efforts toward exemplary communication with and treatment of colleagues.

Prior to the COVID-19 pandemic, studies showed that a work-from-home model actually increased productivity. One such study, by Stanford economist Nicholas Bloom on a 16,000 employee NASDAQ-listed travel agency based in China, demonstrated that working from home yielded a 13% increase in performance, and 9% more minutes per shift including fewer sick days. Moreover, employees reported greater work satisfaction leading the company to embark on an optional home or office model with almost half of the employees choosing to work from home. Ultimately, company gains increased by 22%.[89]

Studies done during the COVID-19 pandemic also showed the positive effects of working from home on worker productivity. In a survey of workers aged 18 to 74, 71% said they saved commuting time, 39% stated they had fewer meetings, and 61% reported less distractions than working within the physical office. Business leaders are discovering that many of the traditional office processes simply are not necessary for productivity.[90]

A chief executive of Splunk, an online learning company, stated that remote working led to actual gains within the organization. Meanwhile at Chegg, an online textbook rental company, 86% of employees reported having better productivity due to reduced commuting and not having boundaries in the workday.[91]

The biggest challenge can be distractions because often I pass the whole day realizing that I should have finished the work earlier. To prevent this, I have started time-driven deadlines now and force myself to finish it. Fortunately, my employer is kind and very empathetic about all employees. We have shifted from in-house to remote work completely, but the family-friendly environment is there.

(continues)

(continued)

> As a writer, I must say my productivity has increased. It may sound odd, but I feel more creative when I am working alone. Another good thing: we sell technology products, so our sales have boosted a lot.
>
> —*Sameed, content strategist, Hong Kong*

Businesses across the globe have been experiencing these gains. A 2020 Work from Home IT Impact study polled 500 IT professionals at companies with 1,000 employees in the United States, Germany, France, Ireland, and the United Kingdom. The study found organizational improvements with 63% reporting an increase in employee productivity.[92]

As businesses searched for ways to promote collaboration and communication remotely, they embraced technologies such as Zoom and Microsoft Teams. As we began to lockdown in March 2020, shares in Zoom surged by about 50% due to investor expectations that businesses and schools will continue using these services even after the pandemic.[93] Stella Olsson, a sales manager with Altria, said that Zoom has allowed her to connect with her team. "It works very well for me and the team, allowing us to keep in touch at all times and even more so when we are in quarantine time."

Microsoft is also observing increased use of its collaboration tools, with the company reporting a surge in active users in the month of March. Skype saw a 70% uptick of users. Other video communications products such as Cisco's Webex had roughly 50 million meetings in March alone, while LogMeIn, Inc. had increased use up to 10 times from pre-COVID-19 levels.[94] These technologies have expanded communication channels, helping to redefine the scope of employment relationships. With video technology, the quality of inter-company communications can flourish. That said, a debate remains about whether digital engagement can totally replace in-person engagement, especially for best results for productivity and feeling part of the team.

Employees need regular and frequent exchanges with supervisors and coworkers when working remotely. Silence makes employees feel isolated and disconnected from their employers, which can negatively affect employee morale and productivity. Company leaders need these remote communications platforms to keep employees connected to the company and each other. Employee engagement is a top priority for senior executives, who know that having a high-performing workforce is essential for growth.[95]

The Harvard Business Review Analytic Services surveyed business leaders and the findings confirmed that digital engagement can be quite challenging as a long-term solution to in-person engagement—particularly with the loss of social capital by employees. The survey found that just 24% of respondents reported their employees as highly engaged, although 71% of business leaders rank employee engagement as crucial to organizational goals and success.[96]

This disconnect exemplifies the need for companies to find meaningful and compassionate ways to improve engagement with their employees. One way of doing this is offering opportunities to take courses, speak at or attend external seminars on their areas of expertise, and gain advanced degrees or certifications. These learning, speaking, and knowledge-sharing opportunities fall into the professional development category.

A survey of employees across three generations, including Gen X, baby boomers, and millennials, showed that 70% of respondents said job-related training and development opportunities affected their decision to stay on the job and 87% of millennials stated that professional development was crucial in their decision to stay or leave a job.[97]

Other effective strategies include supporting employees in their new work-from-home environments, providing a patient transition period, and acknowledging employee frustrations. Some companies have offered reimbursements for the cost of telephone and internet as additional incentives to employees who are adjusting to working from home.[98]

Within the traditional business community, the assumption has largely been that remote workers are less productive than those working in an office, but numerous studies have shown otherwise. Prodoscore, a visibility software company announced data on remote worker productivity and work trends since the pandemic started. The data on 30,000 US-based users showed there was a 47% productivity increase during March and April 2020. The data also showed that telephone calling increased at 230%, e-mail activity was up to 57%, and chats were up 9%.[99]

I've been working from home now for about four months and, at first, there was definitely far too much micromanagement taking place. Our manager scheduled way too many meetings on matters that could have easily been resolved over email, which we all understood as being a method to make sure we really were at our computers.

This created an enormous amount of pressure in the team, particularly as even if we were actually working—which everyone appeared to be, given that the outputs weren't changing—there was a feeling of having to "prove" the extent of our work. It also seemed to encourage a feeling of enormous stress in the team, especially due to the threat that if we stepped away from our computers for even a moment at home, we'd be "caught."

This frustration eventually spilled over during one such meeting when one team member told the manager fairly bluntly what the team thought of this method of work. Further discussions have taken place since then and, fortunately, our manager has significantly scaled back his micromanagement. The work has continued to be successfully performed, despite the fact we'll all be working from home for the foreseeable future. This has apparently reassured our manager that our work can still be done in these conditions. Although time will tell if this continues in the right direction, the change in management style has done wonders for our team's stress levels and productivity.

—*Anna, personal finance expert based in the Nordic region*

Management at a Distance: Trust Versus Micromanagement

For many organizations, the onset of COVID-19 transformed the relationship between managers and their teams. Supervisors were forced into a new workplace dynamic, where management within a shared physical environment is no longer an option. Unfortunately, this new work-from-home environment has brought with it an abundance of complaints about managers trying to control and monitor workers too closely.[100] This type of behavior indicates an absence of trust between managers and their team members, which can be detrimental to a company's bottom line.

Though individual employees respond differently to being micromanaged, in general this style of management tends to have negative consequences, although some employees may take it as a challenge to work harder at earning their manager's trust. Although this may not seem like an undesirable outcome, these types of workers eventually tire of trying and burn out. Other employees may become so dependent on being micromanaged that they fear taking initiative or making moves without the explicit direction of approval of a supervisor. This type of environment discourages professional growth and stunts employees' potential within the company.[101]

> Since this global pandemic started and affected our work, my manager started to micromanage everything, which was not [his style] before. In the past, he would usually allow us to handle our own clients and deal with adversities but lately, he became more flustered, which I will admit affects negatively on my performance.
>
> This pandemic situation, plus a work environment that is so pressuring, heightens the anxiety I am feeling. . . It was all so draining, but then I realized that this difficult situation has different implications and effects on each [person], and my reaction to the situation can worsen it.
>
> What I did was talk to my manager to tell him how he was overdoing things and how I think it affects everyone in the workplace. Eventually he realized too that it was all due to the anxiety, feeling he had to be the most rational in the group. It was fixed right away.
>
> —*Ricardo, financial advisor in the United States*

A third category of micromanaged employee has an outwardly negative response, resisting direction, being unpleasant, and maybe even arguing with the manager. Not only can that person's own performance suffer, but this type of reaction can also affect other team members in a negative way.[102] Managers who choose to leverage a micromanagement style may be "penalized" by their team's response and lack of performance.

Trust works both ways. Micromanagement demonstrates the distrust that a manager has for team members, while also breeding distrust in the team member toward the manager. Organizations that develop effective strategies to build bilateral trust between managers and employees will see stronger work relationships as well as performance.

> Since we've had to switch to remote work, it's been chaotic getting up to speed with the new procedures and requirements. After being used to working at the office for many years, it's been a difficult transition for most of us employees to adapt to working from home. The fact we are being put under a microscope by management now that we are working remotely is not helping, especially considering many of us have worked here for a long time and thought we had gained enough trust to avoid being micromanaged...
>
> For me personally, it has actually increased my productivity a little, which I suppose is good. On the flip side, those small gains don't justify the general anxiety and stress I feel on a daily basis from being constantly monitored. I have to be mindful about what
>
> *(continues)*

(continued)

I type, which pages I open, and how I interact with my coworkers on a daily basis. . .[If] I don't move my mouse for a certain period of time, I will be deemed "inactive" by my manager. It's psychologically taxing to work under these conditions for prolonged periods and it's only a matter of time before I have a full-blown panic attack!

—Aleksandra, content strategist based
in the Balkans

Let's look at some examples of steps employers can take to nurture the well-being of their workers:

- Share best-practices with employees via articles that help workers think about building the skills necessary to be healthy and productive at home. This includes establishing skills that may not come naturally to companies and employees who have typically worked within a traditional office environment.[103]

- Actively address the burnout that is affecting so many employees during COVID-19. The exchange of ideas within teams can help employees navigate through the challenges of the pandemic while encouraging mental well-being.

- Provide financial and technical support to employees as they work from home, including resources to help with the setup of computer monitors and phones, to help workers feel supported.[104]

- Offer access to virtual counseling and therapy through the company's EAP.

Corporations Compassion Culture

Connecting Compassion with Profitability

A review of corporate profitability for the first six months of 2020 suggests that an apparent correlation exists between the implementation of corporate mental wellness programs and increased profits. March 23, 2020, was a difficult day for the global markets, with the S&P 1200 hitting its lowest point all year of 1012.[105] The S&P 100 hit a low of 1040 that day, and the FTSE All World index hit a low of 253.[106] This is the same time that nations worldwide started to quarantine, shutting down businesses and instituting stay-at-home orders.

Over the next three months, the business world began to figure out the new normal, which included mental health and wellness initiatives for many businesses. Those three months also brought about significant changes to world markets. By June 30, the S&P 100 had rebounded to 1427.[107] The FTSE rebounded to 346 on the same day, and the S&P 1200 to 1386.[108]

Companies worldwide have been incorporating mental health support into the work environment. *The Financial Times,* one of the world's leading news providers, is mobilizing a network of mental health ambassadors and partnering with an EAP for one-on-one counseling. PwC offers employees access to well-being coaches, as well as an online community for employees to connect with each other to discuss challenges they face with the pandemic. Global technology company TransferWise offered its 2,000 employees counseling sessions and half off the cost of virtual counseling with Headspace. And EY—a global assurance, tax, transaction, and advisory company—is offering 24/7 access to mental health care professionals and virtual coaching sessions.[109]

The leaders of these corporations recognize that compassion toward employee mental well-being is not just compassionate, it is also profitable. Wellness policies make employees feel appreciated and valued. They demonstrate a company's concern for its workers and commitment to their well-being, which boosts employee creativity, drives company loyalty, and positively affects the bottom line.

A survey by the American Psychological Association found that employees who feel valued are more likely to report greater levels of engagement, satisfaction, and motivation to do their jobs well. Conducted among 1,714 adults, more than 90% of workers who reported feeling valued said that they are motivated to do their best at work and 88% reported feeling engaged within their working environment.[110]

Companies around the world are providing blueprints for successfully evolving a company into the post-COVID-19 era. They show us that business leaders in small and large firms alike need to communicate compassionately with their employees, clearly emphasizing the connection between creativity and inclusion to generate greater revenue.

In my joint interview with Rebecca Henderson of Harvard University and Trevon Logan of Ohio State University, they discussed why firms don't commit to a people-centered way of doing business. They point to a perceived cost to the firms.

"Behaving authentically and putting employee welfare in front of profits doesn't come for free. It's seeing money as a means to an end, instead of treating people as means to ends. That requires financial and emotional commitment," says Henderson.

Logan adds that some leaders find it easier to operate in an enterprise with no emotional attachment where they can "treat people as machines."

"Some firms feel they don't need the productivity and the innovation. They can kind of make do, just set up the system, and let it run. This type of management doesn't challenge. They don't have to give away power and don't have to be emotionally engaged."[111]

Micromanagement and resistance to innovative business structures must be eradicated for companies to evolve. Successful companies are thinking outside the box to improve employee retention and performance. They recognize how power sharing initiatives that promote trust through team collaboration improve the bottom line. Business leaders can no longer rely on authoritative power and in-person engagement. They need emotional intelligence to interact and manage effectively, both during crises and in the aftermath.

The business culture will continue to evolve, even after COVID-19 no longer poses such an existential threat. To stay afloat and profitable, businesses will have to either evolve toward compassionate employee policies or lose the social license to do business. Two things are happening in this climate: employees are awake and the world is watching. Companies must step up to meet the challenges uncovered during the pandemic. Then they must take those organizational successes and permanently implement them into the fabric of their operating models. The companies that take this approach will be the ones still standing post-COVID-19.

Chapter 4 Takeaways

- In 2020, the physical environments where we have traditionally done business experienced dramatic and probably permanent changes. To operate profitably in the new physical environment, managers need to adopt new behaviors and implement new leadership tools.

- During the COVID-19 crisis, some employers addressed employee concerns with compassionate initiatives centered on physical safety and mental wellness. Others ignored the unique needs and concerns of their employees, leading to business interruption and, in some cases, serious reputational damage.

(*continued*)

(continued)

- Workers are increasingly organizing and using their voices to change the way their companies conduct business. Specifically, many blue collar workers and gig economy workers banded together to express dissatisfaction with working in hazardous environments for nonlivable incomes and a lack of flexibility.

- Worker challenges to management emphasized the power and agency of employees, which will likely continue into the future.

- Enterprising companies and workers used innovation and creativity to continuously build their business in challenging economic times. These companies took steps to demonstrate compassion for their employees and ensure that they felt included.

- Firms that effectively responded to employee mental well-being concerns saw a payoff with loyalty and productivity, which outweighed the cost of implemented programs.

References

1. https://www.theguardian.com/world/2020/may/11/manual-workers-likelier-to-die-from-COVID-19-than-professionals
2. https://www.supermarketnews.com/issues-trends/ufcw-over-11500-grocery-workers-affected-first-100-days-pandemic
3. Ibid.
4. https://www.newsweek.com/amazon-worker-safety-osha-complaints-coronavirus-COVID-19-1505429
5. https://www.bbc.com/news/technology-53079624
6. Ibid.
7. Ibid.

8. https://finance.yahoo.com/quote/AMZN/history
9. https://www.cdc.gov/nchs/nvss/COVID-19.htm
10. https://cepr.net/us-should-release-occupational-data-in-COVID-19-death-reports/
11. https://www.pewresearch.org/fact-tank/2020/05/06/telework-may-save-u-s-jobs-in-COVID-19-downturn-especially-among-college-graduates/
12. https://www.cdc.gov/coronavirus/2019-ncov/community/organizations/business-employers/bars-restaurants.html
13. https://www.usatoday.com/story/money/2020/04/29/amazon-instacart-workers-plan-may-day-protest-over-COVID-conditions/3049180001/
14. Ibid.
15. https://carolinapublicpress.org/36708/as-COVID-19-spread-in-nc-meatpacking-plants-workplace-complaints-piled-up/; https://www.bbc.com/news/53137613
16. https://www.cnn.com/2020/04/26/business/meat-processing-plants-coronavirus/index.html
17. http://www.ufcw.org/2020/05/08/trump-order-fails-to-increase-coronavirus-testing/
18. https://www.cbsnews.com/news/chicken-plant-foster-farms-california-health-officials-order-closed-COVID-19-deaths/?ocid=uxbndlbing
19. https://www.bing.com/search?q=medical+workers+contracting+COVID&cvid=e8fb4172a7e34e4ca64b3495d480e502&FORM=ANAB01&PC=LCTS
20. Ibid.
21. https://act.nationalnursesunited.org/page/-/files/graphics/0920_COVID19_SinsOfOmission_Data_Report.pdf
22. https://www.ama-assn.org/practice-management/physician-health/how-pandemic-casts-physician-burnout-new-light
23. https://www.theguardian.com/us-news/2020/may/15/us-nurses-doctors-mental-health-coronavirus
24. https://www.wsj.com/articles/amid-COVID-19-nyc-teachers-union-says-city-must-do-more-for-safe-reopening-11596718862
25. https://www.sciencemag.org/news/2020/07/school-openings-across-globe-suggest-ways-keep-coronavirus-bay-despite-outbreaks
26. https://www.npr.org/sections/coronavirus-live-updates/2020/08/19/903927057/nyc-teacher-unions-prepared-to-strike-if-safety-demands-are-not-met
27. https://www.nytimes.com/2020/07/29/us/teacher-union-school-reopening-coronavirus.html
28. https://www.cnn.com/2020/09/29/us/new-york-schools-reopen-wellness/index.html
29. https://www.insidehighered.com/news/2020/08/12/hundreds-colleges-walk-back-fall-reopening-plans-and-opt-online-only-instruction

Evolution of Companies Post-COVID-19

30. https://www.washingtonpost.com/; https://thehill.com/changing-america/well-being/prevention-cures/512399-unc-chapel-hill-shifts-to-remote-learning-as
31. https://www.reuters.com/article/us-uber-wage-study/mit-study-that-found-low-pay-for-uber-drivers-to-be-revisited-idUSKCN1GF0RL
32. https://www.npr.org/2020/04/07/829264795/coronavirus-and-the-gig-economy
33. https://www.cnbc.com/2020/06/11/instacart-raises-new-funding-now-valued-at-nearly-14-billion.html
34. https://www.vox.com/2017/1/10/14220872/instacart-pay-cuts-2017-wage-reductions
35. https://www.vox.com/2019/2/6/18213872/gig-economy-instacart-tip-theft-contract-workers
36. https://www.ft.com/content/4e827588-4b0b-41d9-80c4-515fcc798771; https://www.pymnts.com/gig-economy/2020/san-francisco-da-files-lawsuit-against-doordash-for-employee-mistreatment/
37. https://www.nytimes.com/2020/11/13/opinion/prop-22-california-gig-workers.html
38. https://www.ft.com/content/4e827588-4b0b-41d9-80c4-515fcc798771; https://www.pymnts.com/gig-economy/2020/san-francisco-da-files-lawsuit-against-doordash-for-employee-mistreatment/
39. Ibid.
40. https://slate.com/technology/2020/03/gig-economy-instacart-doordash-amazon-coronavirus-first-responders-delivery.html
41. https://www.nytimes.com/2020/03/17/parenting/seattle-child-care.html
42. https://www.nytimes.com/2020/06/23/parenting/parental-burnout-coronavirus.html
43. https://www.chicagotribune.com/coronavirus/ct-hacks-for-working-from-home-parenting-coronavirus-tt-20200320-au4edkf25varlfoil4wvldxlt4-story.html
44. https://www.unicef.org/coronavirus/7-ways-employers-can-support-working-parents-during-coronavirus-disease-COVID-19
45. https://www.autoblog.com/2020/04/23/automakers-resuming-production/
46. https://www.cnbc.com/2020/04/09/how-businesses-are-planning-to-bring-workers-back-after-coronavirus.html
47. https://www.businessinsider.com/elon-musk-thank-you-note-tesla-workers-2020-5
48. https://www.nytimes.com/2020/06/04/us/virus-unemployment-fired.html
49. https://www.washingtonpost.com/business/2020/04/30/republican-states-unemployment-benefits/
50. https://www.nytimes.com/2020/06/04/us/virus-unemployment-fired.html
51. https://www.dailykos.com/stories/2020/5/8/1943564/-Ohio-asks-employers-to-report-any-employees-refusing-to-return-to-work-so-benefits-can-be-cut-off

52. Ibid.
53. https://www.nytimes.com/2020/06/04/us/virus-unemployment-fired.html
54. Ibid.
55. https://www.forbes.com/sites/hanktucker/2020/05/03/coronavirus-bankruptcy-tracker-these-major-companies-are-failing-amid-the-shutdown/#2da0cb923425
56. Ibid.
57. Ibid.
58. https://www.bls.gov/opub/mlr/2014/article/consumer-spending-and-us-employment-from-the-recession-through-2022.htm
59. https://voxeu.org/article/coronavirus-pandemic-and-us-consumption
60. Ibid.
61. https://www.forbes.com/sites/jasongoldberg/2020/03/29/the-impact-of-COVID-19-on-us-brands-and-retailers/#548957511452
62. https://www.uschamber.com/series/above-the-fold/new-poll-says-1-4-small-businesses-brink-of-permanent-closure
63. https://www.usatoday.com/story/money/2020/05/12/american-brands-that-might-not-survive-the-coronavirus/111680774/
64. https://fortune.com/2020/05/20/coronavirus-employees-workers-mental-health-benefits-COVID-19/
65. https://www.businessinsider.com/companies-offering-more-mental-health-benefits-amid-coronavirus-2020-4
66. https://www.washingtonpost.com/health/coronavirus-is-harming-the-mental-health-of-tens-of-millions-of-people-in-us-new-poll-finds/2020/04/02/565e6744-74ee-11ea-85cb-8670579b863d_story.html
67. Ibid.
https://www.forbes.com/sites/alankohll/2020/04/20/5-ways-to-support-your-employees-mental-health-during-a-pandemic/#7fec4d6e6892
68. https://www.businesswire.com/news/home/20200409005169/en/New-Data-Ginger-Shows-70-Percent-Workers
69. https://www.forbes.com/sites/bryanrobinson/2020/08/22/upsurge-in-depression-and-suicide-among-american-workers-during-the-pandemic-and-what-needs-to-be-done/?ocid=uxbndlbing#d6b66badb535
70. Ibid.
71. https://www.prnewswire.com/news-releases/39-of-employees-feel-less-productive-during-the-COVID-19-pandemic-employers-have-responded-with-mental-health-support-and-workday-changes-301089875.html; https://clutch.co/hr/resources/employee-health-affected-by-COVID-19
72. https://fortune.com/2020/05/20/coronavirus-employees-workers-mental-health-benefits-COVID-19/
73. https://clutch.co/hr/resources/employee-health-affected-by-COVID-19

74. https://www.forbes.com/sites/alankohll/2020/04/06/how-one-company-is-taking-care-of-employees-during-COVID-19/
75. Ibid.
76. https://www.entrepreneur.com/article/294143
77. Ibid.
78. Ibid.
79. https://www.shrm.org/ResourcesAndTools/hr-topics/benefits/Pages/top-ways-employers-hold-down-healthcare-spending.aspx
80. https://www.businessinsider.com/companies-offering-more-mental-health-benefits-amid-coronavirus-2020-4
81. https://stories.starbucks.com/press/2020/starbucks-transforms-mental-health-benefit-for-us-employees/#:~:text=Starbuckspercent20Transformspercent20 Mental percent20Health percent20Benefit percent20for percent20U.S. percent 20Employees.,sessions percent20with percent20a percent20therapist percent 20or percent20coach percent20each percent20year
82. https://www2.deloitte.com/us/en/insights/topics/talent/workplace-mental-health-programs-worker-productivity.html
83. https://www.who.int/mental_health/in_the_workplace/en/
84. https://www2.deloitte.com/us/en/insights/topics/talent/workplace-mental-health-programs-worker-productivity.html
85. https://www.cdc.gov/workplacehealthpromotion/model/evaluation/productivity.html
86. https://www.forbes.com/sites/kevinharrington/2015/05/13/corporate-wellness-health-wellness-and-an-improved-bottom-line/#7e3276efe82b
87. Ibid.
88. https://www.wellsteps.com/blog/2020/01/02/workplace-wellness-statistics-wellness-stats/
89. https://nbloom.people.stanford.edu/sites/g/files/sbiybj4746/f/wfh.pdf
90. https://www.nytimes.com/2020/06/23/business/working-from-home-productivity.html
91. Ibid.
92. https://sectigo.com/uploads/resources/Wakefield-Research-White-Paper-Report-for-Sectigo_V2.1.pdf
93. https://www.marketwatch.com/story/zoom-microsoft-cloud-usage-are-rocketing-during-coronavirus-pandemic-new-data-show-2020-03-30
94. Ibid.
95. https://hbr.org/resources/pdfs/comm/achievers/hbr_achievers_report_sep13.pdf
96. https://www.linkageinc.com/leadership-insights/when-work-from-home-stops-being-optional-how-to-effectively-manage-remote-teams-during-COVID-19/;https://hbr.org/resources/pdfs/comm/achievers/hbr_achievers_report_sep13.pdf

97. https://hbr.org/resources/pdfs/comm/achievers/hbr_achievers_report_sep13.pdf

98. https://www.linkageinc.com/leadership-insights/when-work-from-home-stops-being-optional-how-to-effectively-manage-remote-teams-during-COVID-19/

99. https://www.businesswire.com/news/home/20200519005295/en/Prodoscore-Research-MarchApril-2020-Productivity-Increased-Led

100. https://knowledge.wharton.upenn.edu/article/COVID-19-teaches-us-importance-trust-work/

101. https://www.omniagroup.com/micromanaging-your-employees-why-its-bad-and-how-to-stop/

102. Ibid.

103. https://www.linkageinc.com/leadership-insights/when-work-from-home-stops-being-optional-how-to-effectively-manage-remote-teams-during-COVID-19/

104. Ibid.

105. https://www.spglobal.com/spdji/en/indices/equity/sp-global-1200-industrials/#overview

106. https://www.spglobal.com/spdji/en/indices/equity/sp-100/#overview; https://www.investing.com/indices/ftse-all-world-historical-data

107. https://www.spglobal.com/spdji/en/indices/equity/sp-100/#overview

108. https://www.investing.com/indices/ftse-all-world-historical-data; https://www.spglobal.com/spdji/en/indices/equity/sp-global-1200-industrials/#overview

109. https://www.mhanational.org/blog/8-employers-supporting-employee-mental-health-during-COVID-19

110. https://www.apa.org/news/press/releases/2012/03/well-being

111. Interview with the author. Henderson Rebecca, Why firms don't commit to a people-centered way of doing business, 30th Sept.

Inclusion and the Bottom Line

A Broken Structure

I nclusiveness, coupled with a respectful curiosity about our differences, allows for valuable learning opportunities and opens doors to the exploration of different perspectives. These days, all or nearly all corporations repeat the mantra that diversity is "the right thing to do." But words without deeds will not make real progress.

Without clear strategies and goals, business leaders lack the foundation for success. True inclusion in the senior management ranks, as well as at the pipeline recruitment level, requires commitment and a willingness to actually do the work. Unfortunately, many companies still maintain a limited view of what true representation looks like. But firms with a track record of authentic inclusion will reap economic benefits.

In 2020, the world saw what Black Americans long knew about continued violence and lack of respect for Black life and liberty with the horrendous deaths of Ahmaud Arbery, Breonna Taylor, and George Floyd, among others. Corporations responded as they always do, with rhetoric about "standing with Black Americans." So-called black-outs, where brands replaced their logos with black boxes as a visual display of solidarity, overtook businesses' social media pages. Publicity departments released carefully crafted statements about their firms' "commitments to change."

But it was different this time. Words were no longer sufficient. People demanded accountability.

The killings of Arbery, Taylor, and Floyd all occurred in the United States, but the impact reverberated globally. In Europe, the European Union (EU) released a resolution denouncing racism,[1] while in Japan, there was push back on media caricatures depicting stereotypes of protestors and discussions about widespread poor treatment, particularly of biracial Japanese people, emerged.[2]

The path to corporate and social accountability for inclusion and ethical treatment was laid. There was no turning back.

In the same way Chapter 4 outlines why successful firms plan and promote health and well-being, here we identify why successful firms plan and promote diversity, equality, and inclusion. Further, the chapter will clarify how these improvements benefit productivity and the bottom line, examining such topics as these:

- Employee discrimination: Not just an American corporate problem
- Regulatory enforcement and legal consequences
- Diversity, equity, and inclusion: From hot trend to corporate culture
- Lack of diversity in the C-suite
- Improving corporate culture
- Talking the talk, walking the walk
- Investors and change
- Hiring bias
- Quantifying true supplier diversity
- Quantifiable hiring goals
- Promoting fairness for agricultural and domestic workers
- The corporate DNA of slavery

Employee Discrimination: Not Just an American Corporate Problem

Harassment and the unfair treatment of people of color has been a constant in corporate America and in corporations around the globe. Racial and ethnic discrimination are not unique to the United States. People of color have contended with these obstacles around the world for generations.

The European Network Against Racism (ENAR) reports were completed between 2012 and 2013 to gather information about racial and ethnic employment discrimination throughout Europe. Researchers looked at Eurozone countries including Austria, Denmark, France, Germany, and the United Kingdom. The reports found ethnic origin to be the most widely perceived grounds for discrimination across the EU.[3] It also found that 39% of Europeans believe that skin color or ethnic origin disadvantage minority job applicants.

When questioned about personal discrimination experiences, 27% of Europeans belonging to an ethnic minority group reported feeling discriminated against. The reports revealed that Muslims, Black Europeans, and people of African descent are among the groups most vulnerable to employment discrimination. In Ireland, Black Africans reported workplace discrimination at rates seven times higher than their White counterparts. Meanwhile, research by the Centre for Social Investigation at Nuffield College at the University of Oxford found that Black Britons and people of South Asian origin–particularly Pakistanis–face labor market discrimination at rates unchanged since the late 1960s.[4]

The Equality Act 2010 is a UK legislation that offers legal protections from racial discrimination in the workplace; it simplified a number of existing regulations to streamline them into a single law.[5] The Richemont race discrimination case was one highly publicized matter that arose out of an Equality Act violation. The court found that a Black employee of Richemont (UK), which owns luxury brands including Cartier and Montblanc, was spied on by her employer, bullied by coworkers, and denied the opportunity to progress due to her race.[6]

The court also determined that the company's preference for White Europeans was an act of direct discrimination, having no Black staff member in senior-level positions or within the human resources department. HR teams had no equality and diversity training and there were no Black staff members at a senior level or on the HR team. When the employee complained about the bullying and harassment she faced from other workers, she was told to look for another job and accused of being a troublemaker. The judge ruled in favor of the employee and awarded compensation for her traumatic and humiliating experiences with the company.[7]

Unfortunately, employment discrimination is a common experience among people of color living in London. As mentioned in Chapter 2, I interviewed an Afro-Caribbean man in the United Kingdom, Idris, and his experience is one many people of color will recognize.

For an African Caribbean person, they can think of any reason that's legitimate to reject someone of color. I know this is just my own personal opinion, but for me, it was more about the "personality" fit, my face didn't fit. For instance, my name is considered a very non-characteristically Caribbean name. So no one would know [my ethnicity] until I go into the interview. I have been in situations where I've been very, very taken aback by the interviewers. They almost fall on the floor when they see me.

These challenges are hardly limited to Europe. The Indigenous population of Australia has faced decades of racial discrimination in the employment sector. A survey by TNS Social Research found that 31% of non-Indigenous people between the ages of 25 and 44 have witnessed employment discrimination against Indigenous Australians, and 56% believe that Indigenous Australians have a more difficult time succeeding within their country. The survey also found that 24% of respondents believe that employment discrimination occurs without the initiators being aware that their actions are wrong. Of the respondents 1 in 10 admitted that they would likely act in a similar way by discriminating against Indigenous Australians in a workplace environment.[8]

In 2009, the government of Australia created the Fair Work Ombudsman (FWO), an autonomous department under the Ministry of Employment, charged with ensuring a safe and secure workplace environment. Their first racial discrimination litigation resulted in the Federal Circuit Court fining of an employer for a total of $211,104. The case involved a Tasmanian hotel operator who was found to have paid his White Australian employees appropriate wages while underpaying Malaysian employees by more than $28,000. The federal court found the hotel breached racial discrimination provisions of the Fair Work Act when he exploited the Malaysian workers and forced them to work extra hours without pay.[9]

This was the first case brought against an Australian employer based on racial discrimination against employees. "This employer knew that all staff were lawfully entitled to minimum award pay rates but chose to pay the Malaysian couple significantly less than Australian staff because of their race, which is unlawful and completely unacceptable," said Fair Work Ombudsman Natalie James. "Our success in this case is a warning to any employer tempted to make employment decisions based on race: the Fair Work

131

Inclusion and the Bottom Line

Ombudsman can and will seek penalties for discrimination as well as pursuing any unpaid entitlements, and we will do so via court action if necessary."[10]

Regulatory Enforcement and Legal Consequences

In the United States, the Equal Employment Opportunity Commission (EEOC) is the federal agency responsible for enforcing federal laws prohibiting discrimination or harassment against a job applicant or an employee. Started under the Civil Rights Act of 1964, the agency has seen more than a million complaints regarding workplace discrimination. Throughout the 1970s, the EEOC accumulated a backlog of 100,000 charges for investigation.

President Ronald Reagan appointed Clarence Thomas as chairman of the Equal Employment Opportunity Commission (EEOC) in 1982. As a staunch opponent of Affirmative Action, his appointment to one of the federal government's leading civil rights agencies was controversial to say the least.[11] Instead of filing increased numbers of class action discrimination suits, which are considered to be more impactful for communities, Thomas chose to shift the focus of the agency toward individual discrimination suits. This disappointed civil rights groups who were fighting for broad systemic changes.[12] After three decades of shrinking percentages, the wage gap between Black and White men became stagnant in the 1980s, signaling fewer promotions and hiring for Black workers.[13] The widest gaps in employment between Blacks and Whites occurred during the 1980s, under Thomas's tenure leading the EEOC.[14]

The 1980s also saw a number of large-scale racial bias lawsuits hitting the media. In 1983, a Black McDonald's franchisee filed a discrimination lawsuit against the company, alleging that Black franchisees were prohibited from operating restaurants within predominantly White communities.[15] Following news coverage of the allegations, the fast food giant experienced a significant dip in stock prices from 1983 to 1984 before rebounding in 1985.[16] And should you think that this issue was put to bed in the 1980s, similar allegations resurfaced in 2020, with more than 50 former franchisees filing suit against the corporation.

Oil giant Texaco settled a racial discrimination lawsuit in 1996, agreeing to pay $175 million to affected employees. The case began with four workers in 1994 but ballooned to over 1,400 plaintiffs. Secretly recorded tapes of Texaco executives allegedly making racist remarks were made public, significantly damaging the company's reputation. Texaco experienced more than a $1 billion in losses during the lawsuit's duration.[17] It was not until the company announced the terms of the settlement agreement that its stock rallied.

General Electric (GE) has faced two major race discrimination lawsuits. The first occurred in 2005 when Black managers accused the company of paying them less than their White counterparts, denying them promotions, and using offensive terms to describe Black workers. Though the case settled in 2006, the company came under scrutiny again in 2008 when more than 50 Black workers filed a lawsuit against the company for racial discrimination, alleging that a manager was allowed to repeatedly refer to them with racial slurs, deny bathroom breaks and medical attention to Black workers, and fire others because of their race.[18] The company settled the suit in 2010 for $3 million.[19] It's interesting to note that GE also faced considerable economic turmoil in 2008, with profits in its financial sector dipping 44%.[20]

Diversity, Equity, and Inclusion: From Hot Trend to Corporate Culture

The 2000s brought about an increase in the number of diversity, equity, and inclusion (DEI) offices in corporations nationwide. Many

C-suites added chief diversity officers (CDO) to their organizations. Pinterest hired its first CDO in 2016, and Uber did so in 2018 in response to numerous high-profile claims of racial and gender discrimination within the company. WarnerMedia added a chief diversity and inclusion officer to its team of executives in 2019.

DEI initiatives created a specific division for identifying and implementing best practices across functions and businesses. These corporate evolutions helped to move DEI from an item on an HR checklist to a necessary aspect of doing business.

Successful DEI involves taking a clear and honest view of a company's current situation to identify areas for improvement within hiring, promotion, and the company culture. It includes underrepresented groups within these discussions and moves the conversation outside of the human resources office so that every department and level of leadership becomes an active participant. An effective DEI program needs the involvement and commitment of C-level executives, which often represent the least diverse areas of a company.[21] DEI offices act as advisors to senior leaders, while still having a large degree of independence.

DEI leaders are tasked with leading their organizations, but they must ensure each stakeholder in the business takes responsibility for compassionate, inclusive treatment once diverse talent is in the door. This requires a proactive strategy that educates employees about diversity and the reasons why the company is taking steps to craft a more inclusive and equitable environment. These dialogues and trainings must take place consistently to reinforce the company's commitment. DEI leaders must move stakeholders beyond buzz words and rhetoric and toward diverse and inclusive culture.

Even the most iconic progressive companies have to put in conscious effort to create diverse environments. Ice cream makers Ben and Jerry's have earned a reputation as a corporation committed to equality and compassion. "In businesses, in a lot of ways, you treasure what you measure," said CEO Matthew McCarthy. "You measure what you treasure. If you don't put goals around these things, they simply don't happen."[22] In 2016, after acknowledging the lack of diversity within their ranks, the company issued the following statement, "Our work starts inside our own company. We aspire to become a more equitable and inclusive business—and to build a culture that makes diversity the real source of our strength. We have formed an equity team to lead that work, and we are well on our way."[23]

Starbucks has also worked at establishing itself as a brand committed to equality. (For more on Starbucks' conscious attempts to become more inclusive, see Chapter 1.) As of 2019, their workforce makeup was 54% White and 46% people of color.[24] The company strives to increase the number of people of color at the vice president and senior leadership levels: 33% of their vice presidents are people of color, as are 15% of Starbuck's senior leaders. The company has also achieved 100% pay equity across races for all people performing similar work in the United States.

Though they have been the subject of several allegations of racial discrimination and the lack of maternity protection, sportswear company Nike has made an effort to take on difficult social justice conversations. In 2017, the company launched a diversity campaign featuring athletes such as LeBron James, Serena Williams, and Victor Cruz. In 2018, the company came out in support of embattled NFL player Colin Kaepernick by making him the face of an international advertising campaign.[25] Faced with widespread protests and viral videos of people setting fire to their products, Nike leadership doubled down on their support for Kaepernick and the message behind his protests. The commitment led to some significant financial gains. Following a small dip in the price of their shares, the company's stock surged 33% hitting an all-time high.[26]

In response to allegations of discrimination, Nike announced measures to increase diversity within the company, including leadership accountability and crafting business opportunities for women and racial minorities. More than 10,000 managers worldwide underwent mandatory diversity and unconscious bias awareness training.[27] A newly created diversity talent acquisition team worked to identify diverse candidates for all open positions within the corporation. Nike also crafted mentorship programs for women and minorities. Additionally, after facing public scrutiny on financially penalizing pregnant athletes, Nike amended their contracts with athletes to protect athletes' compensation during pregnancy.[28]

Outside of their corporate offices, Nike has a proven track record of community advocacy and inclusion-driven program funding. Their N7 fund "leverages the power of sport to create positive change for the next generation of Native American and Aboriginal youth."[29] The company also offers grants and scholarships to minority communities across the country and around the globe.

Lack of Diversity in the C-Suite

In the midst of the COVID-19 pandemic, as the everyday hustle of life slowed down and so many people sat in their homes with nowhere to go, we were inundated with videos revealing heinous attacks on Black citizens. These disturbing images led to widespread participation in protests, racially focused policy discussions, and demonstrations of social media solidarity by corporate leaders. But for many companies, these public outcries and commitments did not match what was actually happening around their boardroom tables.

As conversations began, people of color were invited to share the negative experiences and challenges of working in corporate

America. Although these discussions have been occurring for decades among Black people and other people of color, the invitation to speak directly to the White people who head these corporations and make real decisions about the directions of these companies was a new occurrence. Out of these conversations emerged painful realizations about the parallels between the mistreatment of people of color in public places and the embarrassingly low numbers of people of color in C-suite and executive positions. As discussed in Chapter 3 (but reiterated here again), White males still hold the majority of executive positions such as CEOs, managing directors, and financial officers. They hold about 85% of these well-paid boardroom positions though they only represent 38% of the American workforce.[30] Boardroom diversity positively affects company profitability and employee job satisfaction by providing a valuable connection between company executives and non-executive employees.

As of 2019, the Latinx population was the largest minority group in the US, but only held a small fraction of executive positions. Studies show that Latinx representation is very similar to the representation of Black executives and slightly lower than the representation of Asian American executives (see Table 5.1). The gap that exists between the labor force and executive representation is most significant among the Latinx community.[31]

Table 5.1   Labor Force Representation Versus Executive Level Representation

	Labor Workforce (%)	Executive Positions (%)
Latinx	17	4.3
Black	13	3.2
Asian	6	5.9

Inclusion and the Bottom Line

Improving Corporate Culture

Conversations about corporate diversity also inspired dialogue about the microaggressions and unethical behaviors that drive people of color out of companies or keep them positioned in lower levels of corporations, as introduced in Chapter 2. Here, we go into greater detail. *Psychology Today* defines microaggressions as "the everyday verbal, nonverbal, and environmental slights, snubs, or insults, whether intentional or unintentional, which communicate hostile, derogatory, or negative messages to target persons based solely upon their marginalized group membership."[32] Some examples of microaggressions are a White employee not including a coworker of color in relevant communications; an Asian American being complimented for speaking "good English"; a Latinx employee who is praised for being "well-spoken"; and touching of a Black woman's hair without permission.

Some of these actions and comments may be deliberate, but oftentimes they happen unconsciously because someone is ignorant as to the inappropriateness of their behavior. But deliberate or not, if left unchecked, microaggressions can have damaging effects on workplace culture.[33] Companies need to make all employees aware of how these behaviors point to their own biases and prejudices, ultimately fueling a corporate culture of exclusion.

Any company with a true commitment to diversity should mandate implicit bias and microaggression training for all employees. Those who have been the target of these actions need to feel empowered to speak up when they occur. For decades, employees of color have suffered in silence out of fear of job loss or being labeled a troublemaker. They have allowed these microaggressions to go unchecked because they feared the repercussions that they may face if they complained or went to HR with their concerns.

One glaring example that we saw during the pandemic stemmed from rumors about the origins and spread of the virus. As politicians insistently referred to COVID-19 as "the China virus," Asian Americans of all backgrounds were blamed as carriers. Unconscious bias looms, and when unchecked, biases toward certain groups affect our hiring, promotion, and inclusion decisions.

The events of 2020 have created a unique opportunity for corporations to have these conversations openly and honestly in order to raise awareness and make clear what actions will not be tolerated within the workplace. Meaningful dialogue and communication are key to the reduction of microaggressions within the corporate environment. Conversations about mutual respect helps employees become more aware and thoughtful about their actions, providing them with the knowledge and techniques to mitigate microaggressions (for more practical advice on preventing microaggressions, see Chapter 8).

Talking the Talk, Walking the Walk

Corporations need to do more than make statements and dedicate a page on their website to diversity. The construction of an inclusive, equality-driven, and compassionate corporate culture requires specific plans to reinforce beneficial behaviors and reduce destructive ones. Real quantitative commitments to Blacks and other underrepresented groups is needed to encourage trust and confidence and build a compassionate, solution-oriented environment. Yes, the racial unrest of 2020 has been disturbing and an eye-opener for some business leaders, but will these public displays of support come with real structural change?

Blackout Tuesday was a perfect example of corporations placing trend over substance. In response to the murders of George Floyd, Breonna Taylor, and Ahmaud Arbery, two Black women sought to disrupt the work week and call attention to the systemic racism that exists within the music industry.[34] They proposed that all members of the music industry refrain from conducting business and place all-Black pictures on their social media platforms for 24 hours.

It didn't take long for the entertainment industry to join in the protest, with celebrities announcing their plans to participate. Then, out of the blue, we saw large and small companies alike placing Black pictures on their social media platforms, supposedly in support of the protest. But many people of color viewed these outward actions as disingenuous, especially because many of the "participating" companies continued conducting business on that day. It felt like these organizations had coopted the protest for their own gain instead of truly taking a stand.

On the upside, Blackout Tuesday brought about corporate social media support for Black employees in numbers we hadn't seen before. Many companies went beyond the usual pro-diversity paragraph on their homepages by enforcing behavior-driven practices for the use of language and inclusion. For example, Rocket Companies, Inc. announced a six-point diversity and inclusion plan, detailing the company's commitment to hiring and developing diverse talent, facilitating conversations with the Detroit Police Department and community stakeholders, and advocating for equality.[35]

Nestlé hosted a series of employee listening forums on race, inclusivity, and allyship. They used the information gathered during these conversations to develop plans for addressing racial inequity within the company and their communities. According to the Nestlé website those plans will include linking executive pay and performance to diversity and inclusion outcomes, mandating unconscious bias training for all people leaders in 2020 and all employees in 2021, and donating $1.75 million to the National Urban League, United

Negro College Fund, and other organizations focused on racial equity. Starbucks gives another example of leaning in on diversity. The chain announced in October 2020 they're targeting 30% of US corporate employees and 40% of their retail and manufacturing employees to be people of color by 2025, further, executive compensation for SVPs and higher will have a diversity metric consideration.[36]

Some of the corporate changes we saw even centered on offered products and services. Johnson & Johnson said it would stop selling skin lightening creams, which are among their most popular products in Asia and the Middle East, acknowledging that these products represented lighter or White skin as preferable to darker skin. A unit of PepsiCo, Inc. announced that it would retire the name and image of Aunt Jemima after acknowledging the popular pancake branding represented racial stereotyping.[37] The makers of Uncle Ben's and Cream of Wheat announced similar decisions to "evolve" their product brands.[38] The corporate owner of Eskimo Pie ice cream announced plans to change the product's brand name and marketing.[39]

Perhaps one of the biggest product evolutions of the year occurred when Dan Snyder, owner of Washington Redskins, announced that the team would no longer use the derogatory name and image that it had carried for decades.[40] "Today, we are announcing we will be retiring the Redskins name and logo. [Owner] Dan Snyder and Coach Rivera are working closely to develop a new name and design approach that will enhance the standing of our proud, tradition rich franchise and inspire our sponsors, fans and community for the next 100 years."[41] For years, team leaders adamantly refused to make this change despite consistent requests from the Native American community. It was not until their corporate sponsors, in light of the 2020 racial injustice protests, placed pressure on the team that they finally agreed.

141

Inclusion and the Bottom Line

Investors and Change

Influencing the diversity and equality decisions of a large corporation is no easy task. It either takes a widespread consumer boycott, like we saw with Gucci and Prada in response to their items featuring racially inappropriate blackface images, or media pressure that threatens a company's reputation.[42] But there's another group that is well positioned to influence diversity and compassion at all corporate levels, including the C-suite. Institutional investors, representing pensions, hedge funds, mutual funds, and others, pool loads of money together to invest into corporations. These are not individual investors who invest a few hundred dollars here or a couple of thousand dollars there. These investors put millions of dollars into the hands of corporations. As such, they have influence with the board and C-suite, including how they govern the business. If these institutional investors use their power to insist on diversity at the top levels of corporations, changes will occur.

A 2019 McKinsey study focused on the relationship between diverse executive teams and financial performance found companies in the top quartile for cultural and ethnic diversity outperformed those in the bottom quartile with 36% greater profitability.[43] Studies consistently prove that companies with diversity in senior leadership significantly outperform their all-White, all-male counterparts.[44] Diverse leadership translates to better financial performance and stronger innovation, which translates to higher profits. So, why wouldn't institutional investors push for these changes?

A *Harvard Business Review* article discussed the influence that these investors could have in diversifying venture funds. "Chief executive officers, chief investment officers, board members and trustees of large institutional investors—many of whom claim to care about diversity and inclusion—can make a meaningful difference by holding venture capital funds accountable."[45] Just as institutional investors enthusiastically promote greater sustainability within companies, such as reducing their carbon footprints and using less plastics, they can exercise the same level of influence over ensuring greater inclusive practices within executive boardrooms.

Most retail investors don't have enough shares to make quite the difference. But institutional investors tend to be larger and more organized. So if there is an issue that they really care about, not only can they push the company on it, but they can organize other like-minded individuals in their network. In some cases, especially when it relates to small and mid-cap companies, it's very easy for an institutional investor to own 10 percent, then they really have votes to change the board completely, [or] to change management.

Companies are required to track diversity statistics. The issue is disclosure. As an investor, you first need the data to be able to know what's happening. And very few companies currently provide racial statistics, even though by law they're required to collect that data. So you are seeing more institutional investors are starting to demand that data. It's always harder to find that data on racial diversity.

It's our job as institutional investors to continue to engage companies to make sure they're focusing on [diversity] issues—not only because it's the right thing to do, but because there is real risk of capital loss. [We must] continue to push for better disclosures on issues

(continues)

(*continued*)
like diversity and inequality and on policies and strategies that companies are using to address this issue.

—*Juliette Menga, CFA director, chair of
ESG/Sustainable Investing Committee at Aetos
Alternatives Management*

Hiring Bias

In 2017, Harvard Business School reported on a survey with 1,600 résumés from Asian and Black entry-level applicants in 16 US locations. Some résumés included clues to the race of the applicant, others removed clues or "whitened" their résumés. The outcome? Of the applicants who left racial clues, 10% of Black applicants and 11.5% of Asians received callbacks. Whitened résumés received a much-higher rate of callbacks: 25% of Black candidates and 21% of Asians got callbacks.[46]

This makes the case for scrutinizing old approaches to hiring and recruiting. A growing number of companies are using technology, data, and incentive programs to change the behavior patterns that prevent equality, inclusivity, and compassion within the recruiting, promoting, and outsourcing processes. For example, artificial intelligence (AI) and tech systems are gaining popularity as are diverse hiring panels to mitigate unconscious bias and create more compassionate and equality-driven corporate environments.

The assumption is that AI can fairly screen for candidates that best match the company's needs without the conscious and unconscious human bias that creeps into candidate evaluations. However, some people see cracks in the theory about AI's objectivity. In an interview in *The Guardian,* Cathy O'Neil, author of *Weapons of Math Destruction,* explains how AI can actually reinforce biases, particularly when there is a blind belief in AI's objectivity without challenging AIs transparency. She believes opinions play a role in building algorithms and the technology could be "using people's fear and trust of mathematics to prevent them from asking questions."[47] Despite the reality that there continues to be a need to evaluate and question how AI is created and used, 79% of recruiting and hiring managers believe that AI will play a role in their jobs in the future.[48]

The WePow app is a talent engagement software that helps organizations reduce the time and cost of hiring employees by using live video interviewing technology.[49] The company also claims that the platform works to level the playing field for candidates by increasing consistency and transparency in the recruitment process. With video, everyone has the same initial experience, instead of being subject to different tones or environments from interviewers. Also other people at the company can have access to the video—as opposed to in-person interviews, which are only seen by those in the room at the time. This helps ensure visibility into any potential issues.

Outmatch is another hiring software that is designed to improve hiring strategies by using AI to speak to candidates' fit and potential, instead of just relying on human interaction that may contain possible biases.

XOR is a recruiting tool that uses an AI chatbot to screen candidates, schedule interviews, and answer questions. Their AI capabilities have helped companies such as IKEA, McDonald's, Mars, Exxon Mobil, and Manpower Group recruit and retain talent more effectively.[50]

Pymetrics is a company that uses AI to vet potential employees. It involves a process in which current employees take a series of gaming tests. The resulting algorithms are then used to build a persona of the best candidate for the position. Candidates take similar tests to see if they are a match. With data from the game results, AI-based algorithms match candidates with the company's top performers. Pymetrics was founded in 2013 by two neuroscientists who set out to remove bias in hiring and make it more efficient.[51] The entire process occurs blindly without the collection of demographic information regarding gender or ethnicity.

Companies such as Unilever, Accenture, and McDonald's have already implemented Pymetrics as a part of their job application process.[52] Unilever counts its partnership with Pymetrics as a success, particularly in terms of increased ethnic and educational diversity.[53] They reported receiving applicants from significantly more schools, including community colleges. Their hiring pool also achieved greater gender inclusion with less skewing toward male applicants.

Companies are also implementing diverse hiring panels to mitigate unconscious bias and create more compassionate and equality-driven corporate environments. Diverse hiring panels bring different perspectives and unique experiences to the hiring process. These panels include a small group of people across business disciplines internally and from diverse backgrounds (race, gender, and so on). I've participated in diverse panels consisting of four interviewers of different racial and gender backgrounds, representing different parts of the firm. We all had specific questions to ask the candidate. Questions were transparent and accompanied a rating system.

Candidates appeared more comfortable and welcomed. They also had the opportunity to ask us questions about our area of the business. After the interview, we sent the candidates' answers and our ratings to the administrator handling the HR or business side. This approach was also beneficial in that it allowed candidates to see the company's commitment to diversity and inclusion for themselves during their interviews.

In 2014, technology giant Intel began requiring panel interviewers for any new hire to include at least two women and/or members of underrepresented minorities. Since implementing this policy, the company has witnessed a drastic increase in the diversity of new hires.[54] In 2016, 45.1% were women or people of color, up from 31.9% in 2014. The company counts this as progress toward their corporate goal of an employee population that fully represents the percentage of women and underrepresented minorities in the overall technology workforce.

"Implementing diverse hiring panels has enabled us to cast a wider net at the outset of the hiring process and systematically help reduce unconscious bias in our hiring," says Danielle Brown, Intel's vice president of human resources and group chief human resources officer in an interview with *Working Mother*.[55] "Unless we bring a diverse set of perspectives to solve the most difficult technical problems, we are not going to reach our full potential as a company."

Quantifying True Supplier Diversity

Employees are not the only entities that corporations hire and onboard. Vendors and suppliers are "hired"—in the sense that they are contracted—and must engage corporations as their customers. From janitorial services to cafeteria workers to tech suppliers, vendors exist throughout most corporations. Equality in their onboarding and treatment should also be part of an equitable environment.

Supplier diversity has become part of these important conversations as companies look more closely at their records on this issue. In 1961, President Kennedy created the Council on Equal Opportunity by executive order. It mandated that federal contractors hire people regardless of race, creed, color, or national origin. It also required these contractors to take active steps toward removing obstacles to equal employment opportunity. President Lyndon Johnson's Executive Order 11246 took this mandate a step farther by requiring federal contractors and subcontractors to "identify and correct" any barriers to equal employment opportunity, and where appropriate craft goals to measure success toward achievement of that goal.[56]

These actions at the federal level helped to introduce quantifiable measurements as a tool for greater employment diversity. Since that time, quotas and affirmative action programs have existed within the United States, in one form or another, to address historical discrimination in contracting, employment, and education. Mandates such as these are important because the federal government is the largest employer in the United States—not only do its policies affect the lives of millions of employees but also they influence private sector decisions. The battle over the legality of these mandates has been hard-fought since 1961 and it continues to rage on today.

The National Minority Supplier Development Council (NMSDC) connects certified minority business enterprises with corporate members to provide them with advanced business opportunities.[57] In response to the negative impact that COVID-19 had on Black-owned businesses, the organization started the "In This Together" campaign. It includes a collection of initiatives and supply chain programs to expedite recovery within the Black business community. The council asked their corporate members' C-Level executives to "fortify and recommit to their organization's utilization of minority businesses." Companies such as Coca-Cola, AT&T, Kellogg, and the Walt Disney Company have all pledged their support.

Mark Westfall, chief procurement officer and head of supplier services for The Coca-Cola Company, stated, "The Coca-Cola Company and our bottling partners have a longstanding commitment to the growth and development of diverse suppliers. The Coca-Cola Company has consistently grown our commitment and spend with diverse suppliers over the 45+ years since our Supplier Diversity program began. We are proud to partner with NMSDC and in 2020 will continue to financially support NMSDC's MBE [Minority Business Enterprise] economic inclusion and parity initiatives while growing our overall diverse supplier spend."[58]

Target is another corporation with a proven track record of promoting racial equality among their suppliers. Between 2016 and 2018, the company increased its business with diverse suppliers by 64.4%, with a goal to continue ongoing investments in diverse suppliers.[59] The company's website states, "Target's proud to work with an ever-growing roster of diverse suppliers that are at least 51 percent owned, controlled and operated by women; Black, Indigenous and People of Color; LGBTQ+; veterans or persons with disabilities... That includes the products we carry and services like construction, facilities maintenance and more that keep our stores, distribution centers, headquarters locations and other sites running smoothly."[60]

In late 2019, Target's commitment to a diverse supply chain came under attack when its holiday commercials featured products created and manufactured by a Black female-owned company. Honey Pot is a feminine product line that is sold in Target stores and on their website. Bea Dixon, the Honey Pot founder, appeared in the company's commercials stating, "so the next Black girl that comes up with a great idea could have a better opportunity."[61]

Many customers, particularly White women, took issue with the fact that Dixon specifically mentioned "Black girls" within the ad and began flooding the Target website and Honey Pot's portal with negative baseless reviews and insults. Target reacted to the negativity with a statement that it was "proud" to work with Dixon and her company. Supporters of Honey Pot rallied around the company, ultimately resulting in a 30% increase in sales that benefitted the company, as well as Target.[62] For weeks, the Honey Pot line of products consistently sold out on the Target website.

149

Inclusion and the Bottom Line

Quantifiable Hiring Goals

Supply chains are not the only area where quotas have emerged as a viable diversity tool. Private firms are also embracing quantifiable numbers to increase diverse hiring practices and promotions. Many of America's biggest corporations have publicly proclaimed their commitment to diversity for decades, spending billions of dollars to hire diversity officers, ramp up recruitment efforts, and advertise their efforts to the public. Yet, even with all of these efforts, Black people still only made up about 3.2% of executive senior leadership positions in 2019.[63]

In response to these disappointing outcomes, some companies have implemented quantifiable goals to encourage employment of non-White and ethnic minorities through racial quotas.[64] In the weeks following the George Floyd protests for racial justice, several large corporations, such as Delta Airlines, announced the adoption of workforce quota policies. Wells Fargo & Co. announced plans to increase Black leadership to 12% following their settlement of federal allegations of bias in their hiring practices. Fashion company Ralph Lauren Corp. announced an initiative to ensure that 20% of its global leaders are people of color.[65]

Similar to supplier diversity quotas, hiring quotas also evolved out of the 1960s presidential executive orders. Though these programs face considerable criticism, experts say they are effective at meeting diversity goals. "Companies that write affirmative-action plans, which set goals, see more progress toward diversity than companies that don't," said Frank Dobbin, a professor of social sciences at Harvard University.[66]

On the other side of the argument, some experts assert that corporate quotas can have a detrimental effect on a company's culture. Those hired under these programs may be stigmatized by their coworkers who assume that they have gotten their jobs or promotions unjustly.[67] These feelings may lower employee engagement and lead to job negativity, because employment and societal gains for one segment of the population may be perceived as losses for another segment of the population.

Opponents of quota programs argue that all hiring or promotion that occurs based on anything other than skill or merit is unacceptable. They point to nonminority individuals who gain employment or opportunities through nepotism or a social connection, such as having attended the same college as the person who makes hiring decisions. Although studies do show that these types of employment practices can also lower productivity and employee engagement, one glaring difference still remains. When an individual benefits from nepotism or association, the skills and qualifications of that individual may be brought into question. However, when an underrepresented person benefits from quotas or an affirmative action program, the skills and qualifications of an *entire race of people* may be brought into question. The underlying stigma suggests that no person of color could possibly have the appropriate background to hold these positions but for a quota system. Critics argue that this is where the true problem with quotas lies.

The implementation of racial quotas may also invite legal challenges. Yet, although the Supreme Court has looked unfavorably on quotas used by public employers, it has consistently upheld their constitutionality when used by private companies.[68]

Another quantifiable measurement tactic that has been championed in recent years involves referral bonuses. Employee referral programs provide monetary bonuses to employees who refer diverse qualified candidates. The results of these initiatives have been mixed. Intel began offering $4,000 bonuses to employees who refer women or minorities in 2015. The company did subsequently experience increases in the diversity of their hiring practices, though there is no proof of a direct correlation. Facebook also tried using monetary

151

Inclusion and the Bottom Line

incentives to improve diversity in their recruitment, but the program has reportedly been unsuccessful at netting significant results.

Workplace quotas are not unique to the United States. Globally, India's "reservation" policy is widely acknowledged as the world's oldest affirmative action policy.[69] Adopted officially in 1950, it was designed to address the prejudices of India's caste system by establishing quotas for education, the workplace, and government positions. The quotas, which vary across India, have been partly successful. In 1965, Dalits, who are considered the lowest rung of the Hindu caste system, occupied 1.6% of the most senior positions in the civil service. By 2011, that had risen to almost 12%, just 4% lower than their 16% population share in India. Yet, despite this progress, the widespread oppression of Dalits remains within India's social structure.

Race quotas have also been woven into Malaysian society. In the 1970s, sweeping changes were introduced to ensure that the majority Malays would no longer be discriminated against. These quotas still exist within Malaysia's public sector, though they have become contentious. Although the number of Malays in universities or on company boards has increased, some suggest that only the financial elite have benefited from the quotas, leaving out the poor majority and ethnic minorities.

Promoting Fairness for Agricultural and Domestic Workers

The struggle to increase both equality and equity does not only take place in the board room. People of color within the agricultural and domestic industries are some of the most underpaid and exploited workers in the country. These individuals put in long, physical hours to provide food for our tables and maintain our homes, yet they are often overlooked within discussions about employment fairness and equality.

The US Homestead Act of 1862 helped expand the settlement of western America through land grants. The Civil War–era legislation allowed citizens, including former slaves, women, and immigrants, to become landowners. However, the Homestead Act gravely affected the Native American population. The government took their land and sold it, leaving nothing for the rightful owners.

This legislation was one step in a long line of racially discriminatory actions within the agricultural industry. Farmers of color have faced decades of policies and actions amounting to millions of acres and hundreds of billions of dollars in lost wealth.[70] Resulting from decades of government-sanctioned discrimination, these losses have resulted in numerous lawsuits against the federal government.

Segregation has always been a part of the US agriculture industry. A recent study found that racial and ethnic disparities still exist within the industry when it comes to land and money.[71] From 2012 to 2014, White people comprised over 97% of nonfarming landowners, 96% of owner operators, and 86% of tenant operators.[72] They also generated 98% of all farm-related income from land ownership and 97% of the income that comes from operating farms.

Yet, farmers of color comprised less than 4% of owner operators. They were more likely to be tenants than owners. They generated less wealth from farming than their White counterparts and owned less land and smaller farms. Latinx farmers comprised about 2% of nonfarming landowners and about 6% of owner operators and tenant operators, well below their 17% representation in the US population. They also comprised over 80% of farm laborers, a notoriously undercompensated position within the US farming industry.[73]

The Fairness for Farm Workers Act amends the Fair Labor Standards Act of 1938 with respect to agricultural workers. The bill requires employers to compensate agricultural workers for hours worked in excess of their regular hours at an hourly rate that is not less than one and one-half times the employee's regular rate.[74] For employers with 25 or fewer employees, overtime pay requirements will take effect in 2024.

Congress is also considering legislation to address the injustices faced by the domestic workforce, which is an industry primarily composed of women of color who cook and clean private residences and immigrant workers who maintain the grounds. These are the people who help millions of working families manage the responsibilities of their daily lives by caring for children, aging parents, and households. In many ways, the domestic workforce makes it possible for other workforces to exist.[75]

Of the 2.5 million domestic workers in the United States, 90% are women, women of color, and immigrants. The basic labor rights of these workers have been problematic for generations. Rooted in the legacy of slavery and economic exploitation (see Chapter 2), domestic care work is often viewed as not being "real" work.[76] Nannies, housekeepers, and caregivers have been largely excluded from labor laws, leaving them without the benefits of overtime, unemployment benefits, or even a minimum wage. They have been left out of workplace safety regulations and the right to organize. Some employment laws, such as those prohibiting discrimination and sexual harassment, leave these workers out by default due to the unique nature of their working environments. As a group, these workers have some of the lowest wages in the country, which has resulted in many domestic workers living in poverty and often tolerating abuse for fear of retaliation.[77]

The Domestic Workers Bill of Rights, which was introduced by US Senator Kamala D. Harris (D-CA) and US Representative Pramila Jayapal (D-WA), recognizes the value of domestic work and the individuals who perform these important tasks. It "addresses the exclusions of the past, creates a framework for safe and dignified work environments, and sets concrete protections for the whole care sector. This bill aims to fix many of the loopholes in labor law and create new, innovative solutions to the unique nature of domestic work."[78]

Long-overdue worker protections, such as the Fairness for Farm Workers Act and the Domestic Workers Bill of Rights, help establish trust in the government to protect worker rights. Government agencies have the legal right and power to penalize companies that do not meet minimum hiring and employment standards. These fines can have a lasting effect, affecting the bottom line, as well as a company's reputation. As businesses not only meet but go beyond government policies, they will also gain the trust of their employees as they move toward more fair, unbiased work environments.

The Corporate DNA of Slavery

Our current economic system carries the genetic code of its predecessor: the colonial slave trade.

You may have read that sentence and thought, "Oh, she means that it was capitalism that brought slavery to our shores, and therefore today's capitalism is inevitably a descendent from those bad old days." And yes, I do mean that. But although that sentence can be read figuratively, I am also speaking quite literally. Companies that are still in business today—firms you probably engage with all the time—have direct ties to slavery in their pasts. Though it is an uncomfortable conversation to have, business leaders must consider how the "DNA of slavery" continues to affect corporate culture.

Evidence of this is found in lawsuits and court decisions surrounding substandard pay, hostile environments, and aggressions, from England to America and beyond. Evidence is also directly found in the history of some of the country's most successful corporate enterprises.

- Aetna, Inc., one of the nation's largest insurers sold policies in the 1850s that reimbursed slave owners for the financial losses brought on by the deaths of their enslaved workers.[79] In 2002, a company spokesperson stated, "Aetna has long acknowledged that for several years shortly after its founding in 1853 that the company may have insured the lives of slaves. We express our deep regret over any participation at all in this deplorable practice."

- New York Life Insurance Company also sold insurance policies to slaveholders.[80] Historians suggest that more than 300 of the company's first 1,000 policies were written on the lives of slaves.

- The Wachovia Corporation disclosed that two of its predecessors also owned slaves and accepted them as payment.[81] Ken Thompson, former Wachovia chairman and chief executive officer, stated "On behalf of Wachovia Corporation, I apologize to all Americans, and especially to African Americans and people of African descent. We are deeply saddened by these findings."

- Brown Brothers Harriman, one of the oldest private investment bank and securities firms in the United States, owned hundreds of slaves and lent millions to southern planters and cotton brokers, essentially financing the slave industry.[82]

These are only some of the businesses that benefitted from the forced labor of Blacks in America. Historical records also indicate that many of the first railroad companies used slaves to lay their train tracks.[83] Some of the nation's most prestigious clothing makers worked with slave owners to procure cotton from their plantations.[84] Even more troubling is the thought of how many thousands of other organizations benefitted from loans and business arrangements with these corporations. Yet, as these companies continue to profit from enterprises started or advanced by slavery, the conversation about reparations is labeled as absurd and unreasonable.

Course-correcting calls for more than empty acknowledgments and apologies. It must also include swift economic redress for Black workers and deliberately creating compassionate cultures where divisive language, aggressions, and exclusions are checked and rendered intolerable. The new corporate culture will no longer stand for the vestiges and legacy of slavery in our workplaces and economic systems.

The Gap, Inc. clothing company is one example of a corporation that is doing the work to establish a reputation for inclusion and opportunity. The company's This Way Ahead program helps youth (ages 16–24) who face societal barriers to employment secure their first job.[85] Gap recently announced the renewal of their sponsorship of Harlem's Fashion Row (HFR), an arts and entertainment organization that aligns brand partners with emerging designers of color within the fashion industry. As listed on the company's website, "Our strength comes from our ability to work together—weaving together people from different races and backgrounds. We shouldn't let ourselves be divided, and we must continue working toward freedom for everyone, without exceptions."[86]

Gap's commitment to inclusion and racial equality has been an asset to their brand, their reputation, and their bottom line. As numerous clothing brands struggle to stay afloat post-COVID-19, Gap is seeing significant recovery, with their stock no longer selling at a discount.[87] They have built a community and customer loyalty that has seen them through this challenging year. Even with the closing of their physical locations, their online sales remained strong.

Askinosie Chocolate is another example of a company that has successfully integrated social and racial justice into their culture.

Started in 2005 by a former criminal defense attorney, Askinosie uses profit sharing and financial transparency to honor and benefit the people of color who grow their cocoa beans.[88] Working with farmers in Tanzania and the Philippines, the company does not simply pay these communities fair market value for their harvests. "Most of the communities surrounding the cocoa farms are brimming with potential, but there also is room for us to invest in their greatness," states the company's website. "We translate financial statements and profit share with our farmer partners, all of which leads to empowerment and economic development."

In addition to paying the farmers above the fair trade value for their cocoa beans, the company also shares their profits with them. "At the end of the selling cycle, which also happens to be the time to inspect the new crop, we visit the farmers and pay them directly, in cash."

I had the opportunity to speak with founder and CEO Shawn Askinosie. He talked about the decision to create a transparent relationship with the company's suppliers. "Every time I visit the farmers, we translate our financials into their language so they can understand—year over year—what our income and expenses are ... as they relate to the cocoa beans that we turned into chocolate."[89]

We also spoke about the level of introspection CEOs and business owners must commit to in order to drive a culture with compassion, inclusion, and equality. He explained that introspection among business leaders is extremely important. "It is from the introspection in the awakening of our hearts that we confront, wrestle, deal with ... these biases and everything so that it trickles down to things like financial transparency. And recognizing that though we make our effort, and we aspire to these virtues, that they aren't perfect. They are imperfect, and we embrace that."[90]

In the coming years, employees, customers, media, and shareholders will continue to expect the following from brands: increasing numbers of Blacks and other people of color in senior roles, reimagining supply chain diversity programs, and eradicating microaggressions within the workplace. Discriminatory behaviors and cultures can escalate into racially biased confrontations, with tragic endings, in public spaces. Variations of this same behavior and culture exist in corporations. Failure to meet the social demands during what is considered the largest civil rights movement worldwide will result in decimated brands, damaged reputations, and declines in sales.

Chapter 5 Takeaways

- Despite equal employment laws and so-called legal protections, harassment persists, especially unethical conduct and behaviors built into corporate culture.

- Business goals are measurable, scalable, and flexible to evolve over time. Committing to goals in hiring and promoting people of color should be approached in the same way.

- Quantifiable commitments promote decisiveness, commitment, and build transparency, as well as a foundation for compassionate, creativity-driven workplaces.

- Companies who create quantifiable plans see positive growth in both their numbers of underrepresented groups and marketplace response (share price, sales increase).

- The confluence of the 2020 murders of George Floyd, Breonna Taylor, and Ahmaud Arbery with the growth of #BlackLivesMatter led to corporate dialogue with employees on how they could better support Black workers. Tangible results include increased adoption of AI to limit bias in hiring, intentionality in supplier diversity programs,

(continued)

(continued)

renewed interest in quantifiable goals for recruiting and hiring practices, and a focus on promotions into executive positions.

- Institutional investors emerged as a business stakeholder influencing businesses to act inclusively. Their leverage includes large amounts of investment dollars infused when a company is brought into a portfolio or the reverse if a company is removed from a portfolio due to unethical treatment.

- Today's workplace carries the DNA of slavery. Evidence of this is found in substandard pay, hostile environments, and aggressions. Corporations must own this and resolve it immediately to continue to evolve.

- Corporations must confront the damages that continue to exist with economic redress and creating inclusive, compassionate cultures in which divisive language, aggressions, and exclusions are checked and rendered intolerable.

References

1. https://www.dw.com/en/eu-declares-black-lives-matter-condemns-racism/a-53878516
2. https://www.nytimes.com/2020/07/01/world/asia/japan-racism-black-lives-matter.html
3. http://cms.horus.be/files/99935/MediaArchive/publications/shadow   percent20 report percent202012-13/shadowReport_final.pdf
4. https://www.theguardian.com/world/2019/jan/17/minority-ethnic-britons-face-shocking-job-discrimination
5. https://www.gov.uk/guidance/equality-act-2010-guidance
6. https://www.thetimes.co.uk/article/luxury-goods-giant-richemont-uk-spied-on-black-worker-it-victimised-2htkm9zwm
7. Ibid.

8. https://www.beyondblue.org.au/docs/default-source/research-project-files/bl1337-report---tns-discrimination-against-indigenous-australians.pdf?sfvrsn=2/

9. https://www.hcamag.com/au/news/general/employer-fined-in-landmark-racial-discrimination-case/152463

10. Ibid.

11. https://www.washingtonpost.com/archive/politics/1990/02/05/eeoc-chief-faces-scrutiny-as-court-nominee/7f5ea600-1f44-4dfb-9289-d107aae4b06f/

12. https://apnews.com/b419883e871b5117649d1f3fdacf6f95

13. https://www.nytimes.com/2020/06/25/opinion/sunday/race-wage-gap.html

14. https://www.pewresearch.org/fact-tank/2013/08/21/through-good-times-and-bad-black-unemployment-is-consistently-double-that-of-whites/

15. https://www.foodandwine.com/news/former-mcdonalds-franchisees-sue-for-racial-discrimination

16. https://www.macrotrends.net/stocks/charts/MCD/mcdonalds/stock-price-history

17. https://money.cnn.com/1996/11/15/companies/texaco_settle_a/

18. https://www.thoughtco.com/big-companies-sued-for-racial-discrimination-2834873

19. https://www.al.com/live/2010/11/general_electric_settles_racia.html

20. https://money.cnn.com/2008/10/09/news/companies/ge_earnings/

21. https://www.payscale.com/compensation-today/2018/12/diversity-and-inclusion-success

22. https://www.cnbc.com/2020/06/09/ben-jerrys-ceo-business-must-be-held-accountable-in-fighting-racism.html

23. https://www.benjerry.com/whats-new/2015/journey-about-racial-equity

24. https://www.starbucks.com/responsibility/community/diversity-and-inclusion/aspirations

25. https://www.cnn.com/2018/09/04/us/colin-kaepernick-nike-sneakers-intl/index.html

26. https://www.cbsnews.com/news/nike-stock-price-reaches-all-time-high-despite-colin-kaepernick-ad-boycott/

27. https://www.businessoffashion.com/articles/news-analysis/nike-looks-to-transform-troubled-workplace-culture-with-new-diversity-initiatives

28. https://www.cbsnews.com/news/following-backlash-nike-will-change-its-pregnancy-policy-in-future-athlete-contracts/

29. https://www.communityimpact.nike.com

30. https://www.fastcompany.com/90456329/this-is-where-there-are-the-most-hispanic-executives-and-its-not-where-you-think

31. Ibid.

32. https://www.psychologytoday.com/us/blog/microaggressions-in-everyday-life/201011/microaggressions-more-just-race

Inclusion and the Bottom Line

33. https://www.forbes.com/sites/janicegassam/2018/12/28/how-microaggressions-in-the-workplace-can-thwart-diversity-and-inclusion-efforts/#eb30d3d1ce16
34. https://www.theshowmustbepaused.com/
35. https://www.detroitnews.com/story/business/2020/08/24/rocket-accountability-diversity-inclusion-plan/3428343001/
36. https://www.wsj.com/articles/starbucks-ties-executive-pay-to-2025-diversity-targets-11602680401
37. https://www.moneycontrol.com/news/world/what-changes-are-companies-making-in-response-to-george-floyd-protests-5432891.html
38. https://www.freshdaily.ca/food/2020/06/uncle-bens-rice-racist/
39. https://www.nytimes.com/2020/06/20/business/dreyers-eskimo-pie-name-change.html#:~:text=Eskimo%20Pie%20Corp.&text=The%20name%20attached%20to%20Eskimo,considered%20racist%20or%20culturally%20insensitive.
40. https://www.msn.com/en-us/sports/nfl/the-washington-redskins-are-no-longer-the-washington-redskins/ar-BB16EB4d
41. https://news.sportslogos.net/2020/07/13/washington-redskins-retire-name-and-logo/
42. https://www.cbsnews.com/news/spike-lee-boycotts-gucci-and-prada-over-blackface-items-2019-02-08/
43. https://www.mckinsey.com/featured-insights/diversity-and-inclusion/diversity-wins-how-inclusion-matters
44. https://hbr.org/2020/08/institutional-investors-must-help-close-the-race-and-gender-gaps-in-venture-capital
45. Ibid.
46. https://hbswk.hbs.edu/item/minorities-who-whiten-job-resumes-get-more-interviews
47. https://www.theguardian.com/books/2016/oct/27/cathy-oneil-weapons-of-math-destruction-algorithms-big-data
48. https://www.hirevue.com/blog/hiring/5-recruiting-strategies-to-increase-workplace-diversity
49. https://www.wepow.com/en/
50. https://www.capterra.com/p/191163/XOR-AI/
51. https://fortune.com/2019/12/27/ai-bias-hiring-recruitment-tools-replace-resumes/
52. Ibid.
53. https://www.mic.com/articles/180001/can-artificial-intelligence-and-computer-games-improve-hiring-diversity-heres-why-the-jury-is-out
54. https://www.workingmother.com/diverse-interview-panels-may-be-key-to-workplace-diversity
55. Ibid.
56. https://www.aaaed.org/aaaed/About_Affirmative_Action__Diversity_and_Inclusion.asp

57. https://nmsdc.org/about-nmsdc/
58. https://nmsdc.org/corporate-america-stepping-up-to-support-black-and-minority-businesses/
59. https://corporate.target.com/corporate-responsibility/diversity-inclusion/supplier-diversity
60. Ibid.
61. https://www.businessinsider.com/honey-pot-company-founder-online-trolls-racism-target-commercial-2020-3
62. Ibid.
63. https://www.bloomberg.com/news/articles/2020-09-01/can-quotas-fix-diversity-these-major-companies-hope-so
64. https://www.chicagotribune.com/business/ct-biz-black-jobs-racial-hiring-quotas-20200901-4c3jlnc5mzb4bflnm7egljvm7e-story.html?ocid=uxbndlbing
65. https://www.bnnbloomberg.ca/racial-quotas-start-catching-on-with-major-u-s-employers-1.1487800
66. https://www.chicagotribune.com/business/ct-biz-black-jobs-racial-hiring-quotas-20200901-4c3jlnc5mzb4bflnm7egljvm7e-story.html?ocid=uxbndlbing
67. https://www.gendereconomy.org/the-debate-about-quotas/
68. Ibid.
69. https://www.theguardian.com/inequality/2017/sep/27/how-well-have-racial-quotas-worked-around-the-world
70. https://elizabethwarren.com/plans/equity-farmers-of-color
71. https://www.eater.com/2019/1/25/18197352/american-farming-racism-us-agriculture-history
72. Ibid.
73. Ibid.
74. https://www.congress.gov/bill/116th-congress/house-bill/1080?q=percent7B percent22search percent22 percent3A percent5B percent22HR+1080 percent22 percent5D percent7D&s=2&r=1
75. https://www.harris.senate.gov/imo/media/doc/ONEpercent20PAGER percent20 National percent20Domestic percent20Workers percent20Bill percent20of percent20Rights.pdf
76. Ibid.
77. https://www.vox.com/2019/7/15/20694610/kamala-harris-domestic-workers-bill-of-rights-act
78. Ibid.
79. https://www.latimes.com/archives/la-xpm-2000-mar-11-fi-7637-story.html
80. https://www.nytimes.com/2016/12/18/us/insurance-policies-on-slaves-new-york-lifes-complicated-past.html
81. https://money.cnn.com/2005/06/02/news/fortune500/wachovia_slavery/
82. https://www.pbs.org/newshour/nation/americas-first-big-business-railroads-slavery

83. http://railroads.unl.edu/blog/?p=32
84. https://www.huffpost.com/entry/slavery-reparations_b_4846078
85. https://www.gapincsustainability.com/people/talent/way-ahead
86. https://www.gapinc.com/en-us/articles/2020/06/united-for-justice-and-equality
87. https://www.fool.com/investing/2020/09/01/gap-earnings-business-stabilizes-as-stores-reopen/
88. https://askinosie.com/
89. Interview with the author. Askinosie Shawn, Decision to create a transparent relationship with the company's suppliers, Sept 7, 2020.
90. Ibid.

Chapter 6

Gender Equity and Company Growth

S ociety generalizes women as inherently more compassionate than men. Consequently, women are labeled as "too compassionate to succeed" in an intense corporate environment. When women demonstrate leadership and decision-making styles that differ from the dominant male culture, they are often criticized and made to feel less than their male counterparts. These prejudiced actions, along with the erroneous thinking behind them, influence the way women are paid, promoted, and treated within the business world.

This chapter discusses various challenges related to gender inequity within the workforce, including these issues:

- The pay gap
- Glass ceiling or labyrinth?
- Intersectionality of race and gender
- Expanding diversity initiatives to include women of color
- Women CEOs building compassionate cultures
- Pros and cons of quotas
- Importance of mentorship and sponsorship
- Impact of #MeToo and #TimesUp movements

- Dangers of neglecting allyship
- Economic and reputational benefits of compassionate leadership

The Pay Gap

Gender inequality is deeply embedded in the business world, which is why pay parity and inclusive treatment must be part of any compassionate and equitable workplace. According to a Pew Research Center analysis of median hourly earnings within the United States, women earned 85% of what men earned in 2018. Though this represents a narrowing of pay disparities since 1980, the gender pay gap has remained relatively consistent over the previous 15 years.[1] Experts attribute the narrowing of the gap to gains that women have made in their work experiences and educational accomplishments. But these gains have not been enough to counter the discriminatory behaviors that contribute to the persistent pay gap between male and female workers.

A 2017 Pew Research Center survey found that 42% of working women reported experiencing gender discrimination at work, compared to 22% of men.[2] Of the various forms of discrimination reported, pay inequality was most common. Although 25% of women reported earning less than men performing the same job, only 5% of men reported the same. These discrepancies have been explained in countless ways, but the analysis often blames women's career and family choices.

For example, it is no secret that motherhood can negatively affect a woman's career path and long-term earning potential. Women are more likely than men to take breaks from their careers for the purpose of caring for children and family members. About 40% of women reported taking either a significant amount of time off or reducing their work hours to care for children or other family members, compared to only 24% of men. About 27% reported quitting their jobs altogether due to familial responsibilities. A 2016 survey found that mothers take an average of 11 weeks off of work for the birth or adoption of a child, compared with only one week for fathers.[3]

Many women report experiencing negative impacts on their careers following the birth or adoption of children. Women's careers often stall when they take leave, because their managers question where their priorities lie. Coworkers sometimes treat them differently, taking their absence as a sign of disinterest or lack of motivation. And the longer the leave, the more serious the impact. Studies show that the longer a woman stays away from the workplace after the birth or adoption of a child, the more likely she is to be overlooked for promotions—resulting in fewer opportunities for management roles and the increased earnings that come along with those promotions.[4]

I interviewed Sophie, a senior manager at a management consulting firm in the United Kingdom, about her workplace experiences after taking maternity leave.

I found out I was pregnant shortly after starting my position. My team turned on me, treating me very poorly. As time went by, I faced microaggressions including bullying by two women in the workplace. I was treated coldly on a daily basis. I was questioned about everything from my work ethic to meeting targets and how I wrote emails. This all occurred even though I had a history of high performance with a successful portfolio, which I developed.

(continues)

(continued)

Many women were leaving due to the rigor in the company. I did eventually leave due to the emotional toll of workplace discrimination of working women and women who are mothers. It was challenging for management to fill my position, and while I was offered a different position part-time at the company, I had faced so much hostility and discrimination at the workplace I chose not to return.

Another factor that may partly explain the gender pay gap is the overrepresentation of women within lower-paying occupations. Across racial and ethnic lines, women account for larger percentages of the low-wage and lowest-wage workforce than their male counterparts. Despite making up less than half of all workers, women are nearly 60% of the workers in low-wage occupations, typically paying less than $11 per hour.[5] Of the lowest-wage jobs paying less than $10 per hour, women account for nearly 70% of the workers.

Although some point to educational discrepancies between men and women in their attempts to explain these differences, when educational attainments are taken into consideration, gender pay discrepancies still persist. Generally, workers with a bachelor's degree earn about double the pay of their coworkers without a college education. Yet, the discrepancy between men and women's earnings *widens* as women attain more education. Among workers with a bachelor's degree, women earn 74 cents for every dollar that their male counterparts make. This is less than the 78 cents that women without college degrees receive for every dollar earned by their male counterparts.[6]

Salary negotiation also plays a role in pay disparity between the genders. Linda Babcock, the author of *Women Don't Ask: Negotiation and the Gender Divide,* states that executives who negotiate their first salaries out of college can earn upwards of $500,000 more over their working lives than those who did not.[7] Her research also found that men who negotiated their initial salaries were able to raise those salaries by an average of 7.4%.

Numerous theories attempt to explain why women are less likely to negotiate compensation. According to Babcock, women are looked on negatively when they seek to negotiate. They may be labeled as "overly aggressive" or a "nag." Women may feel apprehensive about these perceptions, so they choose not to question the offered salary. According to Katie Donovan, founder of Equal Pay negotiations, many companies set aside funds in anticipation of new hires asking for higher compensation. However, only 30% of women initiate salary negotiations compared to 46% of men. These figures equate to almost $2 million in lost revenue over a lifetime for professional women seeking to advance into leadership positions.

Earnings follow workers from one job to the next, and salary history is a standard part of employment applications. When women fail to negotiate their starting salaries, they are less likely to receive equitable earnings down the road. Lisa Maatz, the top policy advisor for the American Association of University Women and one of the nation's foremost advocates for equal pay, noted the importance of salary negotiation to closing the pay gap. As she discussed, when women negotiate salary, the pay gap shrinks—not completely, but significantly, and enough to make a major difference for many working women.

Glass Ceiling or Labyrinth?

Some argue that the failure to negotiate contributes to a "glass ceiling" in corporate America. The glass ceiling is a metaphor for an invisible barrier keeping women and minorities from advancing to leadership positions and high-paying careers. Those who argue for the existence of a glass ceiling point to the inequity that persists among the highest levels of corporate leadership.

But there is another school of thought, which argues against the glass ceiling as an accurate representation of gender inequality within the workplace. As mentioned in Chapter 3, a 2007 *Harvard Law Review* article written by Alice Eagly and Linda L. Carli sought to dismiss the glass ceiling concept.[8] The authors asserted that the mere presence of women in positions of leadership, no matter how small the number, disproves the existence of an absolute barrier for women. They also took issue with the metaphor's implication that the only barrier is at the very top—as though women have equitable access to entry- and mid-level positions. Quite the contrary: Eagly and Carli asserted that the inequity between genders in the workforce starts far below the C-suite level.

The imagery of a transparent obstruction also disturbed Eagly and Carli because it suggests that women are being deceived about the professional opportunities available to them. In reality, at least according to the authors, the barriers to professional advancement are well known to women at all levels of business. As they wrote in the article, "In truth, women are not turned away only as they reach the penultimate stage of a distinguished career. They disappear in various numbers at many points leading up to that stage."

A 2018 *Forbes* article by Terina Allen also questioned the existence of the glass ceiling.[9] Allen's somewhat controversial assertion was that women have contributed to the glass ceiling by not adequately negotiating for themselves and by resisting the acquisition of technical skills. She argued that women get it wrong by shying away from conflict, working fewer hours than men, and demonstrating a greater fear of failure. Allen suggested that women need to pace themselves better, recognizing that the reality of "having it all" simply does not exist.

But the numbers don't lie: whether business leaders believe in the existence of a glass ceiling or not, study after study showcases the severe underrepresentation of women within the upper levels of corporate America. Among the 200 highest paid CEOs in America, only 13 are women.[10] Among Fortune 500 companies, only 39 are women as of 2020, representing only 7.8% of the Fortune 500 CEO list. What's more, this small percentage represents the largest number of women ever included on this illustrious listing. Katharine Graham was the first woman to make the list, after becoming chief executive of *The Washington Post* in 1972.[11] By 1995, the number of women heading Fortune 500 companies had dropped back down to zero, before rising to 24 in 2014.[12]

Eagly refers to the glass ceiling as a labyrinth filled with obstacles and challenges along with way.[13] Although a handful of female CEOs have been able to navigate the maze, most women have been unsuccessful at overcoming the personal and societal forces that contribute to the professional barriers they face. They assert that three things need to happen for women to alleviate some of the external forces that keep them from achieving their full professional potential. First, organizations must recognize and reduce their internal barriers. Second, men need to take an equal amount of responsibility for caregiving responsibilities within families. Last, society needs to expand its limited view of what constitutes effective leadership.

Recent reports have tried to minimize these discrepancies with assertions that female CEOs earn more than their male counterparts. For example, a 2019 *Wall Street Journal* report ranked CEO salaries for the S&P 500. The median pay for all of the CEOs on the list reached $12.4 million. However, the median pay for the 20 women on the list was $13.7 million.[14] While some attempt to hold up these numbers as evidence of improved equity between male and female CEOs, the truth is that these female CEOs accounted for only 4% of leaders of the 2019 S&P 500. That means that, out of the 500 chief executives, only 20 women held these positions. Yes, it is good news that male and female CEOs earn similar compensation, but this does not negate the lack of women represented within these positions.

The lack of female representation does not only exist in C-suites. Women also face significant challenges in reaching management level positions. Only 72 women for every 100 men are promoted and hired to managerial and supervisory positions. As a result, men hold about 62% of manager positions, and women only hold about 38% though they make up a little more than 50% of the US workforce. Pay discrepancies also persist, with female managers earning 81 cents for every dollar earned by males working at comparable managerial levels.[15]

In a report by the EU-backed European Women on Boards, researchers analyzed public data from companies listed on Europe's Stoxx 600 index, which is composed of the 600 highest-valued public firms in Europe. The analysis included 17 countries, with Sweden leading the way with almost 35% of its companies having at least 30% female representation at the board level. The United Kingdom came in with 23%, Poland with 20%, and France at 10%. Germany came in at 0% on the metric. Angela Merkel's success in politics does not appear to have extended to German women in the corporate world.

Intersectionality of Race and Gender

Kimberlé Crenshaw popularized the term *intersectionality* in the early 1990s describing how discourse pertaining to those who are both women and people of color frequently takes shape about one identity or another, instead of about both.[16]

Being a woman and a person of color may come with different workplace connotations and perceptions than being a White woman or a man of color. This intersectionality also plays a role in just how far behind women are in pay parity and overall representation. Women of color are a force in the US economy, generating $1 trillion as consumers, $361 billion in revenue as entrepreneurs, and launching companies at four times the rate of all woman-owned businesses.[17] Yet, they continue to be more adversely affected when it comes to pay and discrimination within the workforce. Facing an intersectionality of overlapping identities, women of color experience discrimination both because they are women and because of their race and/or ethnicity.

Black women made 62 cents for every dollar earned by a White man in 2020.[18] That means that, for Black women to earn the same amount that White men earned in 2020, they would need to work well into the latter half of 2021. It's like a perpetual game of catch up, in which Black women are held back at the starting line. Even when compared to Black male workers, the gender discrepancies are undeniable: Black female workers made 87 cents for every dollar earned by Black men.[19] If we give an example through the gender lens, Black women are paid on average 21% less than White women, according to LeanIn.[20]

Latinx women also face greater pay disparities than their White counterparts. In 2018, Latinx women in the United States earned 46% less than White men and 31% less than White women.[21] To make the same as White men in 2018, Latinx women would have had to work until November 20, 2019, the following year. Education does little to close these gaps, with a 36% discrepancy between the earnings of Latinx women and White men with a bachelor's degree.[22]

For women of color, pay disparities start at a young age. From the age of 16, Black girls are paid 21% less than White males the same age.[23] From the ages of 25 to 54 the gap increases to 32% and increases again to 37% at age 55 when compared to White men. Between the ages of 16 and 24, Latinx girls are paid 11% less than White males their same age.[24] That percentage increases to 35% between the ages of 25 and 54 and 40% at the age of 55.

173

Gender Equity and Company Growth

As with junior levels of the workplace, the inequities faced by White women within the upper levels of organizations are multiplied for women of color. Only two Black women have ever led a Fortune 500 company. Ursula Burns became the first Black woman to lead a Fortune 500 company in 2009 as the CEO of Xerox and Mary A. Winston was the second Black woman to lead a Fortune 500 company, who served as the interim CEO of Bed Bath & Beyond between May and November 2019.

Geisha Williams made history in 2017 as the first Latinx woman named CEO of a Fortune 500 company.[25] She took leadership of PG&E Corp., a $17.7 billion electric utility company after heading its electric operations for 10 years. She stepped down in early 2019, bringing the number of Latinx women serving as CEOs of Fortune 500 companies back down to zero.

The lack of representation does not stop at the coveted CEO position. 2020 Women on Boards is a nonprofit group that advocates for increased numbers of female directors on corporate boards. They report that as of September 2020, women held only 22.6% of the board seats among the nation's largest publicly traded companies in the Russell 3000 Index. Although this represents a 6.5% increase over the previous four years, it still does not come close to the percentage of women in the overall workforce. Of the 26,711 board seats on the 2020 Russell 3000 index, women held 6,034.[26]

In January 2020, Goldman Sachs announced an initiative to only underwrite IPOs in the United States and Europe of private companies with at least one woman on the board. And if you think that was merely some sort of "politically correct" gesture, think again: Goldman CEO David Solomon explained that, over a four-year period, IPOs of American companies with at least one female director on their boards performed "significantly better" compared to those without any women.

Boards typically recruit their directors from individuals who have previously served on other boards, which equates to a relatively small pool of candidates. The inadequate promotion of women and women of color into executive-level positions means that a vast number of highly knowledgeable and experienced candidates are never considered for board of director positions.

Expanding Diversity Initiatives to Include Women of Color

The last couple of decades have brought about a push for gender diversity within corporate America, but women of color are still largely excluded from these metrics. Although the number of women in C-suite leadership positions has grown slightly over the last few years, women of color remain largely underrepresented. This has raised concerns that efforts toward "diversification of gender" at senior corporate levels is actually code for "hire more White women."

There are numerous reasons for these discrepancies, beginning with the unconscious bias that persists in hiring and promotion practices. As the numbers demonstrate, most of the decision-makers are White men. Although overt discrimination may be at play, decisions by the board and senior management are often based on unconscious biases in which decision-makers prefer candidates who are similar to them. Greater diversity on boards and within senior management is a solution for this.

Between 2016 and 2018, 230 new board seats were added to Fortune 500 firms. Across these openings White women obtained 124 seats, Black women obtained 32 seats, Asian women obtained 17 seats, and Latinx women obtained a mere 4 seats. Although data is improving, there is far less research around Native American women on boards compared to other women of color. These numbers raise the question whether initiatives to advance women on boards disproportionally benefit White women. As Maryann Reid asked in her February 2020 *Forbes* editorial, "If White women continue to be the face of diversity, then what is diversity? Is it just about hiring more White women? If it is, then how are women of color benefiting?"[27]

Valerie Irick Rainford, CEO of Elloree Talent Strategies, explained that broad references to "women" in the scope of diversification of the workforce often hinders the progress of women of color. She said that expansive data sets disguise the reality that women of color are still left behind as White women advance.[28] "Not only would disaggregation expose this reality—it would also show that Black talent in particular is the farthest behind and, in some cases, even regressing. Like any other business metric where companies are failing, managers should be held accountable for turning around these results for the company along the entire continuum of recruiting, hiring, developing and advancing diverse talent."

For businesses to truly champion gender diversity within the workplace, leaders must recognize the issues of intersectionality that exist for women of color. They must also identify and address the additional barriers that exist for the promotion of women of color into management and executive positions. For example, of the Black women who seek promotions at the same rate as men, only 64 are successfully hired into management roles for every 100 positions.[29]

Companies can employ several techniques when seeking to reduce gender bias in hiring and promotions while also addressing the underrepresentation of women of color. One technique is to include more options from various racial and ethnic groups when hiring. For example, if a company would like to see more Latinx women represented, they need to consider multiple qualified Latinx candidates to increase the chances that one of them will ultimately be hired.[30] Adding one woman of color to a candidate pool has little effect on diverse hiring.

Xochitl Ledesma, director of learning and advisory services at Catalyst, spoke to *Forbes* magazine about the importance of the selection process.

All involved in the selection process should be responsible for highlighting the implicit biases by taking the following three actions. First, by establishing a shared meaning of diversity, a definition that spreads across experience, age, geography, and other "invisible characteristics." Second, an intentional outline of desired diversity characteristics should be conducted in conjunction with timely metrics for obtaining them. Last, all recruiting and interview processes should be updated to mitigate bias and standardized across all candidates.[31]

Founded in 2008, the company Task Rabbit is a case study in inclusive recruitment with equality and compassion. Task Rabbit contracts freelance workers to complete odd jobs for clients. Former CEO Stacy Brown-Philpot spoke about her commitment to increasing diversity within the company. As a Black female CEO in Silicon Valley, she had a deep understanding about the lack of diversity within the tech industry and she set out to change this dynamic. "I'm focusing on changing the face of technology by creating a diverse company where people feel they can bring their whole selves to work," she stated in a 2019 interview.[32]

Task Rabbit has implemented an actionable approach to greater inclusion for years. Their plan includes four goals: the increase of

Black talent within the company to reflect the population in the United States, the development of a supportive and diversity-friendly culture, the education of staff members on issues of diversity and unconscious bias to support the recruitment and retention efforts, and strengthening awareness of the importance of increasing diversity within the technology industry.[33] Task Rabbit also publicly declared their commitment to increased diversity by signing a Congressional Black Caucus initiative aimed at boosting recruitment of Black workers within the tech industry.

The company's efforts at increased inclusion have been effective. Although Black workers are estimated to be 2% of the work force at most tech companies in Silicon Valley, Task Rabbit's workforce is 13%.[34] With Brown-Philpot in the role of CEO, the company developed a leadership composed of 60% women and a workforce that is 48% non-White.[35]

Unfortunately, the efforts of TaskRabbit are the exception and not the norm in corporate America, though there are some examples of firms that have succeeded in including women—and particularly women of color—in their upper ranks. The dearth of women in C-suite represents a dearth of inclusivity.

When promoting internal diversity, businesses should also consider the significant roles that managers play in crafting an environment that champions gender diversity for all races. Consider these troubling statistics from a 2020 study by Lean In about the state of women of color within corporate America.[36]

- Managers are less likely to help Black women navigate the organizational structure of a company, 24% compared to 30% of White women, 28% of Latinx women, 24% of Asian women, and 28% of women of all groups.

- Forty-nine percent of Black women feel pressure to perform compared to White women at 11%. They also feel as though they are seen as representatives of their race at 50% compared to 9% of White women.

- Managers are also less likely to advocate for new career opportunities for Black women at 29% compared to 37% of White women, 35% of Latinx women, and 35% of Asian women.

- Managers were less likely to provide valuable opportunities for project management to Black women at 36% compared to 43% of White women, 39% of Latinx women, and 40% of Asian women.

- Managers were also less likely to provide the sponsorship needed for Black women's career advancement at 24% compared to 31% of White women, 31% of Latinx women, and 27% of Asian women.

Yet again, there is far less research detailing experiences of Native American women compared to other women of color. Other practices that can effectively improve gender diversity within an organization include developing clear conduct guidelines in the workplace to minimize cases of microaggressions against women of color, training on antiracism and allyship, and the hiring of Black women in clusters to avoid the discomfort of the "only" experience.[37] Microaggressions affect Black women at a higher rate than women of other groups. In fact, 40% of Black women reported needing to "prove" their competence compared to 28% of White women, 28% of Latinx women, and 30% of Asian women. Black women also reported having their judgment questioned at higher rates than other women. More than one in four Black women report experiencing someone at work being surprised at their language skills and professional abilities compared to 1 in 10 White women.[38]

These microaggressions take an emotional and mental toll that is sometimes referred to as an emotional tax—the metaphorical tax being the burden of being different from peers because of gender, race, or ethnicity. Catalyst, a nonprofit organization advocating for female inclusion and equity within the workplace, defines *emotional tax* in this way: "Asian, Black, Latinx, and multiracial employees pay an Emotional Tax at work when they feel they must be on guard to protect against bias. These harmful experiences occur both inside and outside the workplace and prevent employees from being able to truly thrive at work."[39]

In Chapter 2 and the Preface, I shared an experience I had with a manager, who put me in the uncomfortable position of having to constantly evaluate every personal interaction and group meeting contribution to ensure that I wouldn't be talked over or that my comments wouldn't be deemed as unintelligible. This was not merely an emotional burden; it was also wasted time and effort—it was an emotional tax. According to Catalyst, 58% of Black women experience an emotional tax within the workplace and are always on guard to protect themselves against discrimination, unfair treatment, and bias.[40]

Women CEOs Building Compassionate Cultures

Corporate culture does not change overnight. It requires a convergence of factors that slowly shift a company's day-to-day patterns, adjusting the culture in the long term. This process requires a critical examination of a company's current culture, acute awareness of different types of leadership styles, and intention behind creating advancement opportunities for women. These factors create an environment for equality, inclusion, and compassion. When this type of environment exists within a company structure, it lays a groundwork that welcomes women and empowers them to work at their highest capacity.

Among the world's wealthiest nations, the United States remains one of the only countries that continues to struggle with compassion in the workplace. For example, America has no clear national policy for leave for new mothers and makes no requirement for paternity leave, which further exacerbates the gender discrepancies that exist within the workplace. In Finland, each parent gets 164 days (7 months) and single parents get 328 days.[41] In Denmark, new mothers get 18 weeks of maternity leave at full pay while fathers get two weeks off and an additional 32 weeks, which can be used by both parents at their discretion.[42]

Under the leadership of Denise Morrison, the Campbell Soup Company changed its leave policies to provide employees with 10 weeks of fully paid maternity and paternity leave intended to give parents flexibility while their children are young.[43] We'll discuss more about family leave strategies in building a compassionate and equitable culture in Chapter 9.

Ulta Beauty is headed by CEO Mary Dillon. The company offers a work environment that creates lasting career opportunities for their employees, reflects a diverse community, and supports work-life balance.[44] They maintain an open communication policy that encourages associates to speak up about internal problems or concerns without fear of retaliation.

Gender is only one arena in which corporations can make strides toward compassionate governance. Northrop Grumman, headed by CEO Kathy Warden, topped the Disability Equality Index (DEI) for five years in a row and was awarded a "Best Place to Work for Disability Inclusion."[45] The award recognized the company's exemplary policies, strategies, and initiatives that have resulted in quantifiable outcomes in disability inclusiveness in the workplace. In 2019, *Corporate Responsibility Magazine* placed Northrop Grumman on its "100 Best Corporate Citizens List" for outstanding environmental, social, and governance transparency. It also made DiversityInc's Top 50 Companies for Diversity list for the 10th year in a row.

"At Northrop Grumman, we remain steadfast in our commitment to embrace all dimensions of diversity and inclusion so this recognition is particularly meaningful," said Warden. "It starts with the tone at the top—leaders at all levels are held accountable for understanding and demonstrating the core tenets of diversity and inclusion. And as the diversity of our teams has increased, so has our performance."[46]

Despite some abysmal numbers in areas of the globe, there are examples of the tone at the top being crafted by a female leader. One of Sweden's biggest banks, Svenska Handelsbanken AB, got its first female chief executive officer in 2019.[47] Carina Åkerström spoke about diversity and inclusion strides being made by the bank. "In Handelsbanken we strive for an inclusive corporate culture with trust and respect for the individual—both our customers as well as our employees. This demands that questions regarding gender equality and diversity are taken seriously. When we mix people with different genders, age, backgrounds and views, we can meet each other and our customers with greater understanding and therefore create trust and good relationships."

Meanwhile, Deloitte Australia has been continuously recognized for its compassionate commitment to its staff, placing eighth on LinkedIn's list of best Australian companies to work for in 2019.[48] One of their most successful initiatives has been a program called Inspiring Women. Initiated in 2003, it promotes the development and advancement of talented women in the workplace. With a leadership team headed by CEO Cindy Hook, Inspiring Women has helped recent female graduates advance through the ranks into leadership positions.

The company has also instituted an effective return-to-work program that supports individual workers who have been forced to put their careers on hold for family care or personal reasons. Deloitte Australia also offers preventative and supportive mental health initiatives, complimentary breakfast options, and a lifestyle concierge service for the children of employees.

These are just a few examples of female-led corporations that are taking real steps to better care for their employees. Because there are so few, Fortune 500 companies with women CEOs often find themselves under a microscope of scrutiny regarding employee-centered policies. That said, it is unreasonable to expect a magical change in day-to-day operations when a woman takes the helm. One female leader does not automatically equate to a change in corporate culture.

Pros and Cons of Quotas

We see increasing examples of women advocating for themselves and each other while also welcoming men as advocates. But recalibrating business to reflect parity and equity can alienate some employees and drive insecurities. The desire to quantify progress in hiring inevitably raises the specter of quotas. Do they work? Or do they do more harm than good?

Many European countries have enacted quotas to improve gender representation at the corporate level, particularly on board seats. Norway led the way in 2008 when it required registered companies to have women in at least 40% of board seats or face dissolution.[49] More than a dozen countries across Western Europe followed suit with similar requirements. Belgium, France, and Italy can fine or dissolve noncompliant companies. Germany, Spain, and the Netherlands have legislated similar hiring quotas, but do not sanction for noncompliance. Britain recommends that supervisory boards, who assess, oversee, and analyze the risks of the work of management teams, be 25% female at a minimum.[50] These state-sponsored efforts have proved somewhat successful, with some of the countries seeing a fivefold increase in women among directors of large companies.

In the United States, of course, the notion of governmental interference with the hiring practices of private companies is frequently controversial. As with racial quotas, US companies have consistently pushed against the use of gender quotas, with opponents offering numerous arguments against them. For example, critics assert that quotas fail to advance the primary goal of corporate leaders, which should be improved corporate governance, not social progress.[51] The argument has also been made that quotas are too rigid and restrictive on the ways in which leaders choose to run their businesses.

CJ Bedford advises businesses as an associate director with Grant Thornton UK LLP. She believes that quotas and penalties do not adequately enhance business diversity—she prefers the term *benchmark*.[52] "There is a huge difference between a quota and a benchmark," she writes. "Quotas drive a particular set of behaviors and, inherently, there has to be some kind of positive discrimination in order to enable the change required. Benchmarks, or indicators of what 'good' looks like, can certainly help organizations to make progress in this area without the pressure to either over-recruit or over-promote people who aren't in the talent market yet."

Perceptions around the lack of qualified candidates also impact the argument against quotas. Opponents assert that, as we fight to break down these perceptions, the use of quotas frustrates those efforts. This critique of quotas views them as inherently problematic because they provoke allegations of tokenism and reverse discrimination. Regardless of how qualified a female candidate may be, this argument goes, if she got her position by means of a quota, she will always be perceived as unqualified.

Another argument against quotas is the lack of prioritization of board diversity by investors. A US Government Accountability Office study showed that, unless corporate boards and investors put gender diversity at the forefront of their priorities, true equality will take decades to achieve.[53] It is up to compassionate, strong leaders to speak directly to these fear-based criticisms.

I've interviewed panels of White men on their thoughts and fears on company-wide targets of including more women in senior roles. There was support in general, but also a desire for increased transparency. Initially it seemed insulting. After all, very few people ask for transparency when men are promoted into high-level positions. However, when thinking constructively, transparency all around promotes a healthy environment that serves everyone. Further, speaking with the men on these panels helped me to see things from another perspective, which is valuable in building relationships for career progression.

Importance of Mentorship and Sponsorship

I met my first mentor as a teenage college student. She was an energetic, generous, and accomplished newswoman who volunteered to spend a couple of hours with me each month. Our relationship initially consisted of newsroom visits and getting her insight on which news markets are good places to start a career. Just as my career aspirations transitioned from television news to financial markets, so did our relationship and the type of insight I sought from her. Now, she is a trusted advisor and a close friend whom I call on for advice ranging from work presentations to salary negotiations to personal life lessons. I owe a great deal of the way I approach my work and the way I engage people to her influence. Although most mentorships start in the workplace, some of the best ones take shape when there is mutual respect and appreciation between advisor and advisee.

Many business leaders have begun to recognize the benefits of mentoring and implementing mentorship programs into the workplace. These mentorships are taking on a variety of new and effective flavors. Peer mentoring creates one-on-one relationships between employees working in a lateral level within the organization. The employee with more experience shares their skills and knowledge while also offering support and encouragement to the employee with less experience. Peer mentoring has been shown to encourage employee well-being and can be particularly useful during exceptionally challenging times, like the pandemic.

About 70% of Fortune 500 companies maintain some type of mentoring program as a method of building bridges internally and encouraging successful employees.[54] Employees who participate in mentoring programs experience higher retention rates. They are more likely to progress within the company, earn promotions, and advance in pay grade.[55]

The benefits of mentoring also extend to a company's bottom line. If resourced adequately, and deployed intentionally, mentoring programs can attract potential employees, grow the current workforce, and retain talent. Deloitte's mentoring program has increased its annual revenue to $38.8 billion, representing a 7.1% revenue increase. Boeing, a Fortune 25 company and one of the largest aerospace companies in the world, also offers a mentoring program aimed at developing leaders, as well as attracting and retaining employees. In 2017, the company ranked 30th on the "World's Most Admired Companies" list.[56]

Making mentoring an integral part of the organizational culture demonstrates commitment to employee development. It indicates to employees that management is open to their movement within the larger organization should employees' interest grow beyond their current position. Mentoring helps to broaden the abilities of the mentor/mentee, while introducing junior employees to critical skills.

The benefits of mentoring also strengthen inclusion efforts. According to a study by Cornell University's School of Industrial and Labor Relations, mentoring programs boosted minority representation at the managerial level from 9% to 24%. They also increased retention and promotion rates for women and minorities from 15% to 38% when compared to employees who were not mentored.[57]

"Reverse mentorships" are also extremely effective tools for the furtherance of inclusion. In reverse mentorships, employees spend time—an hour each quarter or every month—educating senior management on cultural awareness and sharing company insight that they may not usually hear from other executives in their inner circle. Mentorships enabling people of color to educate senior leaders can succeed in raising awareness of senior leaders while creating a more inclusive, compassionate environment where people of color are given a voice and seen as experts. Instead of the seasoned White executives serving as mentors, diverse employees serve as mentors to majority group members. The goal is to share various challenges and perceptions while advancing the aspirational corporate goals for inclusion.

For several years, I cocreated and implemented some of these mentorship programs between underrepresented employees and executive leadership members. We labeled them "reverse" because they push against the paradigm that the most senior person who represents the dominant business culture is best positioned to mentor an underrepresented person. The end goal was to ensure senior leaders were in touch with people from different backgrounds. What's more, reverse mentoring helped me gain a valuable skill set: creating long-term relationships between people of different generations, races, and ethnicities.

When establishing mentor opportunities within the workforce, it's extremely important for business leaders to be clear about their goals. Women don't need "mentorship" that focuses on adapting to male culture. Additionally, women of color don't need "mentorship" that focuses on "fitting in" with the majority race. Women benefit from mentorships that promote meaningful dialogues, form lasting professional relationships, and assist them in pursuing their professional goals.

In each business role I've held, mentors have supported me in bringing my best to bear whenever presenting something new and potentially revenue generating. When identifying mentors, I looked for individuals who knew the landscape. First, they had a great deal of familiarity about the market. I may have been an expert on the audience, but they either had some historical knowledge or depth of understanding about human nature that overrode—or at least challenged—my assessment of the customers' needs.

Second, my mentors were keenly aware of the personalities of those to whom I was presenting. Not all of my mentors have been the decision-makers in the room, but they understood the motivations of those who were decision-makers. Understanding what drives senior management teams to say "yes" is a key element to success.

Last, my mentors encouraged me. It can be tricky plunging into a new market, presenting a new product to senior management, or delivering any business item that requires extra money, resources, or time. If it isn't executed just right, it can leave even the best, most-thought out idea dead in the water. My mentors helped me traverse these challenges to reach greater levels of success.

Although most people have some understanding of mentoring, sponsorship is a somewhat less familiar practice. In short, sponsors promote inclusion by getting individuals into the right rooms with the right people. The sponsor advocates on an employee's behalf in scenarios where that employee isn't present. Whereas individuals may not be positioned to speak about their capabilities to senior leaders they don't know, their sponsors are. Though sponsorships have existed for years, underrepresented groups are reaping more benefits as their numbers grow and corporations begin taking growth and promotion concerns seriously. Indeed, sponsors have played key roles in developing my knowledge, relationships, and opportunities, supporting my professional expansion.

Mentorships, sponsorships, and peer coaching groups offer valuable opportunities for women to learn from each other, as well as individuals in leadership positions. Peer coaching services such as The Cru, founded by Tiffany Dufu, and Chief, founded by Lindsay Kaplan and Carolyn Childers, connect women who collaborate to meet their personal and professional goals.[58] For these types of incentives to prove effective within workplace environments, organizational leadership must communicate the importance of mentoring and ensure that managers actively participate in mentoring programs. Conversations between women can lead to trusted relationships and information sharing that shapes not only the career experiences of one woman but also shapes a broader movement.

Impact of #MeToo and #TimesUp Movements

The era of #MeToo and #TimesUp has resulted in groups of women from different cultures proactively organizing to share information critical for career advancement, including awareness about pay equity and the prevalence of sexual harassment within workplace environments. The peer-to-peer component of these movements replaced speaking about such behaviors only behind closed doors with exposing it publicly. This act of organizing and sharing is compassionate activism at work. Although these movements first gained widespread notoriety in artistic circles, the impact on corporations has changed the way business is done both domestically and internationally. The movement empowered women to expose sexual harassment and violence within the workplace. The result has been more mindfulness about the need to operate inside legal parameters and a greater awareness of consequences for not doing so.

The #MeToo movement reminded employers of their legal duty to be vigilant regarding policies and cultures that affect women's civil rights and worker's rights generally.

Gender Equity and Company Growth

This is an account from Mary, the female cofounder of a small start-up company about the emotional abuse and sexual advances she has endured at work.

In my prior role, I worked at an organization in sales where I was the only female on the team. Microaggressions used within the office and accepted by other team members created a hierarchy where I was seen as more of a support staff person versus an equal leader in the team.

I began receiving emails from coworkers berating my work. A standard was then created where my peers would cut me off while I was speaking at meetings.

I found out that the company was promoting my male colleagues and giving them incentives to relocate. I also faced issues with wage disparity as my male coworker earned more than I did despite the fact I had more experience and stayed longer in the company. In addition, I was also performing higher with better sales numbers, hitting my KPIs more than others.

The straw that broke the camel's back was the sexual harassment I experienced within the workplace. A coworker began touching me inappropriately. I did go to human resources and filed a complaint, although I did not want to open a case at the time. HR then violated my privacy and told the person who harassed me that a complaint was filed against him. This made my experience at work worse. No one would talk to me and my work was de-credited making it very challenging to keep working at the company.

> I tried to call attention to the company on the issue and I reached out to other women to see if they were having similar experiences. I found the issues I faced were common among other women who felt they had no decision-making powers even with leadership roles. Eventually, I found a different position with a different company.

The #MeToo movement has resulted in numerous positive outcomes, but it also brings up some important questions about intersectionality and the experiences of Black women within the workplace. The #MeToo phrase was coined by a Black woman named Tarana Burke who had experienced sexual abuse in her personal life. She began using the phrase in 2006 as a way of bringing together women with similar experiences and empowering them to stand up for themselves. Over a decade later, it became a viral hashtag when actresses such as Alyssa Milano coopted the phrase and began using it on social media when posting about sexual abuse allegations against Harvey Weinstein. It quickly became a widespread national and global movement, even outside of the entertainment sector. Author Sylvia Ann Hewlett explains that although media accounts and examples in the business world aren't as high profile as those in Hollywood, sexual harassment results in legal expenses and loss of key employees and revenue that could bring a corporation to its knees.[59]

As with other discussions about issues of gender equality and inclusion in the workplace, the #MeToo movement too frequently left Black women out of the conversation, focusing instead solely on the experiences of White women.[60] And yet, Black women's testimonies and campaigns against sexual violence and sexual exploitation have resulted in some of America's most prominent movements. Black women have played significant roles in helping to establish the safe spaces and crisis centers that so many women rely on today.

Actress Jane Fonda briefly spoke about this issue in a statement about the movement. "It's too bad that [the visibility of #MeToo] is probably because so many of the women that were assaulted by Harvey Weinstein are famous and White and everybody knows them. This has been going on a long time to Black women and other women of color and it doesn't get out quite the same."[61]

Crystal Feimster, a historian and assistant professor of African American Studies at Yale University, has also addressed this racial divide. "We must examine why it took privileged, elite White women to speak out before the public paid attention to issues that affect all women... If we can hear Black women, especially poor Black women, everybody benefits. If the benchmark becomes the treatment of poor Black women, it is a win-win for everyone."[62]

For White women and business leaders who are interested in true allyship, they must start with listening, sharing, and honoring the narratives of Black women, instead of ignoring or modifying them.

#MeToo has also had a significant impact on global businesses. The Male Champions of Change (MCC) group was founded by members of some of Australia's biggest pension funds, banks, and miners. It issued a statement asserting that firms should work at preventing sexual harassment instead of simply responding after it occurs. The group, which consists of mostly male business leaders with some female executives, also spoke out against the use of non-disclosure agreements to prevent employees from speaking out about their experiences. "As managers we have a collective responsibility to denounce any form of harassment and misconduct," said Simon Rothery, CEO of Goldman Sachs in Australia.[63]

These statements were made in response to several high-profile harassment cases in European corporations. AMP Ltd. demoted the head of its funds management unit, Boe Pahari, following concerns

Corporations Compassion Culture

about alleged inappropriate conduct in 2017. Board chairman David Murray also resigned in the fallout due to the board's decision to support Pahari's promotion while ignoring allegations about his conduct. Patrick Regan, chief executive of QBE Insurance Group Ltd., left the company following investigatory findings that he had fallen short on ethics and conduct standards.

Equality in the workplace must include equality in pay. Linked to the success of #MeToo and #TimesUp, the Equal Pay movement scaled up quickly. *TIME Magazine* published an article that referred to the "triple threat" for women in the workplace, which includes equity in pay, leadership, and opportunity.

Kimberly Churches, president and CEO of the American Association for University Women, described the #MeToo and #TimesUp movements as a Venn diagram that includes sexual harassment in the workplace, eliminating the pay gap and filling the leadership gap. "It really is about equity in pay, equity in leadership, and ensuring we're having environments in every workplace that are good for men and women. We really look at that as a triple threat for women, and it gets to issues of productivity. If women are faced with sexism and harassing behavior in the workplace, that's taking away time they could be using towards the organization's ROI."[64]

Andrea Jung is the president and CEO of Grameen America and former CEO of Avon. She also spoke on the ways that #MeToo and #TimesUp play a role in gender pay equality. She called it an existential moment for equality, commenting that the two movements are integrally linked to one another. "MeToo also means I should be earning a dollar for a dollar. I don't think this genie can get put back in its bottle. I think this is a defining moment, which can in fact move the needle finally on long-awaited equality in the workplace."[65]

Many companies have started to at least consider the issue of pay disparity in the context of and response to these movements. In 2018, former BBC China editor Carrie Gracie stepped down from her position, citing the gap in how much she was paid compared to her male counterparts. The network's original response was to assert that there was no systemic discrimination occurring within their organization. However, four of the network's highest paid hosts agreed to take pay cuts in the interest of equal pay. As a result, the BBC eventually issued a public apology and gave Gracie all of the money that she had been underpaid.[66] To make progress in resolving issues around harassment and pay, it must take women organizing as well as the presence of allies. Allyship, or support from various races and genders, must be reflected in the social sphere for it to take root in the business world.

Dangers of Neglecting Allyship

Allyship, the process by which people listen and honor narratives of underrepresented people as a means to advocate for them, instead of ignoring or modifying them, will take more than just raising awareness about the issues faced by underrepresented communities. One CNN survey estimated that 48% of US firms reviewed their pay policies as a result of the #MeToo and #TimesUp momentum. This suggests that the movements have had some real success in raising awareness, as well as changing the corporate culture within some organizations. Unfortunately, the movement didn't move every woman toward allyship or basic ethical behavior when engaging people from other diverse communities. Female leaders are just as susceptible as male leaders to the creation and preservation of uncompassionate and even dangerous behaviors in public spaces that may also influence workplaces.

A now-infamous incident between Amy Cooper, who worked as a vice president and head of investment solutions with Franklin Templeton, and Christian Cooper (unrelated) is an example of the opposite of allyship that exists between underrepresented groups.

While walking her dog in Central Park, Amy Cooper (a White woman) became involved in a verbal confrontation with Christian Cooper (a Black man) over the fact that her dog was unleashed. She called the police and falsely alleged that Cooper was threatening her life.

Once the video of her actions went viral, concerned viewers reacted to her racially motivated threats and actions with questions about her competence to hire employees with her clear bias. Her employer responded to the video by terminating her employment, stating that they do not tolerate any racism of any kind.

The fallout from Amy Cooper's actions raises the issue of handling situations when bias is totally conscious. Amy Cooper knew what words to use against Christian Cooper. Even before calling the police, she threatened to do so and tell them that an African American man was "threatening" her.

Amy Cooper used biased language that could have gotten an innocent Black man killed. Biased language used in the workplace may not result in death but could still have detrimental consequences. With this example, it is difficult to make the case that conscious actions taken in public places do not seep into our business interactions.

Economic and Reputational Benefits of Compassionate Leadership

Several start-ups have faced ethical issues that have been damaging to both revenue and reputation. For example, in 2016, Audrey Gelman founded the Wing, a space for women in the gig economy to take meetings and network. The start-up raised more than $100 million from venture capitalists and investors. Yet, despite the outward appearance of promoting diversity, the company and its leadership are mostly White, with the staff and minimum wage earners made up of approximately 40% people of color. Former and current employees also reported poor pay and treatment. The company continues to face backlash and negative publicity amidst the Black Lives Matter movement for its poor treatment of workers of color, laying these employees off with no pay.

The start-up company Away also faced backlash for its toxic work culture. The bad press led CEO Steph Kory to resign. In California, the CEO of tech company Solid8 resigned after a video was released of him making racist remarks against an Asian family at a restaurant.

This is an excerpt from an interview I conducted with Greta, the cofounder of a start-up who faced pay discrepancies and a toxic work culture:

> I worked in financial services as the only female cofounder at a start-up. I consistently faced microaggressions from my colleagues. For example, at a conference I was attending, I found I had to report to one of my **peers** after it was decided—without my participating in these discussions—that he would be my manager. My peers also added criteria that I was required to meet despite the fact that I was a cofounder with equity in the company.
>
> As the treatment worsened, I decided to resign. The exit agreement was lengthy and took some time. During this period, I faced cold treatment at work, including threats from the CEO of the company.
>
> The company felt the impact of my departure. About 15% to 25% of clients did not renew with

> the company. My value was in building and selling products and I had a solid network which eventually came with me after I left the company. Pay parity must be part of inclusion in the workplace; it goes hand in hand with compassion.

As conversations around diversity and inclusion in companies gain traction, there are established companies putting diversity initiatives at the forefront of their company-wide policies. Stryker, a manufacturing and production industry company, has 18,244 employees with 26% minorities, 27% minority executives, 35% women, and 27% women executives.[67] Information tech company Cisco employs 38,990 workers with 48% minorities, 30% minority executives, 28% of women, and 21% women executives.[68] The workforce at Accenture, a professional services company includes 51% minorities with about 32% women executives and 38% women.[69]

These companies recognize the value that gender inclusion brings, both internally from a culture of inclusion and externally from organic media and free promotion. A report from McKinsey & Company found that companies with gender diversity are more likely to have increased financial returns compared to those that are less inclusive. In addition, the quality of discussions and perspectives increases when a company has a more diverse boardroom.[70]

As women continue to encounter challenges in the workplace, it is vital to consistently shed light on what is required for their success. Although many companies are embracing changes that create balanced workplaces for all employees, there is still much more work to be done before women experience full inclusion and equity within the business environment.

197

Gender Equity and Company Growth

Chapter 6 Takeaways

- Intersectionality is a key component of discussions about gender in the workplace, playing a role in hiring, promotion, and economic advancement.

- The marketplace rewards firms that advance women's representation in the C-suite and on boards.

- #MeToo and #TimesUp culture kicked off conversations between women, resulting in trusted relationships, pay transparency, and advocacy.

- Women and men alike fall prey to a corporate culture that prioritizes profits over people.

- We can't turn on our biases in one situation and turn them off in another. Core values and principals always reveal themselves. To be relevant and add value in tomorrow's corporations, values must align with equality and compassion.

References

1. https://www.pewresearch.org/fact-tank/2019/03/22/gender-pay-gap-facts/
2. Ibid.
3. Ibid.
4. https://hbr.org/2018/09/do-longer-maternity-leaves-hurt-womens-careers
5. https://nwlc.org/wp-content/uploads/2017/08/Low-Wage-Jobs-are-Womens-Jobs.pdf
6. https://www.census.gov/library/stories/2019/05/college-degree-widens-gender-earnings-gap.html
7. https://www.huffpost.com/entry/5-reasons-why-you-should-negotiate-your-salary-every-time_b_6510350
8. https://hbr.org/2007/09/women-and-the-labyrinth-of-leadership
9. https://www.forbes.com/sites/terinaallen/2018/08/25/six-6-hard-truths-for-women-regarding-that-glass-ceiling/#1b9ae27b427f

10. https://equalmeansequal.com/the-gender-pay-gap/Equilar%20Executive
%20Compensation%20Survey/%20New%20York%20Times

11. https://www.wral.com/the-fortune-500-now-has-a-record-number-of-female-
ceos-a-whopping-39/19279299/

12. http://www.pewsocialtrends.org/chart/women-ceos-in-fortune-500-
companies-1995-2014/; http://fortune.com/2014/06/03/number-of-fortune-500-
women-ceos-reaches-historic-high/

13. https://sites.psu.edu/leadership/2019/06/29/women-and-the-labyrinth-of-
leadership-breaking-from-the-obstacles/

14. https://www.wsj.com/articles/big-companies-pay-ceos-for-good-performance
and-bad-11558085402?mod=searchresults

15. https://www.payscale.com/data/gender-pay-gap

16. https://time.com/5560575/intersectionality-theory/

17. https://hbr.org/2018/08/how-women-of-color-get-to-senior-management

18. https://leanin.org/data-about-the-gender-pay-gap-for-black-women

19. https://www.payscale.com/compensation-today/2020/08/black-women-equal-
pay-2020

20. https://leanin.org/data-about-the-gender-pay-gap-for-black-women

21. https://iwpr.org/publications/annual-gender-wage-gap-2018/

22. https://leanin.org/data-about-the-gender-pay-gap-for-latinas

23. https://leanin.org/data-about-the-gender-pay-gap-for-black-women

24. https://leanin.org/data-about-the-gender-pay-gap-for-latinas

25. https://people.com/chica/geisha-williams-first-latina-ceo-fortune-most-
powerful-women-2017/#:~:text=Geisha%20Williams%20is%20the%20first
%20Latina%20to%20make,March.%20By%20Stephanie%20Fairyington.
%20September%2025%2C%202017%20

26. https://www.bizjournals.com/bizwomen/news/latest-news/2020/09/women-
gaining-corporate-board-seats-faster-rate.html?page=all

27. https://www.forbes.com/sites/maryannreid/2020/02/18/what-happens-when-
white-women-become-the-face-of-diversity/#537e0c4c287d

28. Ibid.

29. https://leanin.org/women-in-the-workplace-2019?gclid=CjwKCAjwkJj6BRA-Eiw
A0ZVPVubDJ09zo7adYQcpaIYd9hVqEbgqe6rTS0TYwTEDVl4M-JQbeAijExoC9
XUQAvD_BwE

30. Ibid.

31. Xochitl Ledesma, Director of learning and advisory Services at Catalyst, 18 Feb,
2020.

32. https://www.nbcnews.com/know-your-value/feature/how-taskrabbit-s-stacy-
brown-philpot-creating-one-most-diverse-ncna1040096

33. https://blog.taskrabbit.com/cbc-tech-2020-diversity-inclusion-plan

34. https://www.usatoday.com/story/tech/news/2016/04/21/taskrabbit-diversity-inclusion-congressional-black-caucus/83314106/

35. https://www.nbcnews.com/know-your-value/feature/how-taskrabbit-s-stacy-brown-philpot-creating-one-most-diverse-ncna1040096

36. https://leanin.org/research/state-of-black-women-in-corporate-america/section-2-support-at-work

37. Ibid. Johnson, Stefanie K., David R. Hekman, and Elsa T. Chan, "If There's Only One Woman in Your Candidate Pool, There's Statistically No Chance She'll Be Hired," *Harvard Business Review,* April 26, 2016; https://hbr.org/2016/04/if-theres-only-one-woman-in-your-candidate-pool-theres-statistically-no-chance-shell-be-hired

38. Johnson, Hekman, and Chan, "If There's Only One Woman in Your Candidate Pool, There's Statistically No Chance She'll Be Hired"; https://hbr.org/2016/04/if-theres-only-one-woman-in-your-candidate-pool-theres-statistically-no-chance-shell-be-hired

39. https://www.catalyst.org/research-series/emotional-tax/

40. https://www.cnbc.com/2020/07/01/how-corporate-americas-diversity-initiatives-continue-to-fail-black-women.html; Hegewisch, Ariane, and Adam Tesfaselassie. "The Gender Wage Gap: 2018; Earnings Differences by Gender, Race, and Ethnicity," *IWPR* no. C484 (September 2019); https://iwpr.org/publications/annual-gender-wage-gap-2018/

41. https://www.businessinsider.com/countries-with-best-parental-leave-2016-8#:~:text=Starting%20in%202021%2C%20Finland%20will%20give%20all%20parents,the%20amount%20of%20two%20parents%2C%20or%20328%20days

42. https://hbr.org/2018/05/denmark-has-great-maternity-leave-and-child-care-policies-so-why-arent-more-women-advancing

43. https://www.consciouscapitalism.org/heroes/denise-morrison

44. https://s21.q4cdn.com/115747644/files/doc_downloads/gov_doc/ULTA_CODE_OF_BUSINESS_032018.pdf

45. https://www.wherewomenwork.com/Career/1763/Northrop-Grumman-makes-Diversity-Inc-Top-50-list

46. https://news.northropgrumman.com/news/releases/northrop-grumman-named-a-2019-top-50-company-for-diversity

47. https://www.handelsbanken.com/en/sustainability/gender-equality

48. https://www.nowtolove.com.au/lifestyle/career/best-companies-to-work-for-in-australia-55355

49. https://www.economist.com/the-economist-explains/2018/09/03/are-gender-quotas-good-for-business

50. https://www.imd.org/research-knowledge/articles/Diversity-and-Inclusion-a-case-of-targets-quotas-or-freewheeling/

51. https://www.usatoday.com/story/tech/columnist/2016/10/25/women-corporate-boards-quotas-wont-help/91739012/

52. https://www.grantthornton.co.uk/insights/are-gender-quotas-good-for-business/
53. https://www.gao.gov/products/GAO-16-30?utm_source=blog&utm_medium=social&utm_campaign=infographic&_ga=2.108674305.2039339971.1598462062-39058873.1597177911
54. https://www.theatlantic.com/business/archive/2017/06/corporate-mentorship-programs/528927/
55. https://www.forbes.com/sites/nazbeheshti/2019/01/23/improve-workplace-culture-with-a-strong-mentoring-program/#49bdc31676b5
56. https://mentorloop.com/blog/which-companies-mentoring/
57. Ibid.
58. https://www.thecru.com/thoughts/262-cru-founder-and-ceo-tiffany-dufu-on-how-to-build-a-successful-newsletter-strategy; https://www.inc.com/brit-morse/lindsay-kaplan-carolyn-childers-chief-networking.html#:~:text=Chief%2C%20founded%20by%20Lindsay%20Kaplan,foot%20homage%20to%20female%20executives.
59. https://hbr.org/2020/01/metoos-legacy
60. https://www.healthline.com/health/black-women-metoo-antirape-movement
61. https://www.indiewire.com/2017/10/jane-fonda-harvey-weinstein-victims-are-famous-and-white-1201891444/
62. https://www.healthline.com/health/black-women-metoo-antirape-movement#The-health-impact-of-cultural-stigmas-on-Black-women
63. https://www.newsbreak.com/news/2057200948463/australian-business-leaders-respond-to-corporate-scandals-metoo-movement
64. https://time.com/5225969/equal-pay-day-2018-women-me-too/
65. Ibid.
66. https://www.npr.org/2018/06/29/624751428/an-apology-and-back-pay-for-editor-in-bbc-gender-pay-inequity-battle
67. https://fortune.com/best-workplaces-for-diversity/2019/stryker/
68. https://fortune.com/best-workplaces-for-diversity/2019/cisco/
69. https://fortune.com/best-workplaces-for-diversity/2019/accenture/
70. https://www.mckinsey.com/business-functions/organization/our-insights/why-diversity-matters?zd_source=hrt&zd_campaign=2448&zd_term=scott ballina

Elements of a Compassionate Corporate Culture

The previous chapters laid out the historical and current-day challenges, successes, and benefits of creating a foundation of diversity, equity, and inclusion. In this chapter, you'll get actionable advice on retooling your business culture, which involves these steps:

- Sustainable management
- Doing the introspective work
- Leadership styles
- Picking your team
- Getting on track and staying there
- Cultivating an equitable workplace culture
- Employee resource groups as culture creators and advocates
- Transparency and employee leadership
- Recognizing and molding your company's internal language
- Investing in employee education, performance, and health
- Measuring employee performance
- Making separations compassionate

Sustainable Management

Problems with business culture often start at the top with leadership. Employees deserve senior teams who are kind and just, who recognize the concerns of employees, and let employees know that they matter. They need and want leaders who manage with integrity and creativity. In return, employees will go the extra mile to advance the goals of the organization. This symbiotic relationship—an employer who treats workers with dignity and gives them agency combined with employees who feel inspired to give their best every day—is the best way to have a sustainable business.

When people hear the term *sustainable,* they tend to picture environmental sustainability—and certainly that's an important use of the term. In the context of this book, when we talk about sustainable businesses, we don't only mean a company's impact on the environment (that said, the environmental aspect of sustainable business will be addressed in Chapter 10). Looking beyond environmental impact, we also are referencing a firm's impact on employees, on investors, and its overall impact on society.[1] Sustainable business, viewed from this more broad social perspective, includes these issues:

- Corporate values that align personally and professionally
- Empowering employees' professional growth
- Aligning compassion, inclusion, and equality toward all stakeholders
- Revenue generation

One of the first steps that firms can take to meet these emerging expectations is to create a workplace that reflects equity and inclusion. Companies that fail to address this priority run the risk of becoming obsolete.

Doing the Introspective Work

Leaders have a responsibility to serve and support others. To do so effectively will require some introspective work, which means examining your own biases, motives, and perspectives about others. Unfortunately, this step is often overlooked in favor of examining practical business questions such as "How can we enhance this product?" and "Do we need to make some employment changes?" From employees to business stakeholders, leaders are constantly placed in positions to analyze the actions of others. But successful leadership also requires an analysis of *your own* behaviors. Clearly, it is important to look at products and services judiciously, but just as much attention should be given to your own agenda, including how it will affect your employees and the marketplace more broadly. This introspective work is valuable for every type of leadership, and whether you are a manager or a CEO this step can be tailored to your particular level.

Regular introspection helps leaders align their actions with their personal truths, reinforcing confidence in their abilities to innovate, make decisions, and execute ideas. A 2017 article published by the Boston Consulting Group explained that critical thinking leads CEOs in addressing immediate challenges and reflective thinking provides clarification of the big picture.[2] The same goes for mid-level management—your team may be smaller, but you are still their leader and need to think and act like it.

Don Jacobs, CEO of PLS Learning, an organization that offers graduate-level courses to educators, stated, "Self-reflection has become a habit for me, and I find that I do it with much less effort these days. It's become more of a state of mind (perhaps to distraction). But I've found that my understanding of my experience is deeper when I take the time to actively reflect. I'm more effective, more deliberate."[3]

From an organizational perspective, leaders need regular introspection to assess whether their workplace behaviors match their personal thoughts and values. Robyn Ward, CEO of FounderForward, has also spoken on the importance of self-reflection and its impact on others. "Being self-aware is knowing who we are and how we show up, what our strengths are, what our weaknesses are. . . It's the core of authenticity—and authenticity leads to trust." She stressed the importance of leaders taking time at the end of each day, month, and year to consider how they showed up within the workplace. "You're not just reflecting on what you've done, but also how you're thinking and feeling. Also, you're a mirror for your team, regardless of the level you're at. Think about how much you will elevate your team by instituting time for self-reflection."[4]

In doing the introspective work, you must assess the roles that fairness, trust, and a love for what you do will play in governance. You must be honest about your commitment so you can find the North Star that will guide your leadership through the most challenging times. You can then craft a professional mission that truly reflects your highest purpose in life.

For some CEOs, that purpose comes from their religious beliefs. Joel Manby, CEO of Herschend Family Entertainment, owns and operates 26 theme parks and attractions across the United States. He said that although he is able to achieve his personal mission statement in his own endeavors, he is also able to achieve it in a growing, profitable business. "I define personal success as being consistent [with] my own personal mission statement: to love God and love others."[5]

Other CEOs place their highest value on the experience of what they do on a daily basis and how it makes them feel. The mission statement of Sir Richard Branson, founder of the Virgin Group, is "to have fun in [my] journey through life and learn from [my] mistakes."[6]

A personal assessment helps CEOs make vital decisions about the type of leaders they want to be and the culture they envision for their organizations. A personal assessment is a self-evaluation helping you understand your strengths, improvement areas, and attitude as a leader. Importantly, you can develop and understand how to leverage strengths to be a more effective leader. Analyzing your strengths and areas for improvement is key for self-development, whether you're leading a small team as a supervisor, line manager, or team leader, or if you're a managing director or CEO leading a business.

This assessment can include simply writing down your strengths, improvement areas, and prioritizing how you can leverage those strengths to improve your performance in leading a team or a project. For an even greater range of information, ask direct reports, colleagues, and managers to share their thoughts on these areas, or use a professional tool created especially for this. For example, Myer-Briggs is a popular personal assessment tool focusing on greater self-awareness and awareness of others to improve decision-making and communication.[7]

This introspective work helps you identify your innate leadership style, as well as adopt components of other styles that may benefit you and your organization.

Leadership Styles

Different people handle their leadership responsibilities in different ways. Analysts have identified a number of clear styles, a few of which include servant, democratic, transformational, and autocratic.[8]

Servant leaders use their leadership skills to promote a greater good. They have identified their purpose and they actively work to weave it through every aspect of the organization. Servant leaders can be powerful forces. Their passion and commitment make their vision so bright that others not only see it but they enthusiastically work toward it too. Servant leaders' values can inspire other leaders. The former chairman of Starbucks Corporation Howard Schultz was often described as a servant leader.[9] His innate belief in the company's commitment has helped the organization through some extremely rough times.

Democratic leaders strongly rely on the skills and expertise of their teams to move the company forward.[10] They consistently ask for feedback and examine the answers received to encourage consensus. Democratic leaders have a knack for creating environments where employees feel like a valuable part of the organization. They empower employees by placing a lot of trust in them, which helps to develop employee confidence while also cultivating worker confidence in leadership. The former CEO and Chairman at Coca-Cola, Muhtar Kent, was known for his democratic leadership style.[11] He earned a reputation for considering input from others when making key decisions, and he ran the company with an inclusive style that reflected his personal commitments.

Transformational leaders use creativity, innovation, and passion to inspire movement toward seemingly impossible goals.[12] They are consistently focused on finding solutions and preventing problems before they arise. They are visionaries who often see possibilities before anyone else, so they need the charisma and presence to inspire others to work toward goals that may not be immediately obvious to others. Steve Jobs perfectly exemplified a visionary style of leadership. His unique approach took creativity and innovation to levels previously unseen or even imagined.

Autocratic leaders operate from a place of complete power and don't invest in power-sharing with others.[13] These are the type of leaders that most workers have experienced at one time or another. They confidently give directives that employees are expected to follow without questioning or second-guessing.

Autocratic leaders can be extremely effective when moving organizations through challenge and crisis. When quick and resolute decisions must be made, autocratic leaders are well-suited to make them.

Autocratic leadership styles are usually found in organizations that operate from the top down where the focus is on results and the bottom line. Martha Stewart has often been characterized as an autocratic leader.[14] Her authoritarian style has been credited with helping her build a successful brand that extends several highly competitive industries.

No leadership style is perfect. That's why many leaders choose to combine various aspects from several styles. Also, social factors may affect leadership style. I spoke about the evolution from top-down to bottom-up management culture with entrepreneur and owner of the NBA Dallas Mavericks Mark Cuban. "Top-down culture is fading. It's really becoming a bottom-up culture again, because of the pandemic. Where the rubber meets the road to use all the cliches ... where people really have an impact on your business, or where your employees touch your customers, and talk to them and listen to them and commiserate with them. So, in terms of building a good culture, you've got to have a culture that allows you to trust your employees from top to bottom to do things."[15]

He went on to acknowledge the challenges of implementing a bottom-up culture within an organization. "Now, they're going to make mistakes. I've had horrible things go wrong where I've trusted people, but at the same time when it works, it's incredible because [employees] love working, and their customers love doing business with you. A culture that's enabled and diverse allows itself to find new ways of doing business. It becomes a lot more agile and resilient than a culture that is very staid and stuck in old ways."

Companies such as Ernst & Young and IBM actively include employees at various levels of the decision-making process. The *New York Times* also moved from a model of centralized power to one of greater collaboration. When the lion's share of decisions were made by managing editors, staff and journalists felt powerless and undervalued. Management recognized the potential in giving

209

more freedom to the team for collaboration and decision-making. Although implementing this bottom-up model took some time, staff members say that it has resulted in a more productive and satisfying workplace.[16]

Doing the work to identify your own strengths and then choosing leadership styles that complement the business as a whole can be a valuable differentiator for you and your enterprise.

Picking Your Team

The same introspection that goes into adopting a leadership style should also occur when building an effective team. The most successful leaders—from supervisors to CEOs—acknowledge their own shortcomings and address them by building teams that can fill in those spaces. A collection of "yes people" cannot help CEOs grow as leaders. They will not challenge you to expand your capabilities, perspectives, and insights because they focus solely on seeking your approval.

If leaders have limited experience in certain areas, they should have executive team members who possess the skills they lack. Leaders need the confidence and humility to bring on people who may be more skilled or knowledgeable than they are.[17] To take an extreme example: if your entire executive team comes from a sales background, you'll miss out on valuable expertise that could be provided by people with marketing, product development, or administrative backgrounds.

Cuban talked about the importance of leaders keeping a group of people around them that broadens their skill set. "So, typically, you want to hire people first that are not like you. And when I say not like you, that encompasses a lot of different things. I'm a ready, fire, aim guy. I'm not detail oriented, so I need somebody who is very detail oriented to be, you know, my CEO or my partner in something because that complements my skill set."[18]

The executive team also offers a valuable opportunity for creating gender balance and diversity within the entire organization. Diversity at the top drives inclusion throughout the entire organization. Recall the study mentioned in Chapter 5: in 2019 McKinsey found companies in the top quartile for cultural and ethnic diversity outperformed those in the bottom quartile with 36% greater profitability.[19]

Cuban spoke about the value of having a diverse executive team. "I also learned over time that you've got to hire people that don't look like you because your customer base probably doesn't look like you either. There's probably a significant diversity in what your customers look like, and you have to hire to match what your customer base looks like in a lot of cases. And sometimes you have to be even more diverse than your customer base, because they'll bring newer ideas to you that you may not have thought of."

Getting on Track and Staying There

Once you've gained awareness about your leadership style and have committed to selecting valuable, diverse team members, it's time to focus on the potential positives of achieving goals instead of the potential negatives of not achieving them. Yes, it's important to acknowledge the negatives—the snares, the competition, the negative marketplace forces, the character traits that need improving—but you can't spend all of your energy there. The creator of the Star Wars franchise George Lucas once said, "Always remember, your focus determines your reality."[20] For leaders, focus determines direction. It guides decisions, judgments, and actions, so your focus must be on outcomes that move the company toward success.

Sheldon Yellen, CEO of BELFOR Property Restoration, uses writing to help him stay balanced and focused on his leadership goals. "I truly believe by putting goals and dreams into written words, it helps to hold oneself accountable and to find clarity amidst all the noise. To do this, I've written my favorite inspirational quotes and lists of goals that I keep with me on a folded piece of paper in my wallet. These are constant reminders that stay with me no matter where I go."[21]

By keeping their goals visible and out front, leaders can easily review and consider them on a daily basis, even several times a day. These reminders help you maintain a clear view of what's necessary to reach your organizational goals. Nazar Musa, CEO of the Australian company Medical Media, spoke about the value of constant goal reviews and the insight they provide into the effectiveness of your leadership. "I feel that constant reviews of what we are trying to achieve is the best way to stay on target.[22] I also have weekly hour-long sessions with my senior managers, with the focus being solely on how I can help them achieve what their goals are. I find it's very useful to ask during those sessions how they feel I am performing in supporting them. While the answers can sometimes be tough on the ego, I find it's a very effective way of staying on track."

The goals set by CEOs and managers alike should become a part of who they are as leaders. Just as you can become so tethered to an annual revenue goal that you know it by heart, your leadership goals should become bound to you and your actions.

In my interview with best-selling author Dan Pink, we spoke about how leaders' actions and behaviors set a tone for the entire organization.

I think that in many cases, leaders discount; they overstate how much people listen to them and understate how much people watch them. So if people see you doing this thing, then there's a fighting chance that they're going to adopt it. So part of it is just simply your example. But the other thing is, is some kind of coating. And so to some extent, what I would do . . . if I'm a leader, let's say I'm doing this thing and having more conversations about "why" and fewer about "how" I would exemplify that in my own behavior. But then I would take my people and be transparent and say, This is "what" I'm doing. And this is "why" I'm doing it, you should give it a try too.[23]

Last, self-reflection requires some form of progress checks and benchmarks. The same rigor you use in revenue-generation goals can be applied to your leadership goals as a CEO. It doesn't have to be difficult. Ask yourself questions such as what are my goals, what concrete steps did I take to reach them this month, did I empower a team member as part of my process, or how can I work with someone else on this in order to support their growth? Just as evaluations are used for products and target audiences, evaluations can be used to examine a leader's motives and movement into a more positive, people-focused workplace. Sharing goals is also an effective way to stay accountable. Discuss your goals with someone within the company or an outside business professional whose opinion you value.

The work of self-evaluation provides clarity on how your leadership will affect your organization and how your employees will feel under your leadership. These are necessary factors to creating a workplace culture that reflects compassion.

Elements of a Compassionate Corporate Culture

Cultivating an Equitable Workplace Culture

In Dr. Martin Luther King Jr.'s 1957 "Birth of a New Nation" speech, he talked about the creation of a beloved community where all "respect the dignity and worth" of all people.[24] Respect and dignity must also be at the core of any successful business environment.

Just as leaders do the introspective work to identify personal strengths and weaknesses, you should undertake the same reflection within your organization. This includes taking a close look at the entirety of your employee compensation packages to analyze the appropriateness of salaries and bonuses. You should also review company health care benefits for affordability, coverage limitations, and wellness features. A comprehensive compensation package is the first step to cultivating a corporate environment where employees at all levels within the company feel valued.

Your internal audit should also include supplier contracts. What percentage of your contracts have been awarded to companies owned by women and people of color when compared to contracts awarded to White male–owned business? If applicable, are your suppliers complying with subcontractor diversity requirements? Though suppliers are not technically employers, they are still part of the corporate culture; they should reflect the values you aspire to within your organization.

Robert Reffkin, the CEO of Compass, is one of few Black leaders in the real estate industry. He strongly encourages his company's more than 15,000 real estate agents to spend 15% of their contracts with Black-owned companies or vendors. "They're all small business owners. They generate $90 billion of commissions a year, and they direct $15 billion of spend to other small business owners: photographers, videographers, real estate attorneys, contractors, stagers, inspectors. With 15 percent of the country being Black America, we're encouraging them to spend 15 percent of their spend on Black professionals."[25]

This next step may take some time and a little extra effort, but the payoff is exponentially valuable. Leaders can greatly benefit from forming personal relationships with employees at all levels of your organization. From the early-level managers to the housekeeping staff, get to know the people who work each day to make your visions and goals a reality. For large businesses or departments, leaders can start with small groups. Use coffee dates or video chats to build relationships. Host monthly lunches (virtual or in person) where you meet with a small group of randomly chosen employees. Open forums can also prove valuable. To keep them functional, limit attendance to the first 10 people to RSVP. Leaders can also make themselves available for quick conversations at the conclusion of team meetings. Even if you can't learn everyone's name, get to know a few employees at every level of the organization.

All-hands meetings are also useful at building relationships with employees. AppsFlyer is a marketing analytics platform headquartered in Israel. They flew more than 300 of their international employees to Israel for a week-long relationship-building event. Though costly, CEO Oren Kaniel said that event provided the organization with long-term benefits. The company saw a significant increase in recruitment referrals from employees, saving hundreds of thousands of dollars that would have gone to head hunters and recruiters.[26]

The leadership at Berlin's AppLift mobile advertising platform carried out a similar relationship-building event, flying more than 200 employees to their headquarters to take part in activities that encouraged the organic exchange of ideas and knowledge. In an interview with *Entrepreneur* magazine, AppLift COO, Stefan Bandorf said, "While it's not easy to measure the ROI, we believe that the indicator for success is marked by how we incorporate the learnings and projects into everyone's day-to-day at the office, a lot of the things we develop and discuss at our all-company all-hands [meetings] are still being used today."[27] Even if large social gatherings are not possible,

Elements of a Compassionate Corporate Culture

smaller events and virtual summits can still promote relationships among the various levels of an organization.

From ensuring fair compensation to establishing genuine relationships at every level of the organization, following these steps will help you create and maintain equity and equality.

Employee Resource Groups as Culture Creators and Advocates

When building a company culture, leaders need to look beyond their leadership teams for help. It's important to build relationships with employees who work outside of the board and executive levels. Junior employees can provide valuable insights into what's happening on the ground—information that you may never learn otherwise—but in order for that to happen, they have to feel comfortable. If employees fear retaliation for telling the truth, they won't talk to you.

Ongoing conversations with employee resource groups (ERGs) can be extremely valuable in this regard. ERGs are voluntary, employee-led associations for team members with common interests, backgrounds, or demographics.[28] Pioneered in the 1960s, the first versions of ERGs offered minorities within particular organizations the opportunity to communicate with one another and advocate for themselves as a united front. In the decades since, ERGs have expanded to encompass a variety of shared workplace interests.

ERGs facilitate positive connections between coworkers who may be in different departments or on different teams; this promotes collaboration and company alliances. These inter-departmental connections can help leadership bolster company culture by providing a proven method for supporting a workplace that is inclusive while also providing opportunities for communication and interaction with employees outside of the executive team. It's a valuable form of engagement that supports progress because ERGs can align their specific objectives with the overall goals of the company. When leaders keep the doors open for communication with ERGs, they will benefit from candid conversations about the concerns, interests, and ideas of not only ERG members but also other employees within the organization.

Ernst & Young is a global management consulting firm that has been recognized by Diversity Inc. for its pioneering efforts with ERGs.[29] The organization maintains more than a dozen of them, including groups for working mothers, veterans, cancer survivors, and various other groups. Further, the company encourages each group to advocate for key populations.

Women at Microsoft (W@M) is another widely celebrated ERG success story.[30] The group empowers members by providing valuable opportunities for skill-building and networking toward the goal of breaking glass ceilings within Microsoft, as well as the workforce in general.[31] Led completely by women, W@M also plans recruiting events at traditionally female colleges and maintains working relationships with women-owned suppliers.

ERGs help leaders align with internal stakeholders on what the organization should stand for within the industry and in the marketplace. I cannot overestimate the value of setting goals and benchmarks for yourself and your team based on the mission and key values of the organization. Create a clear value statement and share it with ERGs within your organization (more on the value of ERGs in Chapters 8 and 9). Encourage employees to commit to upholding and living out these values and mission.

Former Pratt & Whitney CEO Bob Leduc uses periodic conversations with employees to reinforce the company's culture and

(continues)

Elements of a Compassionate Corporate Culture

(continued)

values at all levels.[32] In an interview with ChiefExecutive.net, Leduc declared that "I am a firm believer that my job is to define the culture we want, model the culture we want and nourish the culture we want."[33] He explained that it took some time to fully communicate his message, and he relied on senior leadership to help him set the tone.

> It's . . . the job of the broader leadership team to cascade these concepts through their organizations to ensure alignment from top to bottom. And I make a point of reinforcing them constantly in large forums like global employee town hall meetings and executive conferences and in smaller settings like individual performance conversations. I ask my direct reports to tell me what, specifically, they are doing to advance the company's mission and to foster our desired culture. I expect them to ask the same questions of their teams. I really believe that it's not enough to set these expectations once and move on. A constant drumbeat is needed to maintain focus and is especially important during times of change or challenge.

Transparency and Employee Leadership

Frequent information sharing and honest communication must be part of your goal-reaching process. This is transparency and demonstrating it with employees during times of challenges can allay fears.

For example, you should share your views on the current market environment—in good economic times and challenging ones—as a matter of course. Use commentary, town halls, and internal communications that are easy for everyone to understand, avoiding unnecessary jargon. Additionally, true transparency creates power-sharing opportunities for management to entrust employees with making decisions even during difficult company times.

Not long ago, I spoke with a former colleague who was catching me up on how things were going at my old company. He mentioned that they were undergoing significant downsizing. One of our old colleagues who had recently had a baby and lost her husband was one of the people identified for downsizing. Several of her colleagues and peers drew up a plan for how to keep her on board by reducing their hours as a group, and they presented the idea to the managing director. A few even volunteered to go to part-time status for a while to help keep their colleague from being laid off. Imagine the impact if employees more broadly felt the agency to do things like this? It was a warm gesture that also exemplified how employees can easily be equipped to share insight on decisions about the firm.

When leaders champion transparency and frequently communicate with employees about the state of the market environment and the state of the company, employees aren't caught off guard when challenging situations arise. Through ERGs and other internal communities, they can engage with one another to discuss the environment and share their feedback on improving the company's prospects. It's an approach that strengthens the bonds of trust between you as a leader and your employees.

Recognizing and Molding Your Company's Internal Language

Every organization has a certain language and way of speaking that is part of its culture. By this I don't mean industry-specific jargon or concepts. What I'm talking about is *internal language*: a tone, attitude,

Elements of a Compassionate Corporate Culture

and approach to communication that is specific to that company. Internal language starts in the executive suite and radiates out to the entire organization.[34] The internal language of your company's culture needs to accurately reflect your overall mission and values.

Unfortunately, many business leaders fail to recognize problems with their company's internal language. They are shocked when reports of inappropriate language or offensive interactions arise, adamantly claiming they bear no responsibility and don't condone the behavior. Yet these inappropriate behaviors often represent systemic problems within the organization. Just as a cultural climate can promote company goals and objectives, it can also foster an environment that tolerates and even promotes inappropriate internal language. Inappropriate language can also manifest into inappropriate actions. Leaders need to closely review the climate of their organization to determine whether it gives license for employees to speak inappropriately while feeling perfectly comfortable with their behavior. These cultural permissions open the door to unethical and uncompassionate situations.

In an article for *College & Research Libraries News,* Shamika Dalton and Michele Villagran define microaggressions as "brief and commonplace daily verbal, behavioral, and environmental indignities, whether intentional or unintentional, that communicate hostile, derogatory, or negative slights and insults to marginalized individuals and groups." The *micro* refers to person-to-person interactions, as opposed to *macro,* which refers to systemic racism.[35]

This definition is important because it adds additional context to the definitions for microaggressions previously provided in this book, while laying out its specific forms. There are three general types of microaggressions. Microassaults occur when discriminatory behavior or language is used purposefully.[36] For example, coworkers may make a racist joke and claim that the joke is harmless when they know otherwise. Microassaults may also come in the form of a supervisor acknowledging only White employees or workers of color being treated with distrust.

Microinsults involve both verbal and nonverbal behaviors that express insensitivity and demean a person's race.[37] These instances may occur purposely or without the intention of offending. One example is a male coworker asking a Latinx female coworker how she was able to get a promotion, implying that she did not earn the job on her professional merits.

Microinvalidation communications attempt to negate or alienate a person based on race.[38] These are usually accompanied by a denial of racist intention. The belief that we live in a race-free world, thus invalidating someone's experience of a racist statement is one example.[39]

Discuss these types of situations with your employees and make it clear that microaggressions are not part of your culture. Ask employees to submit stories about when they felt spoken to inappropriately or experienced these situations. This can be done during small-group sessions or submitted anonymously. Review these instances with HR for the purposes of understanding context while also validating the concerns of the people who experienced them. Microaggressions are usually subtle, so the best way to bring them to light is to get clear on what was said, when it was said, how it was said, and the specific nuances about the incident.

The general rule is, if you think a behavior might have been racist, sexist, or otherwise discriminatory, it probably was. If appealing to basic human rights and decency isn't enough (and it should be!), consider your company's liability if you continue to have people in your workplace who speak and act in this way. "I didn't think it was racist," is no longer a valid defense in the eyes of many HR leaders and society in general.[40]

Remember, just because conduct may not have been illegal, it was still offensive to the person who experienced it, and both parties should be treated with the utmost respect. Within many corporations,

Elements of a Compassionate Corporate Culture

employees have dealt with legal but unethical conduct for years. But workers of color are now feeling empowered to stand up for themselves and work toward removing these negatives from their workplaces. Aware leaders need to see this shift and support it. Oftentimes, leaders entrust diversity officers, HR representatives, and others to address internal language issues. But the C-suite, followed by each management level, must take the first steps in cultivating a culture where all employees feel as though they belong. A foundational element is language.

Be transparent when auditing your environment but make it clear that you are not conducting a witch hunt. The point is to not start firing employees because they offended someone. The point is to identify and understand those repetitive behaviors that have been embraced as part of the culture and work to correct them. Although the leader can't control the specific behavior of each individual, she can influence the overall environment in which employees make moment-to-moment decisions about how to behave. The overall culture of the place sways people to behave one way or another, and that can stem from the top.

Similar to microaggressions, code words can also threaten a compassionate work environment. These words and phrases exist within the corporate world in general, but business leaders must be willing to recognize them within their own organizations. When people use words such as *difficult, angry,* and *not a good fit* to describe an employee but offer nothing that substantiates or adds credibility to the claim, these are likely code words. For example, imagine a male employee describing a female colleague as "difficult." Is she genuinely hard to get along with? Or is the male employee just upset that she corrected him in a meeting? Code words are often used to deflect blame for a challenging interaction onto the wrong person.

This type of behavior is sometimes also called dog whistling. A phrase commonly used in the political realm, dog whistles are coded messages that may appear innocuous or neutral on the surface, but the person to whom the words are targeted understands that they carry a more malicious meaning. Dog whistling includes statements that are intentionally made to fuel widespread fear or prejudice in others. Therefore, dog whistling may not only mask inequality and bias within your company, it can promote it.[41]

In this age of technology, employee communications extend far beyond the office walls. From social media to emails, the risk of dog whistling within a workplace has never been higher.[42]

As recently as 2005, the federal courts considered whether use of the word *boy* in reference to Black employees evidenced racial bias by a plant manager who made hiring decisions.[43] The Federal Circuit Court ruled in *Ash v. Tyson Foods, Inc.*, that the use of *boy* alone is not evidence of discrimination.[44] However, on appeal, the US Supreme Court disagreed, stating, "Although it is true the disputed word will not always be evidence of racial animus, it does not follow that the term, standing alone, is always benign. The speaker's meaning may depend on various factors including context, inflection, tone of voice, local custom, and historical usage." With this ruling, the Court rejected any notion that a modifier was necessary to make the term *boy* racist.

As a result, US courts now widely acknowledge how code words associated with "dog-whistle racism" can evidence racial discrimination and harassment within the workplace. Some of the words and phrases that the courts have found to evidence racism include "fried chicken," "ghetto," "drug dealer," "all of you," and "one of them." In *Aman v. Cort Furniture Rental Corp.*, the courts considered the statements "don't touch anything" and "don't steal."[45]

As times change, so does coded, discriminatory language. Today's company leaders also need to be careful of phrases such as "not the right fit," "too ambitious," "not well liked," or even "angry." When my manager told me that my "synapses didn't connect," that was a completely new one on me—but what I did know was

223

Elements of a Compassionate Corporate Culture

that her words and unscientific "diagnosis" were inappropriate in our corporate environment. Ban these codes and dog whistles from your professional environment, performance reviews, and one-on-ones. Remember, it is altogether possible for your employees to expose your organization to potential liability under federal law, even when using words and phrases that you may understand as nondiscriminatory.

Investing in Employee Education, Performance, and Health

Leaders need to invest in employee education, performance, and health. Offering educational opportunities that help employees—both personally and professionally—will go a long way toward building loyalty and appreciation. If your organization cannot fully finance educational programs, consider splitting costs with employees. There are also other creative ways to offer support, such as hosting an educational event on company premises. Consider opportunities for employees to act in roles as teachers. For example, I learned coding from a colleague who hosted a course on it at work. These scenarios give employees a purpose beyond their day-to-day activities, while also helping their coworkers build their knowledge and skills.

The company known as SAS offers an excellent example in how educational offerings can help improve the corporate environment. SAS is a leader in business analytics software and services with more than 14,000 employees working in offices throughout the United States and internationally. The company offers various educational opportunities to employees, including leadership programs and a career resource center. Their SAS Academics program for sales and technical enablement provides recent graduates with classroom and on-the-job training to help prepare them for success even before they start their full-time roles. Shannon Heath, SAS senior communications specialist, said, "SAS provides opportunities for growth to keep our employees challenged, motivated, and engaged."[46]

Other firms take different approaches to this same idea. With more than 280,000 employees globally, AT&T maintains the AT&T University, which is an executive-led program focused on leadership and management development. Partnering with Georgia Tech and Udacity, Inc., the company helped create the first-ever online master of science in computer science (OMS CS) and launched several self-paced, fast-track technical credentials called nanodegrees. "We can't depend on just hiring and the traditional educational system as sources for retooling or finding new talent. We need employees who are ready to work in a competitive and more digital world," says Marty Richter, corporate communications manager. "We're focused on aligning company leaders to strategic business innovation and results, skilling and reskilling our 280,000 employees and inspiring a culture of continuous learning."[47]

In addition to offering education opportunities, it's also a wise strategy to promote employees' physical and mental health. There are numerous benefits to these programs: they help ease burdens on employees (which builds loyalty) and enables them to give fuller energy to the business (which increases revenue). In addition to the various strategies discussed in Chapter 4, such as paid sick leave and mental health wellness benefits, leaders can also promote a compassionate workplace by supporting flexible work situations for employees who need it.

COVID-19 proved how creative and flexible management can be if it really needs to. But the question is, why did it take a global pandemic for so many executives to figure this out? Managers have the ability to react, adapt, change, and thrive when it's necessary to avoid a fallout. Why not start using that flexibility and creativity not only in emergencies but also as a means of promoting a new corporate culture? Flexibility is an important component of a

Elements of a Compassionate Corporate Culture

successful company culture for many reasons. It builds trust between the employee and employer. These mutually trusting relationships benefit the entire organization through improved decision-making and engaged employees. Flexibility also fosters satisfaction and happiness among employees by allowing them the time and availability to balance their work and personal lives.

Flexibility improves employee productivity. Though many business leaders have traditionally doubted the effectiveness of flexible work schedules, COVID-19 quickly dispelled the negative assumptions. With flexible work, employees feel empowered and energized, which translates into improved performance.

The goal of enhancing diversity can also be furthered by flexible work options. Remote work capabilities enable you to build a global workforce. They open up opportunities within your organization to individuals living in more remote communities and those with health conditions. Flexible work options are important for attracting top talent—particularly among millennials and Generation Z workers who increasingly expect these options from prospective employers. They want to work for companies that value and promote work-life balance, so leaders who are able to create such environments will be successful at attracting these talented individuals.

The implementation of flexible work options can be a vital part of creating a successful company culture, where your organization attracts up-and-coming talent while also maintaining an environment where current employees thrive and want to contribute to their greatest abilities.

Measuring Employee Performance

Performance reviews and performance improvement plans (PIPs) have long been used in the corporate world as a way of providing feedback to employees and encouraging positive changes. And yet I've rarely seen an employee get on solid footing in response to a PIP, especially given the routine and pageantry around these workplace traditions. It's a mistake to expect that workers will bring their best innovation and effort when under consistent pressure. That is why leaders should strongly consider moving away from this model.

Threatening employee reviews and PIPs are not effective tools at improving the overall culture. Some supervisors even use PIPs as an easy way to separate employees they don't like from the firm. Numerous studies have found performance reviews ineffective at actually improving performance.[48] Rather than serving as valuable leadership tools, they end up being control mechanisms that cause stress to employees and threaten the corporate culture. Feedback is much more effective when given in the moment, not months later. Proponents of performance reviews argue that they are necessary to inform employees of how they are doing, justify compensation decisions, and establish paper trails for corrective employment measures. But each of these goals can be met by other methods.

Performance reviews are intrinsically filled with problems. For one thing, they are unfair in the amount of subjectivity involved. Even in offices with rigid scoring systems in place, all managers have their own personal biases, which may present themselves during these processes. For example, the "similar-to-me" bias refers to the behavior of performance reviewers giving higher ratings to people with interests, skills, and backgrounds that are similar to their own.[49] These tendencies not only make performance reviews hard to trust but also they affect the inclusivity of the workplace as a whole.

PIPs and performance reviews can also feel insulting to the employee being reviewed. When you hire someone to work within your organization, you do so because you trust and value their ability to do the job. Although it is appropriate to let employees know when they behave in an inappropriate manner, it may not

227

Elements of a Compassionate Corporate Culture

be appropriate to tell professionals how to handle the tasks they were trusted to complete. It reinforces the (unproductive) idea that supervisors sit on a higher level of importance than other workers.[50]

When you ask HR people why they still do performance reviews, the answer is frequently, "because we've always done them!" But when you are trying to build a new corporate culture, the most time-honored traditions are often the ones that need to go. Increasing numbers of leaders are doing away with formal performance reviews. In a comparison between 2016 and 2017, the number of employers conducting formal performance reviews decreased from 94% to 91%. The same trend was seen among formal performance ratings, with only 80% of employers using them in 2017 compared to 85% in 2016. Conversely, informal performance check-ins rose to 50% in 2017 versus 42% in 2016.[51]

Deloitte Touche Tohmatsu Ltd. is one firm that has started the process of moving away from formal reviews.[52] Instead, on a quarterly basis, each team leader is asked to answer the following questions for each employee on a scale of 1 to 5:

- I would award the employee the highest possible pay increase.
- I would always want the employee on my team.

Team leaders are also asked to answer yes or no for the following questions:

- Is employee at risk for low performance?
- Is the employee ready for a promotion?

Deloitte's method is just one example of creative approaches to performance reviews—there are numerous others available to company leaders. You can mandate regular meetings and one-on-ones between supervisors and their direct reports on an ongoing basis.

This type of arrangement allows for the identification of issues early on so that they can be addressed before they become serious problems for the company.

Leaders and supervisors can also invest time into enhancing employee strengths. Although this does involve the sometimes uncomfortable task of identifying employee weaknesses, it also supports them in building their skills and using their strengths. Encourage your managers to partner with employees in discussing what the next stages of their careers may look like. Maybe they are interested in transferring to another department where their strengths can be leveraged. Perhaps they have decided that they are not a good fit for your organization. Leaders can help by providing access to a network that supports them in finding an external role that plays to their strengths. Managers and team leaders must support and listen to employees if they want to move beyond perceived issues affecting culture or performance. A review should be a time of reflection and should be a time to ensure employees feel like valued, included team members.

Even if someone's performance needs improvement, no one benefits when a manager addresses an employee in a rude, dismissive, or annoyed manner when they give feedback. As Maya Angelou so eloquently stated, "I've learned that people will forget what you said, people will forget what you did, but people will never forget how you made them feel."

Making Separations Compassionate

In reality, not every difficult situation at the office is resolved with the employee remaining with the firm. When it does become necessary for an employee to separate from the company, consider what part your organization can play in making these changes less contentious. An employee's departure doesn't always have to be filled with hostility. If your company has truly grasped a culture of compassion, the consideration of an employee's well-being doesn't end abruptly when they separate. When it's time to make hard calls and choices that affect people's livelihoods, leaders need to be more open to thinking creatively. Here are examples of how to do that:

- Furlough people to allow the continuation of their health benefits.

- Offer the services of a career-transition company. These firms help former employees prepare for their new career stage by giving LinkedIn profile and résumé writing support, use of office equipment, and a trained professional to consult on opportunities.

- Establish an alumni network, offering former employees a formal platform for engaging each other in a way that's less awkward than a cold email.

- Separate from an individual with grace and dignity. For example, make eye contact and allow that person to speak without talking over her.

A separation is already a trying time for an employee. Doing so in a way that supports employees' future growth and dignity is the way to separate with compassion.

Chapter 7 Takeaways

- Leaders must begin the journey of improving their business by doing some deep introspection. Start with understanding your motives, agenda, and leadership style. Consider what you want your legacy to be with employees and within the wider marketplace.

- Set clear expectations for your leadership.

- Remember, employees have the agency to determine what type of firm they want to work for.

- ERGs can provide C-suite and other senior executives direction on establishing the business's purpose and recommend strategies for supporting one another.

- The HR handbook and one or two lines on your website about a mission are insufficient. A true mission requires action and measurability.

- Reiterate the type of company you want to build and the type of language and behavior that is needed for your company culture to get there. Identify internal language that is insensitive and outline why it should be avoided.

- Rethink how PIPs are used. Allow managers and employees to work together, along with HR, to develop clear plans to move forward.

References

1. https://online.hbs.edu/blog/post/what-is-sustainability-in-business
2. https://www.bcg.com/publications/2017/leadership-talent-people-organization-rewards-ceo-reflection
3. Ibid.
4. Ibid.
5. https://www.skipprichard.com/ceo-joel-manby-on-how-leading-a-company-with-love-works/
6. https://medium.com/@KaitlinZhang/how-to-write-your-personal-mission-statement-with-5-famous-ceo-examples-87185f158c38#:~:text=%205%20Famous%20CEO%20Personal%20Mission%20Statement%20Examples,for%20inspiring%20my%20students%20to%20be...%20More%20
7. https://www.mbtionline.com/en-US/How-it-works/Framework

Elements of a Compassionate Corporate Culture

8. https://www.informa.com.au/insight/leadership-styles-understanding-and-using-the-right-one-for-your-situation/

9. https://www.forbes.com/sites/katecooper/2018/07/03/who-is-the-servant-leader-really-serving/

10. Ibid.

11. https://www.bing.com/search?q=muhtar+kent&cvid=d623998944af4090bce9dd3de17c0b87&FORM=ANAB01&PC=LCTS

12. Ibid.

13. https://www.informa.com.au/insight/leadership-styles-understanding-and-using-the-right-one-for-your-situation/

14. https://www.industryleadersmagazine.com/martha-stewart-living-omnimedia-a-shining-business-empire/

15. Interview with the author. Mark Cuban, Radical Talent Services Inc, August 24, 2020.

16. https://www.projectsmart.co.uk/get-maximum-benefits-of-merging-top-down-and-bottom-up-project-management.php

17. https://www.inc.com/bruce-eckfeldt/great-ceos-surround-themselves-with-best-leadership-team-heres-how-to-create-yours.html

18. Interview with the author. Mark Cuban, Radical Talent Services Inc, August 24, 2020.

19. https://www.mckinsey.com/featured-insights/diversity-and-inclusion/diversity-wins-how-inclusion-matters

20. https://www.forbes.com/sites/rhettpower/2020/05/03/how-to-focus-like-george-lucas/#35430de2510b

21. Ibid.

22. https://www.businessinsider.com.au/how-ceos-set-goals-2018-1#:~:text=%20Here%27s%20how%2012%20successful%20CEOs%20set%20their,is%20much%20that%E2%80%99s%20written%20about%20goal...%20More%20

23. Interview with the author. Daniel Pink, How leaders' actions and behaviors set a tone for the entire organization, August 18, 2020.

24. https://www.youtube.com/watch?v=IeCzzRY_RI8

25. https://www.inman.com/2020/06/08/compass-ceo-calls-on-his-agents-to-spend-billions-with-black-vendors/

26. https://www.entrepreneur.com/article/303589

27. Ibid.

28. https://www.bluleadz.com/blog/employee-resource-groups-to-inspire-you#:~:text=Why%20Are%20Employee%20Resource%20Groups%20Important%3F%201%20Give,Engagement.%20...%204%20Foster%20Diversity%20in%20POVs.%20

29. https://www.bluleadz.com/blog/employee-resource-groups-to-inspire-you

30. https://blogs.microsoft.com/bayarea/2018/04/30/microsoft-employee-resource-groups-creating-community-and-celebrating-diversity-across-silicon-valley-and-san-francisco/
31. Ibid.
32. https://chiefexecutive.net/the-ceos-role-in-shaping-an-organizations-culture/
33. Ibid.
34. https://hbr.org/2012/07/how-language-shapes-your-organization
35. https://crln.acrl.org/index.php/crlnews/article/view/17431/19237
36. Ibid.
37. Ibid.
38. Ibid.
39. https://www.teenvogue.com/story/microinvalidations-are-real
40. https://www.fastcompany.com/3068670/how-to-shut-down-microagressions-at-work
41. https://defendingmanagement.com/2018/11/05/dog-whistle-racism-in-the-workplace/
42. Ibid.
43. https://defendingmanagement.com/2018/11/05/dog-whistle-racism-in-the-workplace/
44. *Ash v. Tysons Foods, Inc.*, 546 U.S. 454.
45. *Aman v. Cort Furniture Rental Corp.*, 85 F.3d 1074.
46. https://www.monster.com/career-advice/article/companies-with-awesome-training-development-programs
47. Ibid.
48. https://www.forbes.com/sites/lizryan/2018/01/14/performance-reviews-are-pointless-and-insulting-so-why-do-they-still-exist/#4bade3172d1a
49. https://www.cultureamp.com/blog/10-performance-review-biases-and-how-to-avoid-them/
50. Ibid.
51. https://www.shrm.org/ResourcesAndTools/legal-and-compliance/employment-law/Pages/more-employers-ditch-performance-appraisals.aspx
52. https://www.washingtonpost.com/news/on-leadership/wp/2015/03/17/deloitte-ditches-performance-rankings-and-instead-will-ask-four-simple-questions/

Your Plan for Creating Inclusion through Compassion

What Works

To achieve true inclusivity, company leaders need to get real about what they are willing to do and the time frame they'll do it in. Change can't wait until tomorrow. There is too much at stake for companies to put off inclusion and fair promotion of people of color until you find the "perfect" diversity strategy. The despair and disappointment felt by people of color has been centuries in the making. The time to act is now. It's important to remember that inclusivity is a core component of compassion. Recruitment and retention are tools by which inclusivity is achieved.

There is no secret formula to inclusivity. Achieving it requires commitment. Building on the shifts in language, values, and behavior that we discussed in previous chapters, we should next leverage those changes to create intentional recruitment, genuine inclusion, and the fair promotion of underrepresented employees as part of the new corporate landscape.

This chapter offers guidance on the steps that leaders can take to further these goals, such as these:

- Take a fresh approach to the hiring processes
- Strengthen your search for talent

- Explore valuable recruitment channels
- Achieve stronger supply chain diversity
- Make the commitment an executive team effort
- Avoid the diversity revolving door: retaining diverse talent
- Bottom-line benefits of inclusivity

Take a Fresh Approach to the Hiring Processes

In a 2020 *Forbes* article, contributor Paolo Gaudiano explained this viewpoint by exploring the six stages of the hiring process.[1] Leadership needs to ensure potential employees are aware the company exists and the company's reputation. Next, leaders must clearly demonstrate how their firm is an appropriate fit for certain skills and career goals. One way to accomplish those two items is to sponsor and volunteer for activities in which employees interact with prospects. Whether it's speaking at a trade organization with seasoned professionals or guest lecturing at a local college, employees in direct contact with prospects is the best way to spotlight your company and the types of skills needed to thrive at the company.

Third, understand that candidates need to think about your organization from a personal perspective to determine whether it's a good fit for them. Perceived culture plays a role in how potential candidates view your organization. Candidates can quickly research your company's reputation and culture to determine whether you maintain a workplace where they will feel welcomed and included. Employers can't change a candidate's perception, but they can influence perceptions when each touchpoint—where a candidate "touches" your brand, from your website to your social media to your sponsorships—contains language, images, and real-life stories that show an intention toward compassionate, diverse, and equal treatment of employees. Attention to these items will improve candidates' experiences at each phase of their hiring process.

If all of these stages turn out positively, the candidate will apply to your firm. You invite the candidate to interview in the fourth stage. This is where you can implement interviewing panels aimed at reducing bias, as discussed in Chapter 5.

IT company Cisco has also used diverse interview panels to attract and interview a more diverse group of candidates. As stated by CEO Chuck Robbins, the company chose to implement diverse interview panels based on research that showed they would improve the likelihood of hiring Black candidates by up to 70% and Latinx and women candidates by 50%. "At Cisco, we are focused on integrating inclusion and diversity best practices in order to deliver innovative solutions in many critical areas, including pay parity and recruiting diverse talent. We are also deeply committed to advocating for inclusion and diversity in our communities, and across our industry."[2]

The fifth stage of the hiring process involves extending an offer for employment. Not receiving a call back from an employer after several weeks is disheartening. Candidates take time from jobs or other responsibilities to participate in and prepare for interviews. Managers should ensure HR contacts call candidates in the weeks following the interview to update them on the status of the job, even if it's to inform them that you will not extend an offer. To leave people uninformed about the state of their candidacy is unacceptable.

The sixth stage is when candidates accept the offer. Gaudiano believes the available pool of talent decreases with each of these stages.[3] Leaders who are adapting to the new corporate culture are gaining more insight into how to recruit diverse candidates (see Chapter 5) and see how their choices about where and with whom they network help them see the full pipeline that exists.

Your Plan for Creating Inclusion through Compassion

Strengthen Your Search for Talent

If your company's recruitment team is comprised mostly of people who don't interact with others outside of a heterogeneous community, or who socialize largely within structures of privilege, they may have no idea how or where to access diverse talent.

Michelle Silverthorn is the founder and CEO of Inclusion Nation. In a 2020 interview, she spoke about ways that leaders can improve recruitment diversity.[4] She explained that one major problem stems from the tendency of many companies to recruit from a small fraction of colleges and universities. "We keep on saying, 'Oh, the pipeline is broken,' but it's not broken. You're just looking in one place... If you haven't been recruiting at HBCUs—[historically Black colleges and universities]—maybe during your next cycle, that's what you do."

As explained by Gaudiano, "You should also know that sometimes the channels through which you advertise jobs can be significantly skewed in terms of the population segments they reach—again, something that a privileged, majority individual is less likely to know."[5] Candidates form a perception of a job before they decide to apply for it, and that opinion is largely shaped by the language used to describe the available position.

In the United States, the term *minority* connotes a lack of clarity for some. It refers to a variety of groups and sometimes doesn't allow the consideration of differences that exist between different cultures. An ongoing debate in the United Kingdom centers on the use of what some see as a racially offensive term in employment advertisements. BAME (Black, Asian, Minority Ethnic) is an acronym that is widely used by the European media and corporate world.[6] Although it was created for the purpose of bolstering solidarity among minorities, it became a term used to lump non-White individuals into one category.

There are technologies to help employers craft racially neutral job advertisements, but a simple way to do this is to commit to removing language that may offend prospects and including language that promotes inclusivity. This is where managers, team leaders, and supervisors who intentionally expand their networks add value. Building relationships with people in various organizations and networking with broad, heterogenous groups can help you tap into diverse talent; listening to their perspectives also gives insight into the type of language that should be used when looking to embrace diverse applicants.

Many company leaders also fail to recognize how unconscious bias negatively affects job candidate screenings. As noted in Chapter 5, numerous studies have proven that résumés with female names and names perceived as ethnic are less likely to be invited for interviews. HR officers and hiring managers need to consider these biases and implement measures that prevent the additional effect of further reducing the pool of appropriate candidates.[7]

Experts say that leaders should also start looking more at the existing talent within their companies, which may require new training sessions to introduce existing employees to management and leadership opportunities. Although some organizations ask employees of color to assist in recruitment through recommendations and referrals, the onus of inclusive recruitment and promotion cannot be placed on the shoulders of these employees. Instead, leaders can partner with company ERGs as one element in a diverse recruitment strategy. As discussed in Chapter 7, ERGs can be instrumental resources for building business culture. In this chapter, we'll see how they can support recruitment too when you recognize all aspects of the value they bring.

Your Plan for Creating Inclusion through Compassion

Explore Valuable Recruitment Channels

The first ERGs were developed in response to the racial strife of the 1960s. Former Xerox CEO Joseph Wilson developed the concept following the Rochester, New York, race riots of 1964. He and his Black employees launched the National Black Employees Caucus to address workplace racial tensions and discrimination.[8] Since the mid-2000s, companies have begun recognizing the value of ERGs in the areas of recruitment and retention.

ERGs can be instrumental resources for your businesses, but to fully support the goals of these groups, and not just use them when convenient, you must get to know their members and leaders. Get on their agendas and communicate with them to ensure that you understand their objectives and what you can do to further them. Let their experiences help influence your leadership. They are on the ground and they have established meaningful relationships with their coworkers. They are likely experts in what it's like to be a professional in your organization, as well as identifying as a member of their underrepresented group. They can share these experiences with prospective employees in their communities and networks.

AT&T's Black ERG, The NETwork, has been celebrated as a highly effective ERG for Black employees.[9] With more than 11,000 members, AT&T credits The NETwork as a major resource for identifying candidates for leadership. In 2015, the company reported an 85.6% retention rate for Black employees.

Jim Norman, vice president of diversity at Kraft Foods, spoke about holding ERGs accountable for organizational initiatives:

So, for instance, if the issue is advancement of people of color, if I have that as a charge, then the African-American, Latino and

---

Asian-American council can work on development issues jointly. There's a recognition that there is some assimilation required and that there are business objectives to be achieved and that there is an aspect of diversity that is of value to the organization and there are some that, very frankly, are not.[10]

He said that company leaders meet with the groups four to six times a year to ensure that they remain committed to the company goals of assisting with recruitment, supporting employee development, and encouraging community inside and outside of the organization. Their support for the ERGs also includes a two-day facilitated meeting between group members and company leaders to discuss people, processes, and results. They also run a Jump Start program with their ERGs that helps new diversity hires navigate the unwritten rules of the organization.

A June 2020 article by Aiko Bethea for the *Harvard Business Review* speaks about the ways that companies can support and encourage Black ERGs. Among the included suggestions, the article notes that the work of ERGs is often done in addition to the full-time job duties of the members, with no additional compensation for their time and effort. "It's time that organizations compensate these leaders for their work," Bethea argues. "In the past, ERGs were primarily a support network for people with shared identities, but now organizations rely on them for recruitment, retention, marketing, strategic guidance, and other business functions."[11]

The proposed compensation could take the form of bonuses or a raise in compensation. It could also encompass all-expense-paid attendance at relevant conferences or paid membership in Black employee associations. "Companies that use their ERGs to recruit Black employees need to make sure they are taking care of their

Your Plan for Creating Inclusion through Compassion

current Black employees. If they don't, they are ultimately adding to the emotional labor of their current employees, who are left to nurture and support their new colleagues when they are subjected to anti-Blackness and inequity."[12]

Another avenue that leaders from supervisors to CEOs can take toward inclusive recruitment, while also eliminating unconscious bias from the candidate review process, is technology. As mentioned in Chapter 5, AI-recruiting platforms provide a cost-effective tool for consistently filling in these gaps. Importantly, leaders who use AI should also work to ensure the tools have transparency and are evaluated and monitored to prevent unwanted biases. In the age of increased remote working, other tech advances can also have an effect on the hiring process.

---

eMedia CEO Anna Murray shared with me her thoughts about how technology will affect the hiring and even onboarding processes in our remote working environment:

> We can be better at screening with our technology that digests resumes. I actually think that physical presence cuts both ways. Presence can be very powerful when the aspect of physical presence is in your favor. People can see physically in the Zoom [video chat] that I'm a woman. But I assert that it's actually a different experience than if someone's sitting next to me. All the things that make me a woman, hair, etc. This presence is downplayed on a Zoom call. I think that the online aspect of what we're doing is probably favoring those folks who found themselves on this subject of unconscious bias in a meeting room.

Corporations Compassion Culture

> I have clients who have a Zoom culture where the video has to be on. And some cultures that are just a voice or audio only. This benefits people who in another circumstance would have faced bias. In terms of onboarding, I know people who started new jobs over the last months [during the COVID-19 pandemic]. In the first week, it's like, oh, shoot, this is different coming in. They're in meetings, like you always are. But they say it was weird, not going to the office and sitting in the office, not having coffee with people, getting to know them.

Strengthening your search for talent is improved by expansive networks, inclusive language, and even embracing new channels. This isn't limited to hiring junior or mid-level professionals but can be used for recruiting senior leaders as well.

There is still a critical need to diversify candidate pools in C-suite and board positions. In Chapter 6, we spoke about Ursula Burns, CEO of Xerox from 2009 to 2016.[13] As the first Black woman to head a Fortune 500 company, she said that in order for corporations to create more diversity in their boardrooms, they have to "change the criteria." Speaking on CNBC's *The Path Forward: Race and Opportunity in America,* Burns said that companies have to expand their screening processes when building out their boards. By specifically looking for candidates who have already been CEOs, Burns argued, they exclude talented Black professionals who have been systematically excluded from these positions.

"You can probably count on two hands the number of candidates you'll get that are diverse," said Burns. "It's a fallacy and a

Your Plan for Creating Inclusion through Compassion

structural form of racism and exclusion to say that the only people who can actually participate are people that have this very narrow set of skills."[14]

Achieve Stronger Supply Chain Diversity

Studies show that strong supplier diversity programs benefit companies in a variety of ways, including new market connections and potential customers.[15] As discussed in Chapter 5, suppliers are vendors from janitorial services to cafeteria workers to tech suppliers. They are onboarded by a business and typically engage with employees.

The important thing to remember is this: supplier diversity programs are not about doing a favor. They are about expanding your network and outreach to open opportunities to deserving suppliers while benefitting your bottom line. If you see these actions as favors, then you still have some internal work to do in the way you perceive the historic and current business landscape.

It's also important to recognize the challenges that come along with making changes to your supply chain. If you're a procurement manager, a third-party alliances manager, or, more broadly, if you influence vendor onboarding in any capacity, this is especially important. Develop a case for change that includes an explanation about why changes are needed at the supplier level and the potential consequences if they do not occur. The statement should also reinforce the benefits that the proposed changes will bring to the company's future and provide guidance for the decision-making process and onboarding of new suppliers.

This type of supply chain change management is a critical function for addressing the internal challenges that often arise when employees resist necessary change.[16] Understand that when one supplier replaces another, there may be a bit of animosity, especially when "breaking up" long-term working relationships. By anticipating these challenges, you can make plans to deal with them.

For example, plans to compassionately address the human aspect of these changes should begin as soon as new supplier decisions are made. These efforts should focus on all procurement and vendor management officers and influencers embracing a smooth transition to new suppliers and modeling the behaviors you expect to see throughout the organization. Once this is done, these plans can trickle down to middle and first-line management and their direct reports for change implementation.

For the suppliers who are new to your firm, outline a plan to support them through onboarding and beyond. Remember, they don't have the advantage of spending years as your supplier, they may not socialize in the same networks as others at your firm, and likely they do not have long-term relationships with people in your procurement or business departments. Plans to support them should include these actions:

- Sharing vital information needed to do their jobs, such as lists and titles of all relevant stakeholders
- Providing a few key contacts (in case of leaves of absence and vacations)
- Clear objectives and measurable expectations
- Periodic check-ins and ensuring availability
- Providing an accurate and up-to-date scope of the project

A truly compassionate culture ensures that new suppliers have all they need to succeed, free of intentional sabotage or unintended roadblocks that arise due to a lack of shared information or long-standing relationships.

According to an article on the University of Tennessee's website, the majority of businesses fail within their first year and about half of those that survive that first year fail within in years two through five.[17] Because diverse suppliers, also known as minority-owned suppliers, are often new and small in size, they are highly susceptible to these potential failures. Your organization can actively invest in developing their diverse suppliers through adequate change management and training opportunities.

When establishing inclusive supplier programs, business leaders can benefit by learning what has worked for others. Look outside your own industry and evaluate the best practices used by other industries. The most effective goals are ones that can be measured and realistically achieved. Those goals may be as simple as developing a system for tracking your current diversity statistics or encouraging your current suppliers to start their own supplier diversity programs.[18] Your company may also choose to develop a repository of diverse supplier names and referrals.

There are many resources for procurement professionals to use when seeking diverse suppliers, such as the National Minority Supplier Diversity Council, the US Small Business Administration, and state government databases. Dun and Bradstreet maintains a database of diversity data collected from more than 400 sources. With more than 5.3 million socioeconomic classifications and more than 20 million small business indicators, companies can find qualified third parties that meet their immediate and long-term needs. Using the Dunn and Bradstreet matching process, companies can determine the diversity of vendors and the amount they spend with diverse suppliers within their current supplier base.[19]

The question of setting spending goals is controversial. Many purchasers wrongly believe that the goal of networking with and onboarding more minority-owned suppliers will conflict with the goal of cost reductions. But in fact, savings and supplier diversity goals can actually exist in harmony. Collectively, these goals can motivate purchasing and procurement teams to find highly qualified diverse suppliers while also maximizing the amount of bidding opportunities granted to businesses headed by people of color.

From broadening your network to enhancing recruitment to improving onboarding processes, bottom-line growth is not the only benefit to the approach outlined here. Reputational value and social license with employees, consumers, and investors are strengthened. Support from a variety of stakeholders does help you implement your approach and succeed in reaching these goals.

Make the Commitment an Executive Team Effort

No matter how strong a leader's commitment to inclusion may be, if her company's executive team doesn't exhibit the same level of dedication, efforts will be stalled. People at every layer of management must serve as agents of change, modeling desired behaviors and supporting necessary shifts to build the desired corporate culture. To successfully drive cultural changes, leaders must craft a detailed plan that looks at where the company is and where it needs to go. Get clear on how your executive or management team can increase their participation and lead with a commitment to inclusion. Share priorities and commitments for hiring, promotion, and retention with your leadership teams to ensure that they play a role in reimagining and rebuilding the culture.

Stakeholders look to their leaders' actions, on or off the job, to exemplify their level of commitment to inclusion. In a 2017 article in the *Harvard Business Review,* Sallie Krawcheck, CEO of Ellevest, spoke about her priorities when establishing an executive team. She decided to hire candidates who could bring in new perspectives rather than those who had similar backgrounds to current members of the team. She said that the benefits of "culture add" should be considered as part of the hiring criteria instead of always focusing on "culture fit."[20]

The same article included statements from Bernard J. Tyson, CEO of Kaiser Permanente, who spoke about the evolution from equality to equity within the company. "Equality says everybody gets equal. Equity says no, everybody gets what they need. Part of building an inclusive environment is not how you're going to change the person. It's how you're going to change yourself and the environment in which the person is going to have to succeed."[21]

According to Kaiser Permanente's year-end 2016 numbers, more than 60% of their workforce, which numbered more than 180,000, were members of racial, ethnic, and cultural minorities, and more than 73% were women. More than 50% of the management and professional positions were held by racial and cultural minorities. Tyson said that they achieved these outcomes through deliberate planning, development of current talent, and outreach within the communities that they serve.[22]

Deliberate planning must also include the creation of regular progress and status checks. Corporations take measurable, quantitative approaches to revenues and client retention all the time—they can also measure, assess, and improve their company's plans for inclusion. These progress checks should extend beyond entry-level positions to include middle and senior executive levels. Research has shown that setting and following through on diversity goals is the most effective method for increasing underrepresentation of minorities.

Omar Ishrak serves as executive chairman and chairman of the board of directors at Medtronic and chairman of the board of directors at Intel. Heading up Medtronic's diversity council, he signs off on all diversity goals, such as increasing the diversity of their board of directors and diversity in their management and executive ranks. The company set a goal of establishing a US-based workforce in which 20% of management and higher-level roles were held by ethnically diverse talent by the year 2020. By 2019, Medtronic had surpassed this goal, with ethnically diverse talent representing 22% of their management positions.[23]

There is a clear financial rationale for ensuring measurable levels of diversity. A 2019 diversity and inclusion article published by research and advisory company Gartner states, "Through 2022, 75% of organizations with frontline decision-making teams reflecting a diverse and inclusive culture will exceed their financial targets."[24] In addition to this bottom-line rationale, society is seeing diversity and inclusion as an equality and humanity imperative.

The setting of inclusion goals was accelerated by the social justice protests that followed the death of George Floyd. For example, HP Inc. plans to double their number of Black executives by 2025. Jeans maker Levi Strauss launched a new diversity plan that includes adding a Black person to their board of directors, striving to achieve 50% persons of color in job candidate pools and increased hiring from HBCUs.[25]

Mozilla announced plans to double the percentage of Black and Latinx representation within its 1,000-person US staff and also increase Black representation in the United States to 6% at the director level and above. Mark Surman, executive director of the Mozilla Foundation, commented in June 2020, "There is no question events of the past few weeks have underlined the need to focus more on racial justice. The collective push of the tech industry is promising and important, but we need to make sure we are collectively held accountable on moving the ball."[26]

But even the best-laid plans will be ineffective at bringing about change without company-wide commitments. Whether you are a supervisor or business unit head, seek a higher level of awareness about your blind spots and how to address them. It may be difficult to get an accurate assessment of your compassion and equal treatment of others from your current subordinates, but previous employees are often more willing to provide open and honest answers. Use blind

Your Plan for Creating Inclusion through Compassion

surveys to ask former employees whether they would (1) actively seek to work with you again or (2) actively avoid working with you again.

I spoke about these strategies in an interview with behavioral scientist Matt Wallaert. I asked him whether corporate leadership can design tests to measure managers' emotional intelligence and ability to promote a diverse workforce. "I think we can root out bad actors," he told me, "the Harvey Weinsteins of the world. We can develop better mechanisms for identifying systematic offenders. But in the fuzzy gray area . . . it's interesting." Wallaert believes we need to move away from identifying "good guys" and "bad guys" when it comes to diversity issues and instead think in terms of areas where we can all improve in various ways.

Although it may be challenging to identify the gray-area people that Wallaert speaks about, compassion and a desire for a diverse team can still be taught. Work with your leadership teams to understand the "right person" for the job is not always the "White person" for the job. This is where language and mindset come into play. Even the term *diversity hire* can be problematic when it creates feelings of "otherness" within the workplace. Historically, male White workers are seen as a baseline or a default for what is normal. Everyone else is seen as "other than," so they require greater scrutiny. This means that in organizations run by all-White leadership, Whiteness typically becomes the standard for appropriate behavior, workplace values, and the criteria for promotion.[27]

This type of workplace is one of inherent tension for employees of color. Their speech and tone are scrutinized. Their headwraps or hairstyles are scrutinized. Their ideas and perspectives are scrutinized. Even the smell of their non-Western food in the breakroom is scrutinized. All of these dynamics stem from a work environment where minority workers are tolerated instead of truly included, which does not support a compassionate workplace.

Wallaert created his own survey called "Work with Me Again," where he collected feedback from former employees and coworkers about his performance as a manager. "I sent 800 people that I've worked with before a survey that basically says would you choose to work with me again ... on a one-to-five scale. One is 'I would actively avoid working with you.' Five is 'I would actively seek out working [with you].'"

The results were enlightening. He said he has scored at about the middle of the scale, so a three on a scale of one to five with his latest version of the project, which he previously iterated five to six times. He says White women in particular found him more polarizing and more likely to give him either a one or a five. He also recognized his tendency to try and "explain the results away."

Wallaert's takeaway from the project as a whole was that the question of what makes a good manager is never going to be completely clear cut:

> I think the best we can do is actually root out bad actors, which I think we're going through a process—as a culture—of doing now. We can try and make every-body better than they are. And that's a better focus than trying to figure out who's incrementally better than the next person and hiring that person. It's going to be hard because [what if] we have a leader that's really good with women, but really bad with people of color? How do we make those trade-offs? I think we have in our minds that it's some smooth gradient, that people will be universally better or universally worse, but that may not be true.[28]

Your Plan for Creating Inclusion through Compassion

Avoid the Diversity Revolving Door: Retaining Diverse Talent

No matter how hard you try, a bucket with a hole in the bottom will never be filled. In the area of diversity and inclusion, this challenge is often referred to as the "diversity revolving door."[29] Since the new millennium, corporations have spent countless dollars and hours trying to attract and hire a diverse array of candidates, but once these individuals become employees, there is no effective plan for retaining them.

Recognize that your supervisory employees may fall short when managing diverse new hires. Although resources abound to assist with inclusive recruiting, far less guidance exists for the purpose of helping managers successfully manage and retain employees who do not look like them. The result may be a lack of communication with new employees of color, for example, in sharing adequate instructions regarding what management expects. In response, new employees may perform inadequately and face termination or become frustrated and leave the company.

Communicate with Managers

One pitfall is that managers may see efforts to retain employees of color as some sort of extra burden or as a favor the company is doing. Leaders need to identify and address this type of thinking. All people of color are just as capable as anyone else of good work when provided with adequate management. Managers' behavior and language should reinforce this fact.

These issues can also be addressed by making your management teams more inclusive. Encourage open communication between White managers and managers of color about their concerns, management methods, and inclusion questions. Not only will individual managers benefit from these discussions but also they are an effective way of reinforcing your overall goals for the company. In addition, diverse new hires will come into an environment where they are just as likely to be managed by another person of color as they are a White supervisor.

Sponsors and Mentors

As mentioned in Chapter 6, sponsorship is one method of promoting the movement of diverse candidates into supervisory positions. These programs have been proven successful at overcoming network gaps and other systemic structures that reinforce inequities. According to a CNBC report, up to 80% of jobs are secured through networking. As the old saying goes, it's all about whom you know, and most people leverage their networks to stand out from a pile of résumés and secure interviews. Unfortunately, some diverse candidates tend to have smaller, less powerful networks available to them; this makes mentoring and sponsorship vital tools for Black and Brown employees.[30]

As mentioned in Chapter 6, although mentors provide their mentees with advice about reaching their goals and ambitions, sponsors take on an active role in advancing the professional career of sponsees. They are generally senior-level leaders who use their network and professional connections to advance sponsees.[31]

The traditional model of informal sponsorship centered on shared interests, such as hobbies, family connections, college affiliations, or social memberships.[32] These connections worked well for some—namely, young and middle-aged White males—to advance their careers and expose them to valuable professional opportunities.

Your Plan for Creating Inclusion through Compassion

But traditional sponsorship both purposely and unintentionally left out most of the workforce.

Current demands for greater racial and ethnic diversity require a new look at sponsorship and how it can be used to further a corporation's inclusion goals. Many organizations rely solely on mentoring programs, upholding them as best practices. Although mentoring is an important piece of the puzzle, the consistent absence of people of color from C-suites brings into question the effectiveness of mentoring in truly advancing diverse employees.

As a relatively recent formal concept, sponsorship is proving to be a highly useful tool for the progression of people of color into executive-level positions. Economist and Columbia professor Sylvia Ann Hewlett serves as CEO of the nonprofit think tank Center for Talent Innovation. The organization's research champions the benefits of sponsorship. According to the Center for Talent Innovation, diverse employees with sponsors are 65% more satisfied than nonsponsored employees.[33]

Business leaders with a true commitment to inclusion should see the opportunity in this research. Informal sponsorships don't naturally evolve within corporate America, largely due to embedded cultural beliefs that White men are best suited for leadership positions. That is why it is important for companies to intentionally establish and promote sponsorships between existing leaders and diverse employees with leadership potential. Encourage and empower these leaders to take a real interest in the career development of their sponsee and advocate for them just as they would advocate for someone they came to know and trust through a less formal connection.

Hugh Welsh is the president and general counsel of DSM North America, a global leader in nutrition, health, and material sciences with sales in excess of $12 billion. He wrote a 2016 article in *Entrepreneur* detailing his personal experience with intentional sponsoring.

In the past few years at DSM, I've taken on four promising employees as my own experiment testing this theory. All were diverse by age, gender and ethnicity and none of them were among the organization's leadership at the time. They did share one trait; I believed they were among the most talented people in our company. The results—all four were promoted, all four moved across different businesses in DSM, a key development goal; and three have already been promoted to the executive ranks in DSM.[34]

He suggested that companies consider connecting talent goals with executive compensation to encourage the adoption of sponsorship arrangements. "At DSM, we already tie sustainability goals to executive bonuses, so adding talent and business development goals as part of incentive payouts is a reasonable next step."[35]

Role of ERGs

Successful sponsorship can also take place within the ERG model. Every ERG should have an executive sponsor who is either in the C-suite or one level away.[36] This individual will advocate for the ERG's initiatives, helping them to overcome obstacles and achieve collective goals. These executives can also get to know the skills and aspirations of the individual ERG members to identify exceptional employees who would benefit from their sponsorship.

Multinational pharmaceutical company GlaxoSmithKline (GSK) maintains a successful ERG program for Black employees.[37] Members of the African American Alliance (AAA) have been able to benefit from executive sponsorships by leveraging the company's reverse mentoring program. The initiative promotes the exchange of information about cultural differences between senior leaders and ERG members. These relationships have provided the company leadership with valuable insight for dealing with inclusion-related challenges and obstacles. In return, participating AAA members have received increased visibility and exposure to senior leaders outside their business unit.[38] GSK leaders credit the reverse mentoring program with providing a structured environment for fostering authentic relationships between employees and senior leaders, which has led to inclusive leadership and increased sponsorship opportunities for diverse employees.

These types of initiatives empower companies to recognize existing minority talent and provide them with the voice they need to excel and advance. Companies that fail to take proactive steps risk losing Black and Brown employees, leading to a "revolving diversity door."[39] The failure to promote these employees also raises a red flag for all people of color who may be considering employment with the organization. With sponsorship programs, companies can do more than talk about driving inclusive recruitment and hiring; they can actually hit the goals they have committed to achieve.

One senior vice president of HR had this to say about her experience with the reverse mentoring program:

> Through my diverse reverse mentoring [DRM] experience, I truly believe I have become a better, more inclusive leader who is constantly curious and wants to learn from others. It has helped me see things in new ways and created a very different type of conversation for me with my team and with other leaders in the organization. My mentors have given me the courage to do some things I would never have dreamed of doing previously and for that I am grateful![40]

Ensure Public Accountability

Open forums and public proclamations have become common practices among corporations in their quests for greater inclusion, and these tactics can be effective at holding employers accountable for hiring and retaining workers of color. In 2020, sports apparel maker Adidas pledged to fill at least 30% of all open positions with Black or Latinx candidates.[41] They also pledged that a minimum of 30% of all new Adidas and Reebok positions in the United States will be filled with Black and Latinx people. Adidas North America president Zion Armstrong and Reebok brand president Matt O'Toole have reportedly worked in close partnership with the company's Black employees to identify necessary steps for meeting these goals and establishing a plan of action.[42]

In June 2020, cosmetics company Estée Lauder made a public declaration promising greater inclusion within their organization. The company pledged to ensure that, within five years, the percentage of Black people it employs mirrors the percentage of Black people in the US population.[43] Company leaders also committed to doubling the amount spent on sourcing ingredients, packaging materials, and supplies from Black-owned businesses and requiring a diverse pool of candidates for all executive director and above positions.[44] They said that these goals will be accomplished through strong partnerships with Black associations and increased recruiting from HBCUs.

Middle Management Influence

Supervisors and managers can have a wide degree of influence over their employees' career growth and professional networks. At this level, day-to-day interactions can support your team members' current and future career goals exponentially. For example, in my first corporate job, I recall my manager taking me with her to executive lunches with vendors who supplied our data or those to whom we sold our products. Before lunch, we'd go to her office and she'd give me a lay of the land about their product, the role of the person, the role's salary range, and industry detail they might share with me. This gave me insight to direct key questions to that vendor or client that furthered my knowledge, while also helping me expand my resources and network of potential future employers. This level of inclusive behavior should be standard performance for middle managers. When you are able to expose your team members to people, projects, or networking opportunities that advance them, don't hesitate.

Leader Networking

For managing directors or C-suite people with a quest to create a more compassionate and inclusive company, it can also be useful for you to network with other leaders—including diverse leaders—who have strong commitments to the same goals. This engagement can take on various forms, including networking groups, professional associations, or CEO Roundtables. Participation in these groups can help you develop additional approaches to re-creating a culture that embraces racial and ethnic diversity, including how to build a diversity imperative into your managers' everyday performance.

Business-owner peer groups have grown significantly in popularity over the last few decades. Membership is typically limited to no more than 15 business leaders who meet on a monthly basis. The confidential nature of these groups provides members with a safe environment for working through challenging or sensitive topics. The benefits of these groups are plentiful, including diverse perspectives, solid reasoning, and unfiltered feedback.[45]

The Business Roundtable is a widely known CEO peer group made up of CEOs from some of the world's largest corporations. In June 2020, the group's chairman Doug McMillon, chairman and CEO of Walmart, announced the creation of a Special Committee of the Business Roundtable Board of Directors to advance racial equity and justice solutions.

"Over the past few days, I have watched with a heavy heart the violence, unrest, and national outcry to end race-based injustice. Our employees, customers, and communities are looking to us to act now. Having spoken to many CEOs of America's leading businesses, I know they share my conviction that this is a time to act to address racial inequality. The pain our country is feeling should be turned into real change."[46]

Bottom-Line Benefits of Inclusivity

The passion, commitment, and dedication that leaders put into shaping a culture that genuinely sets up all employees for success, including employees of color, not only benefits the corporate culture and inclusion of an organization but also has positive effects on the bottom line. Consider these statistics:

- Employers in the top quartile for racial and ethnic diversity are 36% more likely to have financial returns above their respective national industry medians.

- Employers in the top quartile for gender diversity are 15% more likely to have financial returns above their respective national industry medians.

- Employers in the bottom quartile both for gender and for ethnicity and race are statistically less likely to achieve above-average financial returns than the average companies in the data set.[47]

In other words, companies that lack gender, racial, and ethnic diversity don't just fail to outperform their more inclusive competitors,

Your Plan for Creating Inclusion through Compassion

they straggle behind them. These performance differences suggest that inclusion is a competitive differentiator potentially shifting market shares in favor of more diverse companies.[48]

The reasons offered for this outcome are varied. One explanation is the enhancement of creativity that diversity brings. A 2014 article by Katherine Phillips, senior vice dean at Columbia Business School, discussed the effects of diversity on individual workers and companies in general:

> It encourages the search for novel information and perspectives, leading to better decision-making and problem solving. Diversity can improve the bottom line of companies and lead to unfettered discoveries and breakthrough innovations. Even simply being exposed to diversity can change the way you think. This is not just wishful thinking: it is the conclusion I draw from decades of research from organizational scientists, psychologists, sociologists, economists and demographers.[49]

The different perspectives that arise from a diverse workforce can reduce risks and improve innovation within a working environment.[50] We saw the negative response of these risks when fashion industry giants like H&M, Gucci, and Prada faced high-profile backlash for selling products that were considered offensive to people of color. The consequences were severe, with the companies facing global boycotts and protests.[51] In the months following the controversy, H&M's sales plummeted 62% as company leaders found themselves with more than $4 billion in unsold merchandise.[52]

Just as businesses can suffer the financial consequences of being publicly seen as lacking compassion for racial equity, they can also reap the benefits of earning a reputation for demonstrating a commitment to inclusion within their workforce. Businesses that are known for their inclusive employment practices attract a more diverse pool of qualified applicants. They also attract business and loyalty from consumers who seek to spend their money with companies that not only speak about racial equity but actually work toward it.

Chapter 8 Takeaways

- Move toward new ways of hiring and onboarding that call for creativity beyond antiquated HR practices.

- Build measurable goals for recruitment and promotion.

- Improve behaviors toward racially and ethnically diverse groups and keep working on it.

- Your target customer profile includes members of underrepresented groups. Engaging employees who are also members of these groups not only is common sense and ethical but also can be profitable.

- Make inclusive behaviors a regular part of management performance.

- Create opportunities for informal mentoring, planned sponsorship, and external engagement.

References

1. https://www.forbes.com/sites/paologaudiano/2020/03/23/6-ways-diversity-and-inclusion-impact-the-cost-and-effectiveness-of-recruiting/#26eddc787a5c
2. Ibid.
3. Ibid.
4. https://www.npr.org/2020/09/03/909274979/workplace-diversity-goes-far-past-hiring-how-leaders-can-support-employees-of-co
5. Ibid.
6. https://metro.co.uk/2020/07/07/bame-debate-why-terminology-matters-when-talking-about-race-12954443/

7. Ibid.
8. https://www.diversitybestpractices.com/employee-resource-groups
9. https://hbr.org/2020/06/what-black-employee-resource-groups-need-right-now
10. https://www.diversityinc.com/how-ergs-increase-engagement/
11. https://hbr.org/2020/06/what-black-employee-resource-groups-need-right-now
12. Ibid.
13. https://www.cnbc.com/2020/09/08/ursula-burns-ex-xerox-ceo-companies-must-change-board-criteria-for-diversity.html
14. Ibid.
15. https://www.jumpstartinc.org/tips-tracking-supplier-diversity-data/
16. https://www.logisticsbureau.com/7-golden-rules-for-change-management-in-supply-chain-organisations/
17. https://www.nextlevelpurchasing.com/articles/supplier-diversity-goals.php
18. https://www.jumpstartinc.org/tips-tracking-supplier-diversity-data/
19. https://www.dnb.com/products/third-party-risk/supplier-diversity-data.html
20. https://hbr.org/2017/08/what-11-ceos-have-learned-about-championing-diversity?registration=success
21. Ibid.
22. Ibid.
23. https://www.medtronic.com/us-en/about/citizenship/supporting-a-global-workforce/inclusion-diversity.html
24. https://www.gartner.com/smarterwithgartner/diversity-and-inclusion-build-high-performance-teams/
25. https://blog.ongig.com/diversity-and-inclusion/diversity-goals/
26. Ibid.
27. https://www.pollenmidwest.org/stories/confronting-white-supremacy-in-the-workplace/
28. Interview with the author. Matt Wallaert, What makes a good manager is never going to be completely clear cut., August 3, 2020.
29. https://www.tlnt.com/a-12-step-program-for-retaining-your-diverse-workforce/
30. https://www.forbes.com/sites/forbeshumanresourcescouncil/2020/06/12/tackling-diversity-and-inclusion-sponsors-consultants-and-advisors-as-part-of-your-strategy/#4c31a9e42342
31. https://www.forbes.com/sites/forbeshumanresourcescouncil/2020/06/12/tackling-diversity-and-inclusion-sponsors-consultants-and-advisors-as-part-of-your-strategy/
32. https://www.entrepreneur.com/article/274525
33. Ibid.
34. Ibid.

35. Ibid.
36. https://hbr.org/2020/06/what-black-employee-resource-groups-need-right-now
37. https://www.diversitybestpractices.com/erg-spotlight-gsks-african-american-alliances-reverse-mentoring-program
38. Ibid.
39. https://hbr.org/2020/06/what-black-employee-resource-groups-need-right-now
40. Ibid.
41. https://theconversation.com/diversity-pledges-alone-wont-change-corporate-workplaces-heres-what-will-143408
42. https://www.adidas-group.com/en/media/news-archive/press-releases/2020/message-adidas-board-creating-lasting-change-now/
43. https://theconversation.com/diversity-pledges-alone-wont-change-corporate-workplaces-heres-what-will-143408
44. https://www.elcompanies.com/en/news-and-media/newsroom/company-features/2020/elc-commits-to-racial-equity
45. https://www.forbes.com/sites/henrydevries/2016/10/11/10-reasons-to-join-a-ceo-peer-group/#32d2aa7e48c1
46. https://www.businessroundtable.org/business-roundtable-chairman-doug-mcmillon-establishes-special-committee-to-advance-racial-equity-and-justice
47. https://diversity.social/diversity-inclusion-benefits/
48. Ibid.
49. https://www.scientificamerican.com/article/how-diversity-makes-us-smarter/
50. https://diversity.social/diversity-inclusion-benefits/
51. https://www.theguardian.com/fashion/2019/feb/08/courting-controversy-from-hms-coolest-monkey-to-guccis-blackface-jumper
52. https://newsone.com/3786010/hm-earnings-racist-monkey-ad-update-profits-plunge/

Your Plan for Creating Gender Equity through Compassion

What Works

L et's first reiterate an important message from Chapter 8: significant inclusion can only happen when leadership—from supervisor to CEO—gets real about what they are willing to do and the time frame that they'll do it in. Whether we're talking about gender or racial inclusion, promotion, or pay equity, a solid plan for improvement should include strengthening your talent search, exploring new recruitment tools, achieving supply chain diversity, committing to a team effort, and avoiding a revolving door by retaining talent. Gender equity is a core component of your compassion and inclusion strategy.

A plan deeply rooted in commitment and desire for inclusion helps leaders tear down inequities that emerge from generations of systemic workplace bias and build new opportunities for all employees. Here, we continue building out this plan, this time taking into account societal biases and expectations affecting women particularly.

There are still prevalent societal expectations that follow women from their families and home lives into their corporate lives and workplace conduct. In this chapter, we explore some methods to help deliver change and gender advancement:

- Identifying and addressing gender inequity
- Transitioning employees back into the workplace
- Meeting the needs of child-free employees
- Supporting women's leadership and advancement and confronting saboteurs
- Building a gender-inclusive community
- Leveraging data to measure future progress

Identifying and Addressing Gender Inequity

In re-creating your organization to be more inclusive of women— including women in leadership roles—you must first understand the pain points in your old culture that prevented the inclusion of women in the first place. I suggest you take a data-intensive approach, analyzing the most vulnerable areas of your firm that have inhibited women's retention and advancement.

A first step in creating a culture that truly includes women at each level of the organization starts with understanding data about the trajectory of women's careers within your company, from entry level to senior management, and building a realistic view of where the drop-offs occur. One way to gain this understanding is to work with HR to gather data about your workforce. Start simple: how many women are employed at your company? Then use that data to understand percentages of women in senior levels versus those in lower-level roles. From there, you can begin to discuss why such a large number of women at your firm remained in lower or mid-level roles; it's worth discussing this with your HR department, but don't forget to ask the women at your firm as well. Also, you can discuss which aspects of your culture may be derailing women's efforts to progress. (These potential pitfalls will be detailed later in the chapter.) You might find patterns in your firm mirror patterns we've seen more broadly over the decades.

The 1970s and 1980s saw significant progress for women moving into positions of power and authority within the corporate environment. Those advancements stalled in the 1990s, and the last 20 years brought about a virtual standstill. It's a persistent problem that has been debated across the globe.

The discussion on why women remain so dramatically underrepresented typically includes a conversation about women's devotion to family and how these commitments run counter to the steps necessary for obtaining and maintaining high-level corporate positions. This explanation is referred to as the "work-family narrative," and it is the most commonly used justification for the lack of female representation in executive suites.[1]

In a 2012 survey of more than 6,500 Harvard Business School alumni across various industries, 73% of men and 85% of women used the work-family narrative to explain women's lack of equitable progression.[2] But the widespread use of this explanation doesn't make it accurate.

Culture of Gender Inequity

The challenge of balancing work and family is not a female issue; it is a parenting issue that affects both women and men. Of the millions of mothers in America, about 71% of them are part of the workforce, according to the US Census Bureau.[3] However, although society encourages mothers to modify their professional paths to care for their families, fathers are encouraged to focus on advancing their careers. The lack of advancement among professional women does not stem from the challenge of balancing work and family. In theory,

Your Plan for Creating Gender Equity through Compassion

fathers deal with the same issues that mothers do. But in reality, it's the mothers' careers that become stalled. Family responsibilities cause women to accept part-time work schedules and internally facing roles, but men also have family responsibilities. The expectation that those responsibilities should take a greater priority for women is due to a culture of gender inequality.[4]

Work accommodations have long been touted as a valuable resource for working parents. However, working mothers make far more use of these options than working fathers. Though women may experience the immediate benefits of greater flexibility and availability for their families, the long-term effects include the disruption of their career trajectories and the stigmatization of their professional reputations. As stated in a 2020 article in the *Harvard Business Review,* "The upshot for women at the individual level was sacrifices in power, status, and income; at the collective level, it meant the continuation of a pattern in which powerful positions remained the purview of men."[5]

Across the corporate environment—from law firms to tech companies to banking institutions—the result of women taking schedule accommodations results in a permanent detour from the road to advancement and leadership. This occurs for a few reasons. Studies show that, within the workplace, women who opt for a flexible schedule are viewed more negatively and seen as less productive.[6] Even though female employees are actually more likely to excel in their positions when provided with flexibility, their male coworkers tend to categorize them as being able to "to come and go as they please," which can foster feelings of resentment.[7] These opinions—and the inappropriate conduct that may follow—send a message to women that they are outsiders in the corporate environment and do not truly belong.

The characterization of accommodations as measures put in place for the sole well-being of women reinforces the long-standing belief that men and women have specific and separate roles to play within society. It is the idea that females are best suited to care for families and take on caregiving roles, even within the workplace. As such they are expected, and sometimes even pushed, to make choices that place their careers on the back burner for the "good" of their families.

Achieving a work-family balance is not what's really keeping women out of executive suites. What really keeps them from advancing are deep-seated beliefs about the roles of women within society. But corporate leaders adamantly insist that the work-family narrative correctly explains the inadequate advancement of women within their organizations. This perspective supports a false conclusion that the only potential solutions must be geared toward women. But to be a leader truly committed to inclusion, you must recognize the realities, including where the systemic legacies of gender inequality have pervaded your corporate culture.

Ask yourself some tough questions. Do you have a workplace that encourages 24/7 workdays, where employees' ability to advance depends on their availability for work at all times of the day and night? Are schedule "accommodations" geared toward female employees? Before you can build a new inclusive culture, you must get real about where your organization currently stands.

Female-Centered ERGs Create Safe Spaces for Women

We've discussed how ERGs benefit overall worker well-being and racial and ethnic diversity in previous chapters. Female-centered ERGs can be extremely useful at providing insight into your company's current culture.

My own experience bears this out. As chairperson of Women @ Thomson Reuters and Women @Refinitiv Employee Resource Groups, I engaged more than 100 employees for the purpose of creating gender equity and equality. For more than three years, I supported and advocated for initiatives promoting allyship between genders, peer mentoring on salary negotiation, reverse mentoring between underrepresented employees and executive leadership members, and external, cross-financial services industry programs for women's financial literacy.

Other examples of female-centered ERGs can be found at Corning Inc., which operates two global ERGs aimed at professionally developing and supporting the company's female employees. The Corning Professional Women's Forum (CPWF) champions "an environment in which women are valued, promoted, and able to achieve their full potential. The group is dedicated to attracting and retaining women to Corning, and providing opportunities for professional development, networking, and exposure." The ERG includes 23 chapters in 13 countries around the world. Corning's Technology Community Women's Network (TCWN) operates in Corning, New York, to empower women in technology. It offers skill development events and activities throughout the year.[8]

The Women of AT&T (WOA) ERG includes more than 24,000 women in 39 chapters across the country.[9] Among its many accomplishments, the group created a mentoring program aimed at developing internal talent and facilitating relationships between upper management and high-potential women. With more than 72,000 female employees at AT&T, women account for 32% of all of the company's workforce and 35% of managers. "We have frontline employees working side by side with senior leaders, vice presidents, and officers," states Corey Anthony, senior vice president of human resources and chief diversity officer of AT&T. "We engage the Women of AT&T to help us identity the most talented women in our business," Anthony adds. "We look at the people who are taking leadership roles within ERGs, and they get to interact with [our CEO] and senior leaders."[10]

As mentioned in Chapter 8, executives and managers usually don't belong to ERGs; this happens, because they assume they don't have the same firsthand experiences or perspectives as the members. But as a leader at any level you should nonetheless make an effort to participate in their events and make yourself available for engagement. View it as a tremendous listening and learning opportunity. Not only can you learn about issues and needs facing people in your organization but also you can often get an understanding of solutions that are being developed elsewhere that your firm can emulate. For global firms, there may be a particular opportunity to see how other regions are successfully solving gender-specific challenges.

Global Data about Family Leave Benefits

According to UNICEF, Sweden, Norway, Iceland, Estonia, and Portugal offer the best family-friendly policies among 31 rich countries with available data.[11] The United Kingdom and United States rank lower for family-friendly policies.[12] The National Partnership for Women and Families reported that only 19% of US workers have access to employer paid leave. In addition, the Family Medical Leave Act (FMLA) is only an option for fewer than 60% of the workforce. Even for those who qualify, many simply cannot afford to take 12 weeks of unpaid leave.[13] In light of all of this, employers who provide 12 weeks or more paid leave see greater employee retention, which means companies spend less in recruitment and onboarding, while increasing worker productivity.[14]

The Organization for Economic Co-operation and Development (OECD) compared childcare expenses among various countries. They listed New Zealand as the most expensive country, where families with two children pay about 37% of their wages for childcare. Australia, the United States, and the United Kingdom also came in at over 30% of a couple's average salary for childcare.[15] For corporations in areas of the world with less than stellar leave policies, these statistics demonstrate a valuable opportunity for bridging the gap.

Investment into an effective family leave plan can have huge payoffs for a company. The leaders of Australia's Westpac Bank recognized an internal problem in 1995, when only 32% of their new mothers returned to work after having a baby. They set out to fix the issue by launching a paid maternity leave program. Within two years, they saw an increase to 53% returns. Today the percentage of new mothers returning is about 96%. According to Shenaz Khan, Westpac Group general manager, the benefit is well worth the cost. "We are able to retain that knowledge and experience," she said noting that it can cost up to 2.5 times a woman's salary to replace when accounting for recruitment, retraining, and onboarding. "And in specialist roles, where skills are hard to find, those costs are significantly higher."[16]

Transitioning Employees Back into the Workplace

When employees—women and men—do take advantage of family leave options, it's important to examine your company's integration procedures on their return to the workplace. This second step in ensuring an inclusive and compassionate culture is critical: inadequate processes and overlooked microaggressions create a culture of exclusion that alienates employees returning from family leave and discourages the advancement of women into executive levels of your organization. Work with your HR professionals to build a reentry program that meets the needs of your employees. Every situation is different. Some employees take leave for the birth of a child, and others may have adopted an older child. Some employees take leave to care for an elderly family member. Strict and inflexible return policies may not work for every situation.

Embrace Transitions and Re-onboarding Programs

The technology company Intel offers benefits and perks, such as additional time off, special parking, and on-site nursing rooms to help employees and their families' transition after those life-changing moments.[17] Patagonia has accomplished a 100% return to work for women after maternity leave by offering a variety of benefits, including on-site childcare that empowers new mothers to breast-feed infants on demand.[18] Their turnover rate for parents who have children in the program is 25% lower than that of their general employee population.

The twin phenomena of aging baby boomers, coupled with the rise of Gen X and millennials caring for elder relatives and young children, shine a light on issues facing caregiving workers in general, not just those who are transitioning back into the workplace.

Corporations can and should consider innovative policies in this area. Goldman Sachs offers on-site childcare centers in some of their offices.[19] Intuit works with a third-party daycare provider to provide employees with backup and long-term care services at a reduced rate.[20] Prudential Financial Inc. maintains a program in which employees pay a $100 co-payment for a geriatric-care specialist to visit an elderly parent's home and draw up a complete care plan. Employees at publishing company McGraw-Hill can enroll one other adult family member, including an elderly relative, on their health insurance plan at regular family rates.[21]

These programs benefit all genders, while recognizing the obstacles that women sometimes face when balancing work and family. They also benefit the bottom lines of these companies. For example, recognizing the value of on-site childcare

(continues)

(continued)

facilities, the federal government provides a $150,000 annual tax credit to companies in addition to the reduction of up to 35% of unrecovered costs from corporate tax liabilities.[22] The cost is also offset by increased employee retention and improved employee engagement, which translates to higher performance and increased customer satisfaction.

Former Patagonia CEO Rose Marcario estimated that the company recoups about 91% of their childcare program costs. JPMorgan Chase Bank, N.A., has estimated returns of 115% for its childcare program, and global business consultant KPMG found that its clients with on-site childcare earned a 125% return on investment.[23]

Sometimes leaders need outside help to craft effective return-to-work leave policies. Companies such as Mindful Return help employers and new parents successfully transition back to work after family leave.[24] The company says that even with the most comprehensive systems in place, companies often underestimate the value of employees feeling supported during the transition period. The organization partners with more than 60 progressive companies that offer Mindful Return services as part of their leave benefits.

The Manager's Role

Once policies are in place, leaders must ensure that managers at all levels are clear on what is expected of them on an employee's return to the workplace. It is up to leaders to ensure that all managers recognize not only the value of a solid female pipeline but also the role managers must play in maintaining it.

If you have already done the work of communicating your overall goal for inclusion within the company, these conversations with your managers should naturally progress from there. Let them know the business benefits of retaining these women. Then, provide them with the guidance to properly facilitate these returns. Advise them not to make assumptions about what working mothers want when returning to work. Not every mother wants to work part-time or take on fewer duties, and they should not be forced to go in that direction. Encourage your managers to talk with returning mothers one-on-one to determine their needs during the transition. This may require some awareness training, but it's a worthy investment to keep talented professionals within the company.

It's also important for managers to exercise the same level of understanding and compassion for new fathers returning to work. Although society still encourages mothers to handle most of the childcare duties, these traditional roles are constantly evolving, with increasing numbers of fathers taking on these responsibilities. From single-parent households to multiparent households, all genders take up family responsibilities and need flexibility. True gender equality requires that all genders be treated with the same level of respect.

Remind managers that new parents may need flexibility. These transitions must be done in a way that reinforces the employee's value to the organization while also promoting the company's overall goals. Parents shouldn't be made to feel guilty about needing flexibility in their work schedules. By extension, managers should not act as though they are doing these employees special favors. One strategy for addressing these potential problems is providing flexible schedule options to the entire team instead of just new parents, which prevents the singling out of these employees. A department-wide flexibility policy can be extremely useful in this regard so that returning parents and managers have a clear understanding of what's possible and expected. Managers can share with senior executives the data about productivity and retention success of department-wide programs, and this could lead to creating company-wide flexibility programs.

Moody's Corporation is a perfect example of company leadership understanding the challenges of returning to the workplace after a lengthy absence. In 2020, the company was included on the Working Mother's 100 Best Companies list for the fifth consecutive year and the Best Companies for Dads list for the third consecutive year.[25] These accolades were earned with a variety of gender-inclusion policies, notably their RE-IGNITE program, which is a 12-week return-to-work opportunity designed for individuals, especially mothers, seeking to restart their careers after a minimum workplace absence of two years. The fully paid program immerses participants into the Moody's organization, exposing them to hands-on projects, leadership development, and networking opportunities. They also benefit from coaching, support, mentorship, and a chance for permanent employment within the company.[26]

Role of Re-onboarding

Along with flexibility and compassion, workers returning from family leave or a transition period also need re-onboarding to assist them with re-acclimating to the environment. Advise managers to think about what information those employees may need to know. For example, the composition of the department may have changed drastically during their leave. Maybe there were some critical customer, competitor, or marketplace changes that the returning employees need to know about.

Although these return-to-work strategies may sound like a new concept for some business leaders, similar initiatives are actually quite common. Many companies offer these programs to military veterans who return to the workplace after deployment or to injured employees who return to the office after medical leave. It's the same general

Corporations Compassion Culture

concept: easing the return to work after an extended absence. Your firm's language and official policies about leave should match the actual culture of inclusive treatment of returning employees.

These leave options may seem to contradict my previous point about alternative work schedules redirecting women away from the leaderships track, but remember, the point is to offer these options across the board—regardless of gender—and to not push anyone into accepting them. Don't make assumptions about what new working mothers want. Being a new mother doesn't automatically mean that a woman wants to take time off or move away from the advancement track. By making space within your organization for these important conversations, you send a message to these women that they are valued employees.

Successful re-onboarding must be done with a spirit of cooperation. Returning employees should not be made to feel like a burden to others. Dignity and respect must persist in any work environment. This is where your company's internal language (we'll discuss gendered language later in this chapter) and intention must align with the new culture you and your team are reimagining—a culture where compassion and inclusion include ethical treatment of others. Remember that excluding people and a lack of cooperation are forms of microaggression and should be promptly addressed.

Meeting the Needs of Child-Free Employees

Though the conversation about gender equity often centers on working mothers, for many women, the childcare conundrum doesn't factor into their professional needs. About 30% of working women do not have children, which is a substantial segment of the workforce.[27] Yet, these women are often ignored or expected to fill in the gaps when their colleagues need time off for parenting duties. Along

Your Plan for Creating Gender Equity through Compassion

with the steps of understanding the data behind gender inequity and formalizing smooth transition processes, meeting the needs of child-free workers is just as important.

Recognize Importance of Leave Time for Child-Free Workers

When parents are given time off from the office, their single female coworkers—and sometimes their single male counterparts—may routinely face pressure to work late, take on extra duties, or delay their vacations to accommodate.[28] For example, one university professor explained how, when class schedules are assigned each semester, parenting professors receive first choice so they can schedule their classes around their childcare needs. She is routinely left with late evening or even weekend classes as a result. Other examples may include a child-free worker being asked to take their vacations on off-seasons to accommodate for family trips or being treated poorly when asking for a day off to spend time with friends.

Conversations about work-life balance often equate the "life" aspect with personal parenting time. Within the workplace, childcare is widely regarded as the most valuable type of personal time an employee can take, so when nonparents ask for time off, it is considered less important.[29] The assumption is that women with no kids have more than enough free personal time, which makes the work-life challenge inapplicable to them. This is a false characterization. Many times, women without children are expected to shoulder all the responsibility for eldercare in families, which might net out to a greater time commitment. In some cases, women with children may be considered too "busy," especially if there is a child-free woman around; the thought is "what else do you have to do with your time if you're not a mom?" If these women are on a leadership track, they may be working an exorbitant number of hours each week to meet their professional goals, which makes time off valuable and necessary. Even if a child-free woman isn't on the leadership track, her request for personal time should not be scrutinized and questioned.

Society often views child-free women as being less personally fulfilled than mothers. That can lead to the unstated belief that they somehow deserve to be penalized for violating what many consider a social norm.[30] Companies reinforce these dangerous notions when they maintain a culture that formally or informally ostracizes child-free women. In today's workplace, employers could do more to show they value all employees, not just those who are parents.

Many companies have shifted from traditional vacation and sick leave policies to paid time off (PTO) policies that offer all employees an established number of days per year that they can use however they see fit. Although these changes do offer some benefit for child-free employees, there is still more that can be done to make the workplace inclusive for them. Flex-time policies should also reflect consistency for all employees, offered across the board without consideration to parental status.

Sabbaticals and Long-Term Leave

Long-term leave options should also be offered across the board. New parents are generally extended maternity and paternity leave without issue, but other employees without children rarely receive similar opportunities for time off, even to pursue endeavors that they consider extremely important.[31] Consider extending sabbaticals to employees who show an interest in pursuing research or external programs that helps them grow both professionally and personally. For example, an employee may want to do volunteer work in another country for a few months or research a marketplace event. They may even want to take a six-week intensive-study course or take a culturally immersive trip.

Companies can use sabbaticals to recognize long-term service, encourage professional growth, and avoid employee burnout. They also benefit from these offerings when employees return to the workplace recharged, appreciative, and often with newly acquired skills. Their gratitude shows up as improved work product and increased productivity, which can ultimately lead to increased revenues.

A 2018 study by SmallBusinessPrices.co.uk shows the retention value of sabbaticals. Baby boomers, Generation X, millennials, and Generation Z workers across the United Kingdom ranked sabbaticals as their second prioritized work benefit (health insurance was first).[32] According to a 2018 Employee Benefits Report from The Society of Human Resource Management, about 15% of companies offer sabbatical leave. About 5% of those programs are paid sabbaticals and 10% are unpaid.[33]

In furtherance of their commitment to work-life balance, global organization Deloitte offers two types of sabbatical programs. Eligible professionals can choose between one month of unpaid leave for any reason or a paid sabbatical for up to six months in order to pursue professional growth opportunities. Workers receive 40% of their regular salary under the longer sabbatical option. "We are committed to addressing continually the work-life needs of all our people as we recognize its critical importance to fostering an environment where leaders thrive," says Paul Silverglate, work-life managing partner, Deloitte LLP. "The Sabbatical Program is one more way by which we are able to provide our people with the flexibility they need, when they need it."[34]

McDonald's has been offering corporate employees a sabbatical option since 1977. After every 10 years of service, eligible employees can take eight weeks of continuous time off in recognition of their extended service.[35] Timberland offers employees an opportunity for paid community service or a service sabbatical as part of its flexible work environment. Through their Path of Service Program, employees can take between 12 and 24 weeks for volunteering around the world.[36] The UK-based computer software company Arm allows employees to take an extended sabbatical every four years. Their website states, "We actively encourage our people to take time out—it is good for you and good for Arm."[37]

The Swedish government understands the value of offering sabbaticals. Government employees can take up to six months off in pursuit of their entrepreneurial goals. Thousands of workers have taken advantage of this innovative workplace initiative. Referred to as the Leave of Absence for Entrepreneurship Program, it allows all full-time, permanent employees to focus on their businesses with the security that they can return to their job, or a similarly situated position, when the sabbatical ends.[38]

Let go of misconceptions about the childless and child-free in the workplace. If more companies continue to create policies that treat all employees equally regardless of their parental status, it will reflect a growing acceptance of those without children in the workplace.

Supporting Women's Leadership and Advancement and Confronting Saboteurs

Supporting women—all women—in senior roles, means ensuring that their team members understand the importance of group success and respect the team leader. Take seriously any attempts to sabotage or undermine leaders that may occur because people aren't comfortable reporting to a woman or a woman of color. Recall that rarely does anyone use illegal, overt methods to undermine a supervisor's authority. Instead, sabotaging a leader's success is generally subtle and indirect, via actions such as withholding vital information or making condescending comments in front of the team. These instances should be reported and swiftly addressed. Further, sabotage can be unconscious. From political figures to boardroom directors, we've seen instances in which colleagues fixate on a single personality trait or minor part of a woman's presentation. In some cases, people are totally unaware of this type of fixation or the fact that they wouldn't give this same sort of attention to a man in the same position.

Support Women Executives and Root Out Sabotage Efforts

When acts of sabotage are subtle, they can be difficult to identify. Here are some signs of sabotage that may be occurring within your company:

- Employees gossiping or spreading rumors about a coworker or supervisor often indicates an intention of casting doubt on her abilities.

- Team members taking credit for someone else's work; this type of behavior is outright inappropriate, unethical, and dishonest.

- Backhanded compliments and slightly rude or inappropriate comments may seem harmless, but they can cause a coworker or supervisor to experience significant distress.

- Outward hostilities can quickly turn into bullying. These behaviors are often done with the purpose of making the target uncomfortable enough to leave.

- "Anonymous" negative feedback about a coworker or supervisor's performance may signal an underlying motive. When colleagues are genuinely concerned for another, they find tactful ways to communicate their concerns and support one another instead of criticizing underhandedly.

- Leaving colleagues out of the loop on important matters may signal more than just absentmindedness. "Forgetting" to include colleagues in important meetings or to copy them on urgent emails may indicate sabotage.

To weed these types of occurrences out of your organization, believe employees when they make allegations about these incidents and behaviors. Take them seriously and make an effort to investigate the accusations.

In addition to signs of sabotage, it's important to recognize other internal factors that may be indirectly sabotaging or pushing women out of your company, or at least off of the leadership track. For example, many corporate cultures make female leaders feel as though they have to give up their natural leadership style and take on a more "masculine" style of management.[39] On a larger scale, these pressures stem from societal beliefs about the leadership abilities of women.[40] They force women leaders to accept these masculine cultural norms and try to act like "one of the boys," which only helps to normalize these inappropriate assumptions.

"Women" Always Includes Women of Color

As you work to rebuild a more gender-inclusive work environment, be careful not to build a new culture that benefits only White women. Include women of color in opportunities for roles with upward trajectories, such as client-facing opportunities and high-impact projects. Take the same data-driven approach you used to address gender inclusion generally to understand the current numbers of women of color in the firm and in senior management roles specifically.

Recognize the unique challenges that women of color face when taking on leadership positions within your organization. Although all bosses face some level of second-guessing from their workers, Black, Indigenous, Asian, and Latinx women face these difficulties much more often. As members of two underrepresented groups, these women often experience even greater levels of discrimination than their colleagues who only represent one underrepresented identify, such as a Black or Latinx man.[41] They are scrutinized more harshly than their male counterparts and looked at more closely when organizational failures occur.

Peer Networking

As covered in Chapter 8, peer networking and sponsorship groups can be vitally important to help women of all races and ethnicities overcome workplace challenges and move up the corporate ladder. Intentionally build and cultivate networks inside and outside the firm that include women and women of color. Encourage your leadership teams to do so as well.

General Motors maintains a (voluntary) women's network, known as GM WOMEN (Women Offering Mentoring, Expertise, and Networking). This team of women is led by a group known as the "Cabinet," a senior executive team representing a diverse group of women from each of GE's businesses and critical corporate functions. It is also sponsored by two of the company's most senior leadership members.[42] According to the company, instead of talking about mentoring, GM WOMEN focuses on sponsorship. As a company spokesperson stated, "That simple phrasing [change] helped our women shift from just discussion to action, and the women in management positions challenged themselves to become not just mentors, but sponsors."

Women in the workplace need to support each other in word and deed. When trying to rise up into leadership roles, the cultural and systemic hurdles that challenge women make the road much harder to traverse. Close connections with other women who have been there are valuable. They can seek advice and guidance from women who have "been there, done that"—women with personal insight on everything from asking for what you're worth to bringing your unique talents to leadership.

In my interview with Laura Freebairn-Smith, she spoke about women reaching back to help other women advance. "The woman who gets to the top, at least in the last three generations of feminists, had to climb up a male-built ladder," she explained. "That ladder to the top was built by men. All the screws and nuts and bolts, the spacing between the steps the width of the ladder was all decided by a White male paradigm. The problem is, if you climb a ladder like that for years, you get mentally co-opted and think that the ladder is okay. So when I'm teaching to women in particular, I tell them when you get to the top, you change that damn ladder. You make it a triple-wide escalator!"[43]

Another way to explain this is called shine theory, which is the idea that when you help another woman rise, we all shine. We are all better together. As Madeleine Albright said, "There is a special place in hell for women who don't help other women."

One way to encourage connections is to create opportunities for positive engagement between women within an organization. The support provided to women by global law firm Linklaters LLP includes a successful sponsorship program.[44] In 2012, as part of its broader gender diversity strategy, Linklaters began a women's leadership program to increase and retain its pipeline of talented senior women associates. Each participant is assigned a sponsor partner from a different practice area and a different country. The firm says that these practice and geographic distances allow for more meaningful and candid conversations.

Sponsors help their sponsees understand the inner workings of the firm, expand their networking and visibility and promote their brand. Each sponsor also acts as an internal and external ambassador introducing her sponsee to clients and contacts. The nine-month sessions include 25 women, and almost 200 women have been selected since its inception in 2012. The law firm reports that each program cohort shows significantly better retention (12% to 37% higher) than

285

its female peer group. In addition, 19 (10%) of program alumnae have been elected to partner and 34 (17%) have been promoted to counsel.[45]

Slack also provides an example of successful female sponsorship. Rising Tides is a six-month sponsorship program for high performers and emerging leaders who have historically lacked access to this level of support. The goal is to invest in future leaders who will have a positive impact on the Slack organization. Program participants receive career development training, executive coaching, and one-on-one sponsorship with a Slack executive team member, with a focus on building a supportive community of peers.[46] One cohort focuses on female and nonbinary employees with a specific focus on people of color within the US. Another cohort focuses on senior-level underrepresented women and nonbinary employees on the verge of entering leadership roles.

Include Men in Discussions

Encourage male employees to engage with women's ERGs and development groups. Create a clear narrative for why inclusion is important to you and to the business. The organization called Diversity Best Practices published on their website an article by Jennifer London, which discussed the importance of engaging White men as allies in the mission for diversity and inclusion within the workplace.[47] She said that leaving White, straight, cisgender men out of the discussion constitutes a major lapse in judgment. She referenced the White Men's Leadership Study, where White male respondents identified their own exclusion as a major obstacle to achieving true gender inclusivity. She also noted that many respondents reported confusion about whether diversity initiatives intend to include White men.

These misperceptions and misunderstandings exemplify why companies should include men in gender diversity and inclusion efforts. To accomplish this goal, company leaders must first identify the barriers to engagement in order to address issues related to bias and privilege. Leaders should emphasize the importance of inclusion instead of solely championing diversity. Building relationships across gender and selecting influential men to champion inclusion efforts can also help. Encourage women ERG leaders to invite their male managers to leader meetings for the purpose of exchanging concerns and furthering goals.[48]

Goldman Sachs has taken similar steps within their organization by including male participation within their female affinity network groups.[49] The company engages male senior leaders with hosting events, coaching, opportunities to mentor women members, and participation in dialogue about gender in the workplace.

Building a Gender-Inclusive Community

As you work to evolve your company and restructure it with a more gender-inclusive culture, it can be useful to think of your organization as a community. As social beings, we crave a social structure larger than ourselves. Communities bind us together with customs and norms that promote the collective good.[50] In the business realm, a strong community encourages an environment of inclusion, understanding, and compassion. It's a group of people who commit to removing negative patterns and gender-based stereotypes for the purpose of promoting the overall success of the company.

Create Communityship

In 2009, a *Harvard Business Review* article by Henry Mintzberg discussed rebuilding companies as communities.[51] Using the word *communityship* to define the space between individual leadership and collective citizenship, the author talks about the need for leadership that is not egocentric or based in top-down authority. Community leaders reach out to their employees instead of reaching down to them. With communityship, leadership looks more like engagement with responsibilities and duties distributed among managers at various levels of the organization. Community leaders create an atmosphere that promotes trust by using personal engagement to inspire employee engagement and initiative.

Restructuring a company into a community must start with recognizing and addressing the current behaviors that would undermine the transformation. For instance, workplaces where employees are undervalued and undercompensated do not promote a sense of community. An overemphasis on leadership and a tolerance for disrespectful norms also suppresses the community.

Pixar has successfully established a creative community that encourages group collaboration.[52] Speaking to the *Harvard Business Review*, Pixar founder and president Ed Catmull said that even with their reputation for incredible creativity, the company values people above ideas. He stated, "If you give a good idea to a mediocre team, they will screw it up; if you give a mediocre idea to a great team, they will either fix it or throw it away and come up with something that works." Catmull advocates for an egoless work environment where leaders are not afraid to hire people with more knowledge or skills than their own. The company wants to bring together the most gifted work force, which they say will attract even more talented people.

Pixar refers to the quest for an inclusive work environment as its "North Star."[53] Their learning experiences include an annual inclusion summit where employees from all parts of Pixar engage in the work of addressing unconscious biases and other barriers to true inclusion. The employee-led Studio Resource Groups include Women@Pixar, which is designed to foster advancement of female employees and ensure that the company's productions represent an accurate and uplifting female perspective.

Community is also a major goal for social media company Twitter. They have created a team-oriented environment that inspires both individual ideas as well as collaboration. Employees, calling themselves Tweeps, give the company high marks for its compassionate culture that includes yoga classes, rooftop meetings, free meals, and various other rare perks. The company is also committed to its inclusion goals and offers various ERGs.

As explained by the company website, Twitter Parents provides its members with support and community at every stage of the parenting journey "to enable a healthy balance inside and outside of the workplace."[54] Twitter Women fosters gender equality and supports the advancement of female employees within the company, as well as in the tech industry as a whole. The Blackbirds ERG includes "members and allies of the African diaspora." The group also provides additional support for women of color within the organization.

When creating a corporate community, raise awareness about the social gender perceptions that each of us come to work with every day. Position these teachings as "relearning" organizational interaction on the firm's revised or revisited values. Many who practice gender stereotyping in the workplace are not even aware of how their perceptions are affecting others because gender stereotyping is often subconscious. Make it widely known and understood that, within your organization, gender discrimination—even actions that individuals may not have considered discrimination because it is in line with their individual values—is not a part of the firm's values.

Recognize that firm members may need to unlearn certain behaviors and attitudes that play into gender stereotypes. Reassess the sort of language used when describing or referring to women, as well as terminology such as "gentleman's agreement" and "middleman." Terms such as "drama queen" and "mommy brain" may seem harmless in the moment, but this language can perpetuate gender stereotypes within the workplace.

Your Plan for Creating Gender Equity through Compassion

These connections between language and gender can be challenging to untangle. Your workers may have been using these terms for years without realizing the negative connotations that this language carries. Leadership needs to take the lead in making changes. Don't use stereotypes in your language and challenge others when they do.

Of course, inclusivity is not only a question of language. Workplace norms and other subtleties can also promote negative environments. Ensure that the input and feedback of women employees is respected and treated equally to that of their male counterparts. Also take steps to ensure that female employees are not always tasked with notetaking or scheduling meetings. This is the same type of thinking that stereotypes women as "caregivers" or "housekeepers" of the office environment.[55] Women may feel compelled to take on activities such as training, fetching food or coffee, making sure the office is maintained properly, and other similar tasks that are outside the scope of their actual jobs. Take a look at your workplace to identify these types of behaviors and address them. Supervisors and managers, as well as senior leaders should not make assumptions about their female employee's willingness to take on these duties. Implement policies that spread these necessary tasks around to all members of the office regardless of gender.

A study published in the *Journal of Applied Psychology* found that when women refuse to take on these duties in the workplace, they are viewed negatively, while men don't suffer any penalties.[56] In other words, men benefit from refusing to take on tasks that do not benefit their careers, while women are punished for making the same decision. When a man says no, he is seen as being too busy, but a woman is seen as selfish and unwilling to help the company. A study out of New York University found that men performing altruistic tasks, such as staying late to help the team prepare a presentation, were rated 14% more favorably than their female counterparts.[57]

Leveraging Data to Measure Future Progress

As with any other area of your company, data plays an important role in establishing a gender-inclusive community. It is the best way to understand how far your organization has come and how best to successfully achieve your next goal. When I interviewed Debra Walton, chief revenue officer at Refinitiv, she spoke extensively about using data to advance corporate initiatives, as well as some of the obstacles when seeking to identify and collect needed information.[58]

> I think you have to be able to use data. For anything that you're wanting to change, you have to be able to measure it, and if you can't measure it, then you can't manage it. So, by definition, data become a critical input. I think that, as we strive for a more diverse and inclusive organization, being able to measure where you're at right now, [evaluate] what the industry benchmarks look like, and then track how your company is progressing . . . is absolutely critical.
>
> In terms of the issues of ethics and quality, that becomes much more subjective. I think increasingly, you can measure that. I think employee surveys become a really powerful way to measure how well we're doing through the eyes of our employees. We live in a world where pretty much anything that happens in an organization is known to the rest of the world through sites like Glassdoor. So the challenge is how do you take a lot of that unstructured data and turn [that] into data that you can actually use to get measurable insights?[59]

When asked about the next frontier of data in terms of gender equity, she spoke about the progress being made at Refinitiv. "We've done a great job as a company when we launched the Diversity and Inclusion Index, where we took from our 7,000 company database of ESG data to create an index of companies based on their diversity, inclusion, and performance from an agenda perspective. We've been able to use that to really bring a lot of transparency to the issue of diversity inclusion from a gender perspective."

She also spoke about how some corporate leaders are "agitating for" more data to understand the backgrounds/ethnicities of the people they employ. Ironically, some regulators are simultaneously "agitating for" more data privacy, which will make it more difficult for companies to obtain this information. Walton explained,

> One element is making sure companies are disclosing. But the second element, where it is something like sexual preference, how do you know just from looking at your population? We don't know that unless we get disclosure from an individual level. It's easy to look around a company and sit at the front door with a clicker [to calculate that you've] got 40% women. That's great. But you can't do that when it comes to race. And you absolutely can't do it when it comes to gender preference. So for us to use data in a really powerful way, we need to have disclosure.

Seeking gender inclusion for women of color also brings up challenges in terms of collecting and analyzing data. Walton discussed how Refinitiv began tackling their lack of gender diversity in 2012. By 2020, they had accomplished 40% female representation within senior leadership.

> Actually 40% is pretty good by our benchmark standards, but that's taken us eight years. When it comes to other minority groups that we want to see represented on a more equitable basis, the change isn't going to happen overnight. My fear, especially around the issue of Black Lives Matter, is that there is such emotion and such an appropriate

expectation of action, that I think we need more real-time data to show that we're making progress. You can't wait a year to see how [the data] show up in some external benchmark. You want to have [the information] when jobs are being filled . . . how do you gather that data? That's a really important real-time measure that is really critical for people to get some confidence that the leading indicators suggest that we're heading in the right direction.[60]

Measure, Evaluate, Evolve

This chapter began by challenging you to not take assumptions at face value but to gather data to get an understanding of the real reasons women may not be progressing into senior roles. From there, we looked at tactics managers and senior leaders could use to ensure inclusion, from paid family leave programs to benefits you could offer to supporting caregiving to transition policies and ensuring women are supported and not undermined when they earn senior management roles.

Once you've incorporated these ideas, the only way to ensure the progression of gender equity and equality is to measure the data. This measurement can be as simple as a survey where, on a scale of 1 to 5, employees can answer questions such as "Has your firm improved on reducing offensive gendered language?" and "Do you still see microaggressions or subtle discriminatory behaviors toward women?" and "What is your perception of work-life balance for child-free and people with children?" and "Do you see instances in which female leaders are second-guessed more frequently than male leaders?" Another option is to give employees the opportunity to answer these questions in a long-form style, where they give examples of each. The measurement can also take the form of outlining the percentage of women senior leaders you want to have in

293

your organization over the next one to five years and engaging with other firms who have accomplished similar goals to understand the specifics about how they accomplished that.

These types of measuring and information gathering are generally done at the senior management level, but there is also an opportunity for supervisors or frontline managers to conduct their own intradepartmental research. Instead of a formal survey, managers can reach out directly or ask their employees to answer a questionnaire that focuses on gender equity.

Measuring, evaluating, and evolving is the way that businesses improve products, customer service, and even meet investor demands. Measuring, evaluating, and evolving is also needed to ensure that compassionate corporate communities are taking the actions needed to ensure gender equality.

Chapter 9 Takeaways

- Measure composition of women in your firm relative to composition of the broader market. Get data-driven insights to determine your goals for increasing numbers of female leaders and set recruitment and retention targets in the same way targets are set for any business goal.

- Reach out to women in other industries through employee (or business) resources groups to understand how they've succeeded in areas your firm would like to progress in.

- Clarify and meet the needs of women and men as they relate to family and balance. Don't make assumptions on behalf of your employees. Listen to them to understand their specific needs and desires.

- Extend to child-free employees opportunities to engage in activities through sabbaticals or other offerings. Recognize what is important to them. Show that your firm values their contributions by welcoming pursuits that refresh them and may benefit the firm.

- Create safe spaces for sharing specific challenges facing women of color in women's parity discussion. Equity and advancement should always include women of color.

- Prevent conscious and unconscious sabotage by being aware of the signs and swiftly addressing it.

- Measure and review data as a means to improve gender parity and promotion.

References

1. https://hbr.org/2020/03/whats-really-holding-women-back
2. Ibid.
3. https://www.psychologytoday.com/us/blog/happiness-is-state-mind/201805/feminism-changing-the-way-our-society-views-women
4. https://hbr.org/2020/03/whats-really-holding-women-back
5. Ibid.
6. https://fortune.com/2017/02/21/flexible-schedule-women-career/?xid=soc_socialflow_twitter_FORTUNE
7. https://hbr.org/2020/03/whats-really-holding-women-back
8. https://www.corning.com/worldwide/en/sustainability/people/diversity/employee-resource-groups/women-erg.html
9. https://www.diversitywoman.com/companies-that-are-getting-it-right/
10. Ibid.
11. https://www.unicef.org/reports/are-the-world%E2%80%99s-richest-countries-family-friendly-2019#:~:text=Sweden%2C%20Norway%2C%20Iceland%2C%20Estonia%20and%20Portugal%20offer%20the,least%20six%20months%20of%20leave%20for%20all%20parents.
12. https://www.bbc.com/news/education-48612493
13. https://www.nationalpartnership.org/our-work/economic-justice/paid-leave.html
14. https://www.nationalpartnership.org/our-work/resources/economic-justice/paid-leave/paid-leave-good-for-business.pdf

Your Plan for Creating Gender Equity through Compassion

15. https://www.weforum.org/agenda/2019/04/these-countries-have-the-most-expensive-childcare/
16. https://www.theguardian.com/sustainable-business/2017/feb/17/paid-family-leave-transformed-australian-business-its-now-under-threat
17. https://www.intel.com/content/www/us/en/jobs/benefits.html
18. https://www.fastcompany.com/3062792/patagonias-ceo-explains-how-to-make-onsite-child-care-pay-for-itself
19. https://www.goldmansachs.com/careers/benefits-wellness-compensation.html
20. https://www.intuitbenefits.com/covid-19/kids/up-to-5
21. https://www.cbsnews.com/news/elder-care-benefits/
22. https://www.fastcompany.com/3062792/patagonias-ceo-explains-how-to-make-onsite-child-care-pay-for-itself
23. Ibid.
24. https://www.mindfulreturn.com/for-employers/
25. https://www.businesswire.com/news/home/20200915005922/en/Moody%E2%80%99s-Named-to-2020-Working-Mother-Best-Companies-Lists
26. https://womenreturners.com/opportunities/moodys-reignite-programme/
27. https://www.bls.gov/news.release/famee.nr0.htm
28. https://slate.com/human-interest/2013/06/family-friendly-workplaces-are-great-unless-you-re-childless.html
29. https://fortune.com/2015/11/07/truth-about-childless-at-work/
30. https://www.myfatpocket.com/17944/lifestyle/career/the-brutal-truth-about-being-childless-at-work/
31. https://www.psychologytoday.com/us/blog/complete-without-kids/201105/discrimination-against-childfree-adults
32. https://smallbusinessprices.co.uk/best-work-perks/
33. https://www.sabbatic.com/companies-offer-sabbaticals/
34. https://www2.deloitte.com/us/en/pages/about-deloitte/articles/about-deloitte-life-going-places-sabbatical-benefits.html
35. Ibid.
36. https://www.csrwire.com/press_releases/34605-timberland-celebrates-20th-anniversary-of-path-of-service-program-
37. https://www.arm.com/company/careers/life-at-arm
38. https://www.cnbc.com/2019/02/20/sweden-lets-employees-take-six-months-off-work-to-start-a-business.html
39. https://hbr.org/2020/03/whats-really-holding-women-back
40. https://www.catalyst.org/research/women-in-male-dominated-industries-and-occupations/
41. https://gap.hks.harvard.edu/failure-not-option-black-women-effects-organizational-performance-leaders-single-versus-dual
42. https://www.huffpost.com/entry/8-ways-to-make-your-corporate-womens-network-successful_b_57977053e4b0e339c23f90c8

43. Interview with the author. Laura Freebairn-Smith, Women reaching back to help other women advance., July 22, 2020.
44. https://idaabbott.com/wp-content/uploads/High-quality-mentoringdiversity .pdf
45. Ibid.
46. https://slack.com/intl/en-gb/blog/news/diversity-at-slack-2020#:~:text=Rising %20Tides%20Rising%20Tides%20is%20a%20six-month%20sponsorship, historically%20lacked%20access%20to%20this%20type%20of%20support.
47. https://www.diversitybestpractices.com/best-both-ergs-and-inclusion
48. Ibid.
49. https://www.huffpost.com/entry/8-ways-to-make-your-corporate-womens-network-successful_b_57977053e4b0e339c23f90c8
50. https://hbr.org/2009/07/rebuilding-companies-as-communities
51. https://hbr.org/2009/07/rebuilding-companies-as-communities#:~:text=%E2 %80%9CCommunityship%E2%80%9D%20is%20not%20a%20word%20in%20the %20English,one%20side%20and%20collective%20citizenship%20on%20the %20other.
52. https://www.business2community.com/small-business/business-can-learn-pixar-01557578
53. https://www.pixar.com/inclusion
54. https://careers.twitter.com/en/tweep-life.html
55. Ibid.
56. https://www.abc.net.au/life/why-women-are-always-left-doing-the-workplace-housework/11448624
57. https://www.fastcompany.com/3050043/how-to-end-the-office-housework-gender-bias
58. Interview with the author. Debra Walton, Using data to advance corporate initiatives, as well as some of the obstacles when seeking to identify and collect needed information, September 2, 2020.
59. Ibid.
60. Ibid.

The Future

Compassionate Corporate Culture and Sustainable Business

M oving toward compassionate corporate cultures means shifting our mindsets. For those who believe that the role of business goes beyond profit margins and includes the creation of inclusive workplaces that reflect a more compassionate society, we must commit to introspection, ongoing education, and openness. We must value the exploration of why our organizations exist and challenge Milton Friedman's rationale, which was discussed in Chapter 1, that business exists only to make money. We must operate and make decisions in a way that is better for the people inside the corporation, as well as the people outside.

We close the book with an exploration of how leaders can strengthen communities where they do business, making positive social impacts on environmental, social, and governance issues. We'll also look at some plans for partnering with employees, customers, and external organizations to identify and implement social change, the alignment of green business and compassionate business, and redefining the purpose of business. This chapter will discuss these issues:

- Role of environmental, social, and governance on compassionate cultures

- Identifying your company's social responsibility

- Partnering with external organizations

- Interconnection of internal inclusion and external social impact

- Intersection of DEI and sustainability

- Role of business in protecting the environment

- Current coursing through your business

- True purpose of business

Role of Environmental, Social, and Governance on Compassionate Cultures

Beginning in the 1960s, some investment firms became interested in what they called "socially responsible investing." Over the years, that trend has evolved and grown into what is now known as environmental, social, and governance (ESG). ESG is a lens through which people can screen criteria about how a company uses natural resources, engages with society, and governs their firm. These criteria and standards associated with ESG can be used by stakeholders in several ways. For example, companies may obtain their ESG ratings from ESG databases and indices to see how they rank and where they need to improve in specific areas. If they want insight on their performance in employee relations, they can review their scores in subcategories such as labor practices, employee health, and safety and diversity.[1]

Investors can also look at ESG scores for a variety of firms within an industry to determine which firm has policies about use of natural resources, social engagement, or governing that best complement that investor's own portfolio of stocks. An investor may make stock selections based on that ESG information. Additionally, prospective employees can look at a company's ESG scores to understand how seriously that company takes sustainability, diversity, and social impact. So whether you're a company leader, an investor, or even a prospective employee, information about a firm's ESG standing can provide valuable information and insight.

Most people in business recognize a firm's ESG standing as an indication of its impact on environment, society, and governing, therefore providing a way to measure its sustainability and ethical impact. ESG can also predict the future financial performance of the business. The years since 2010 have seen an increasing number of investment funds incorporating ESG factors and the numbers are expected to continue increasing over the decade ahead. Here is a breakdown for each of the three components:

- Environmental criteria include measurements for a firm's waste and pollution, resource depletion, greenhouse gas emission, deforestation, and climate change. It evaluates the impact that a business has on our natural environment.[2]

- Governance criteria measures how corporations govern themselves to include executive compensation, tax strategy, government relations, and board diversity.

- Social criteria can measure a company's treatment of its workers, with particular attention to working conditions, diversity, inclusion, and employee relations. This is the specific area explored within this book. Diversity, equity, and inclusion (DEI) is part of the social component of ESG. As discussed, taking ethical approaches to working conditions, diversity, inclusion, equity, and employee relations will provide your company with a strategic advantage in the marketplace. Companies that score well on the social component of ESG support innovative employees, offer livable wages, and foster inclusive environments and diversity at each level. Corporations, compassion, and culture intersect at the social component of ESG.

As the host of Refinitiv Sustainability Perspectives Podcast, I've interviewed guests ranging from heads of ESG investing at some of the largest asset management firms to C-suite officers at investment banks. I've also hosted academics in the field for the purpose of educating investors on how firms can improve ESG efforts while increasing revenues. I've spoken about businesses and trends that have a measurable ESG impact, as well as businesses that struggle to meet ESG demands of consumers, employees, and investors.

Once C-suite officers, managing directors, managers, and other leaders embrace relationships with people in various levels of the organization, involve themselves in ERGs, and do the introspective work discussed previously, the stage is set for identifying the type of social impact work the firm is positioned to do outside of the organization's walls. The benefits of a company choosing to work toward greater social change are evident in the support and endorsement they gain from consumers, employees, and even investors.

Identifying Your Company's Social Responsibility

When seeking to identify your company's social responsibility focus, it is useful to start with the United Nations' Sustainable Development Goals (SDGs). The SDGs lay out the basic global issues that other organizations across the globe are currently working on. Understanding these issues will help you avoid reinventing the wheel and, taken together, these objectives provide a blueprint for achieving a sustainable future. The SDGs are as follows:

1. No Poverty
2. Zero Hunger
3. Good Health and Well-Being

4. Quality Education

5. Gender Equality

6. Clean Water and Sanitation

7. Affordable and Clean Energy

8. Decent Work and Economic Growth

9. Industry, Innovation, and Infrastructure

10. Reduced Inequalities

11. Sustainable Cities and Communities

12. Responsible Consumption and Production

13. Climate Action

14. Life Below Water

15. Life on Land

16. Peace, Justice, and Strong Institutions

17. Partnerships[3]

As you can see, this list incorporates issues we have touched on throughout this book. Gender equality includes the creation of cultures where women are treated equitably and provided with opportunities for advancement into the upper levels of leadership.[4] Goal 10, reduced inequalities, speaks to eradicating racial disparities and economic inequality.[5] The change that happens on the societal level can influence and lead to greater levels of equality in our workplaces as well.

First, consider these 17 goals and examine which are most important to your business, your employees, your investors, and society as a whole. Think about the ways in which your company affects society and the common good. Identify the pain points where your products (even how they are manufactured or distributed) may affect society in a negative way and what you can do to address that. Then, determine how your brand is best positioned to assist with such issues based on your products and services, as well as your customer segment.

For example, through their AI for Earth program, Microsoft supports a variety of environmental projects, such as the Vector Center, the Freshwater Trust, and the Leadership Counsel for Justice and Accountability.[6] The company has pledged to use technology to analyze water stress and optimize water replenishment investments. By 2030, the company plans to replenish more water than they consume globally by reducing their water-use intensity and replenishing water within water-stressed regions where they operate. A small company probably can't take on a project as big as this, but that doesn't mean it can't do smaller scale works in its own communities.

The US Plastics Pact encourages public-private stakeholders to rethink the way they design, use, and reuse plastics.[7] The initiative brings together companies such as L'Oréal, Target, and others that may have heavy plastic use with government entities and nongovernmental organizations (NGOs) for industry-led innovation. Their goals include 100% reusable, recyclable, and compostable plastic packaging by 2025 and increasing responsibly sourced bio-based content in plastic packaging by 30%. Through these collaborations, companies and governments can meet goals that they would not be able to meet individually. Importantly, a business can actively work to reduce the negative impact its processes have on the environment.

At the same time you are doing this analysis, it is critical to find out what matters to your customers or audience. A survey conducted by the PR firm Edelman found that 70% of consumers are willing to pay more for products and services provided by a business that supports worthwhile causes.[8] In addition, more than half of those surveyed reported a willingness to promote these brands to other customers. This data shows how invested consumers are in the social platforms and efforts of the businesses they patronize. So, why wouldn't you solicit their opinions when choosing your social impact platform?

Use customer and client surveys to help you identify their social interests and worries. Then, use the gathered information to help guide your company's social impact direction.

I spoke with *New York Times* bestselling author Seth Godin about the power customers and large groups of people inside or outside an organization have when they come together to change how businesses operate:

> Patient, consistent speaking up is what changes the culture. That's what's getting measured. So if we look at the progress of women, Black people, people of color, people who had previously been disenfranchised over the last 60 years in the workplace, it's not fast enough. But compared to 1960, there is a significant change. Why did it change? It didn't change, just because the people at the top say "I'm a good person, so I'm going to be more of a human." It changed because consistently and persistently talented folks said, "I'm not going to work here because I don't like what you're doing." And consumers who had a choice said, "I'm not going to buy from you, because I don't like what you're doing." Because people are consistently speaking up about it. And we don't have to just speak up about it in the streets and online. We have to make laws, because

(continues)

(continued)

> that's what capitalism understands: boundaries. And we've got to be really clear about what the rules are. We've got to enforce rules, but it's up to each person to speak up and say, "this is my priority list. And I'm not going to rest until this rule is in place."[9]

Concurrently, ask your internal communities and ERGs to participate in discussions on how the firm can best support the specific efforts you identified. Often times, ERG members have already pinpointed societal areas of concern to them and have begun gathering resources to address those issues. Look at the volunteer opportunities that these groups have already taken part in and consider building off of them at a company-wide level.

Some companies offer volunteer resource groups for employees who want to support specific causes and give back to their communities. Employers often support these groups by matching monetary donations or providing resources for events. While donating to a specific charity or cause can satisfy employees' desires to give back, providing or supporting employee volunteer opportunities can be even more beneficial.[10] Include employees in social impact decisions and assist them in taking on volunteering efforts. It will not only empower them but also give them a personal stake in the company's initiative.

Partnering with External Organizations

Once you have identified a social impact focus for your company and engaged your team and customers to ensure their input and alignment, the next step is to identify external organizations that work in your area of focus. These organizations can help you better determine what the specific needs are and how you can best deploy necessary resources. By partnering with not-for-profits and NGOs, business leaders can learn strategies to strengthen their social impact performance while also creating new business opportunities. Frequently, the expertise and skill sets of corporate leaders differ from those of NGO and not-for-profit leaders. But when they collaborate, their distinct differences can complement one another, helping both partners achieve more together than they could individually.

The partnership between Payscale, Inc. and the USC Race and Equity Center offers a perfect example of corporations and NGOs effectively working together toward a social good. The two have combined their research and technology services to expand pay equity among various industries.[11] This valuable partnership moves beyond a one-time effort by using continuous monitoring and maintenance.

"We want to empower our customers to be critically conscious of gender and racial inequality and be proactive agents of change when it comes to pay equity," Scott Torrey, CEO of PayScale, told *Street Insider* in September 2020. "Our partnership with the USC Race and Equity Center empowers our customers to confidently manage pay equity through access to strategic guidance, insight and ongoing support."[12]

Shaun Harper, founder and executive director of the USC Race and Equity Center, agreed about the importance of the initiative. "Our partnership with PayScale aligns closely with our overarching goal to illuminate, disrupt and dismantle racism in

(continues)

(continued)

all its forms. . . With PayScale, we are more able to help corporations, educational institutions, and other organizations achieve their pay equity goals and implement sustainable practices to minimize pay discrepancies."[13]

A variety of not-for-profits and NGOs, including the United Nations, have taken the lead in trying to influence global policies on women's empowerment and racial equality. To be truly successful, business leaders should create partnerships with these organizations, making them an integral part of their business by gradually integrating them into relevant areas.[14] When done correctly, each party can leverage their skills and resources to advance the common goal. These partnerships also offer business leaders an opportunity to educate themselves and their business members on relevant issues and policies, as well as how employee communities are affected.

In 2007, global insurance company Swiss Re was approached by the international NGO Oxfam for assistance in providing Ethiopian farmers with insurance against risks to their crops from climate change.[15] Oxfam recognized the need, but it was Swiss Re that had the expertise to carry it out. Swiss Re benefitted from the collaboration because it helped meet a goal of expanding its market to developing countries. The partnership also enabled Swiss Re to further its commitment to addressing climate change.

The organizations started with a pilot project in one Ethiopian village. They started slowly to allow themselves time to develop confidence in one another and identify the best approach to collaboration. In 2010, a conversation among organizational leaders brought up a possible connection between current efforts and food security, an issue that Swiss Re was also passionate about. They jumped on this opportunity for expansion, and within five years, Swiss Re and Oxfam were working together on projects in Ethiopia and three West African countries.[16]

When considering a partnership with NGOs, think about what your company brings to the table. For example, you may have tech expertise, an abundance of corporate volunteers, essential funding resources, or leverage with key government actors.[17] In response, the NGO may provide you with advanced knowledge about execution challenges, especially in geographic areas that are unfamiliar. They may additionally offer potential talent from communities outside of your company's reach and valuable relationships with local actors and communities. These relationships can also assist you in establishing your company's credibility and social impact reputation.

A 2012 article by Jonathan Doh for the Network for Business Sustainability provides additional tips for success when partnering with NGOs.[18] He suggests that each entity first embrace their differences and recognize their value. Remember that it is the differences that make collaboration worthwhile. Think carefully about potential NGO partners and what they bring to the table. Consider its culture and mission. Does it complement your company's culture? Just as a good culture contributes to employee-employer relations and productivity, the same holds true for alignment between corporate and NGO partnerships.

The article also suggests that companies assign a specific point person and give that person decision-making authority in relation to the partnership.[19] This shows NGO leaders that you take the relationship seriously and also helps the initiative move along efficiently.

Last, recognize that the partnership will change and evolve over time. Hope that you are entering the relationship for the long run. As with any business relationship, there will be bumps in the road. Interests may change or circumstances outside of the partnership may force changes to occur. Just expect that obstacles will present themselves and be ready to address them, even if it means that the partnership has run its course or turns out not to be a successful match.

The protests inspired by the killing of George Floyd motivated a lot of companies to make large philanthropic contributions. For example, Netflix pledged to shift $100 million to Black-owned banks.[20] Although these monetary donations are admirable, companies should also think about how they can partner with not-for-profits and NGOs for the purpose of making a lasting impact and meeting long-term social impact goals. Change shouldn't be an either-or proposition. Rather business leaders must leverage every tool they have—financing, volunteering—to make as much positive change in as many areas as possible.

Interconnection of Internal Inclusion and External Social Impact

It's important not to make the mistake of thinking you must abandon inclusion and equity issues within your firm to focus on social impact outside it. Rather, you should view inclusion and social impact as interconnected and commit appropriate resources to both.

External pressures from stakeholders, internal risk-mitigation requirements, and the need for organizational and governmental compliance have triggered many businesses to support innovative efforts promoting human rights, addressing environmental challenges, and improving communities.[21]

A recent example of this was 2020's economic downturn. According to the IMF World Economic Outlook, the pandemic had an even greater negative impact in the first half of 2020 than anticipated. In addition, they project the economic recovery to occur at a slower rate than previously forecast. Global growth for 2021 was projected at 5.4%, which was expected to result in a 2021 GDP that was 6.5% lower than the January 2020 pre-pandemic projections.[22]

The impact on lower-income households was expected to be especially severe, likely reversing significant advances made in the reduction of global poverty since the 1990s. As reported in a 2020 *Politico* article, "executives say the disproportionate impact of COVID-19 on the less affluent and people of color—coupled with a younger Wall Street workforce that demands more engagement on these issues—has led them to think it's the right time to put more teeth into what they like to call 'ESG' goals, referring to better environmental, social and governance practices."[23]

In an interview with Leena Nair, CHRO at Unilever, we spoke about the role that HR will play within the economically challenging years ahead. "I think HR leaders will have to prioritize physical and mental well-being, health, and infrastructure in a very, very big way. Secondly, they have to think about the economic impact that's coming. Yes, we're going to have job loss, we're going to have people earning less than they'd like, and HR leaders have a big role in thinking systemically about [questions such as] how do I look after livelihoods? How do I look after people? How do I make sure I'm giving young people a chance?"

She said that HR leaders must think holistically. "They can't just think within the boundaries of their company. They have to think much more broadly to try and connect how they can create more opportunities [and] ensure that the people in their jobs or in their companies are rescaling and upskilling fast. The third area which will dial up in a big way is what we call capacity. Capacity is

(continues)

311

The Future

(continued)

all about ensuring that people are rescaling and reshaping all the agile ways of working . . . that they're all learning."

Nair also spoke about culture and "ensuring that people are being purpose led and ensuring that leaders are leading for performance, leading for inclusion, leading for purpose. The whole area of culture leadership that allows for purpose and performance must be stepped up now."

Nair said "Last but not least is sustainability. How do we contribute to environmental and social goals? We want to be a global leader of sustainability. We want to show the world how a sustainable business can be a performing business. . . And we talk about being a beacon for diversity and inclusion. And those are the kinds of things I think most companies should be thinking about in HR. How do you step up the business to think about sustainability? How do you ensure that we become very, very inclusive as companies? HR has a very critical role to play in capacity, capability culture, enhancing the employee experience, ensuring that leaders are being built with purpose and performance."[24]

Intersection of DEI and Sustainability

Within many companies, DEI officers with internal responsibilities have much in common with sustainability officers with external responsibilities.[25] At the fundamental level, both positions focus on reaching out to disenfranchised communities and implementing collaborative solutions to their company's challenges. They both work toward a business culture that continuously furthers equity and social inclusion, while helping business respond to an ever-evolving marketplace.

As companies added environmental initiatives, they sought talent from within the green industry, which is notorious for its lack of diversity. A 2014 study of several hundred environmentally focused government and private organizations found that racial and ethnic minorities make up less than 16% of staff and board members within environmental organizations.[26] Therefore, the pursuit of greater diversity within a large company's sustainability department, or a small company's network of external sustainability industry professionals who serve as valuable advisors, may quickly become an initiative for the DEI and HR departments.

Gender equality is another shared goal. A gender-inclusive environment can broaden a company's leadership perspective, increase employee engagement, and improve market branding.[27] A DEI officer might focus more on the recruitment and leadership aspects while the corporate social responsibility (CSR) professional may focus more on community empowerment.

Many of the skills used in these departments also overlap. Tasks related to stakeholder engagements, management changes, community relations, and reporting commonly take place within DEI and sustainability roles. This explains why the corporate ESG and social impact efforts are sharing resources and working together.

The Global 100, a list compiled by the research firm Corporate Knights, ranks corporations with revenue in excess of $1 billion based on such key metrics of sustainability as carbon footprint and gender diversity.[28] Danish Company Orsted A/S topped the list in 2020. The first electricity company to earn this distinction, the company completely transformed its corebusiness from a coal-intensive to renewable power provider. By divesting from fossil fuels and investing in offshore wind power, the company saw an 83% reduction in its carbon emissions; half of the company's Global 100 sustainability score is dependent on revenue earned from products and services that benefit the environment or society.

313

The Future

Cisco Systems was the highest-ranking American company on the list, coming in at number 4.[29] Cisco's annual sustainability report also includes workplace culture and diversity as part of its concerns.[30] About 62% of the company's executive leadership team is diverse in terms of gender and/or ethnicity.[31] In FY19, Cisco welcomed a record number of female new hires, reaching an overall total of 31%. It also saw a 4.8% increase in women in director and manager roles. As part of its ongoing effort to increase racial diversity, the company increased Black employee representation to 3.8% and Latinx employee representation to 5.6%.[32]

The Japanese company Sekisui Chemical Co. Ltd. ranked twelfth on the list.[33] Along with its environmental accomplishments, its sustainability report includes a 3.6% increase in female hires between 2018 and 2019, as well as the addition of 15 women to management positions.[34]

Role of Business in Protecting the Environment

Increasingly, business leaders are understanding that the changing climate presents both risks *and* opportunities. In response, they are taking various steps, such as reducing their company's carbon footprints or only partnering with suppliers that likewise demonstrate a strong commitment to climate action.

What your company specifically should be doing about climate may depend on what you've done in the past. For example, companies that have participated in deforestation should develop solutions to mitigate the harm caused by that practice. Almost any company can contribute to the defeat of environmental injustice by simply engaging more directly with the communities where they do business. People inside and outside business are demanding change, making constructive engagement all the more necessary.

This demand for change means firms benefit from driving an all-encompassing sustainability agenda. Luke Manning, Refinitiv's head of sustainability, wrote in an April 2020 LinkedIn post that "if we want to truly progress the climate agenda we need to help everyone understand that tackling it is in all our personal and financial self-interests. It's not just about the impact we are having on the environment, but the impact the environment is having on us."[35]

Firms such as Refinitiv are setting science-based carbon emissions reduction targets in furtherance of long-term goals for sustainability. A firm's industry and region may play a role in its specific contributions, but organizations should use all of their intelligence and investment resources to craft measurable outcomes.

Nearly 300 companies have set greenhouse gas emission reduction targets as part of a global science-based targets initiative.[36] More than 100 have set goals to be powered by 100% renewable energy. Companies such as Microsoft are adopting operational carbon neutrality goals, and other business leaders have chosen to purchase carbon offsets from projects such as reduced deforestation to cost-effectively achieve emission goals.

These leaders are increasingly realizing that addressing climate change just makes good business sense. While they are saving money with the energy and operational efficiency standards that target greenhouse gases yield, they are also experiencing the financial benefits of decreased production costs *and* increased sales.

According to Lila Karbassi, chief of programs with the UN Global Compact,

> As more and more companies see the advantages of setting science-based targets, the transition towards a low-carbon economy is becoming a reality. Businesses now working

towards ambitious targets are seeing benefits like increased innovation, cost savings, improved investor confidence and reduced regulatory uncertainty. This is becoming the new "normal" in the business world, proving that a low-carbon economy is not only vital for consumers and the planet, but also for future-proofing growth.[37]

Companies are taking steps such as consolidating office space, which COVID-19 has accelerated, and optimizing the use of energy-efficient equipment to lower emissions.[38] They are also implementing initiatives such as paperless offices and water-filling stations, which decrease the use of disposable water bottles. In addition, increasing numbers of companies are partnering with third-party vendors for the recycling of paper and composting cafeteria food waste.

As a business leader, make an effort to understand how investing in green jobs and climate change action will support your community today, as well as tomorrow. Evaluate how green economy jobs may help employees get skills with greater job security thanks to the increase of green job opportunities. Consider how your company's commitment can positively affect society while also benefitting your organization's bottom line.

Companies experience numerous benefits from incorporating environmentally sustainable initiatives. For one thing, they will better meet customer expectations.[39] Many shoppers feel it is their responsibility to spend their money only on businesses that demonstrate a commitment to environmental policies. These expectations can be especially seen among millennials and younger generations. By meeting these expectations, companies can improve their reputations and their public image in the eyes of customers, investors, and employees. When businesses go green, they benefit the national economy and support the common goal of becoming an energy-independent world.

Innovations such as efficient light bulbs lower utility bills. EnergyStar appliances and technology help businesses limit their energy use and also leaves money in the budget for investment into employee training and development. In addition, investors like to see companies with ESG solutions already in place, which is an additional benefit. There are also tax benefits for businesses that go green, such as tax credits or deductions for companies that invest in renewable energy and green technologies. Here are some of the financial benefits green businesses can expect:

- A 15% reduction in paper consumption and costs

- A 20% reduction in water consumption and costs

- A 30% reduction in energy consumption and costs

Studies show that companies with green initiatives or green products have witnessed an increase in their profits. Walmart and Target provide great examples. After incorporating green initiatives, including recycling, enhancing transportation to reduce gas, and increasing stocks of green products, they each reported significant increases in sales.

Singapore-based CapitaLand Group has experienced considerable cost savings through their sustainability efforts. Tan Seng Chai, group chief people officer and chairman of the company's sustainability steering committee, said, "We have managed to reduce energy and water intensity (per m^2) by 23.4 percent and 24.1 percent respectively for our operational properties and reduced our carbon emission intensity by 29.4 percent, compared to the base year of 2008. This amounted to utilities cost avoidance in excess of $140 million for CapitaLand since 2009."[40]

Current Coursing Through Your Business

Leaders who listen to and understand the perspectives of their employees, customers, and investors recognize the tide has already shifted toward more environmentally aware business practices that include making a positive social impact as a core business principle. Among the most important components of leading a compassionate corporation is listening and learning. Although this does apply to listening to stakeholders' requirements about sustainability, it can be much broader than that. It can also mean understanding not just what business gets done but *how* employees feel about their work, *how* energized are employees about their work. Knowing *how* employees feel about their jobs gives insight into the current that courses through the business.

In my interview with author and speaker Dan Pink, he talked about a "current" that runs through each organization. "Electricity is a current. It's something that courses through something else and gives it energy. Compassion does that too. Compassion. . . [it's like] an electrical current. It keeps something energized, so it flows through human beings. Compassion could flow through organizations and keep that organization energized."[41]

Maintain ongoing conversations with employees at each level of the organization to gauge the type of current that runs through your organization and how that current is evolving. Determine whether the current is compassion, inclusion, or another sort. Remember that this current is the lifeblood of your business operations, so ensure it sets the tone you want for your organization.

Compassionate business, which Mark Cuban described to me as simply "smart business," means taking care of employees, even in the most trying times.

> I just think it's smart business, if you have the financial wherewithal to take care of your employees to support

them, to help them at home wherever they may need help. Because it's not only your employees, but their family issues as well. And so where you can provide support for people who work for you, or maybe even other stakeholders, I think it's good business because it's an investment, truly an investment that will pay off in the long run.[42]

For employers and leaders who have the financial wherewithal to help employees through these vulnerabilities, financial assistance can be of great value. I know what you are thinking: "Well that's easy for Mark Cuban to say!" But assistance does not have to be overly expensive. If your company lacks the money to offer monetary benefits, consider low-cost but meaningful perks. For example, Shipstation, a shipping software company based in Austin, recently began offering its nearly 300 employees DashPass, a paid subscription to the DoorDash food-delivery service that waives delivery fees on takeout orders. The company has also hosted activities for its staff's kids, such as magic shows and Disney character lunches, to keep them entertained while employees are working.[43] This is what is meant by compassion being the driving current of your business.

Ask your staff members for ideas on how your company can be of assistance to employees during difficult times. Consider appointing a person or a committee to vet ideas and feedback from your team.

On-demand pay is another option being offered by an increasing number of companies seeking to help employees manage financial stresses. These resources, offered through a third-party partnership, allow workers to access their earned wages before payday. They offer a much better alternative than predatory payday loans with their high fees and interest rates.[44]

Under circumstances where companies are forced to let workers go, leaders can offer incentives for transitional staff to stay on and help implement changes. Financial perks can encourage employees to remain with the company and assist with the transition. For example, leaders may offer severance packages of six weeks to employees who want to immediately separate when layoffs are announced. However, if they agree to stay on for a month, they could receive an enhanced severance package of 12 weeks.[45]

If you are forced to separate employees, show your appreciation to build professional goodwill. Consider offering outplacement assistance to workers affected by a layoff. Partner with third-party outplacement services to offer assistance with résumé writing, job-search assistance, or career-transition consulting. Letters of recommendation area also appreciated. When you take the time to help employees find their next role, it encourages a positive transition. This type of goodwill exhibits compassion and shows employees that you care about their future and well-being.

True Purpose of Business

As discussed in Chapter 1, Milton Friedman's theory about the purpose of business asserts that a firm's main responsibility is to its shareholders.[46] Mr. Friedman believed that businesspeople who concerned themselves with "providing employment, eliminating discrimination, avoiding pollution" were "puppets" and that shareholders, as the economic engine of the organization, are the only people to which the firm is socially responsible.

But savvy business leaders recognize that employees and investors demand greater business accountability for racial and gender equality, as well as environmental responsibility. Even before the coronavirus outbreak, investors were increasingly looking at companies through the lens of ESG practices. But in the age of COVID-19, corporate decisions about human capital, customers, and society carry even greater weight. As companies face increased scrutiny during the crisis, ESG factors will now be a key layer of diligence in evaluating an investment.

I interviewed Juliette Menga, chair of ESG/Sustainable Investing Committee at Aetos Alternatives Management. She spoke about how investors are viewing ESG factors. "If you own a company, you can vote on any shareholder resolution. But institutional investors tend to be larger and more organized. So if there is an issue that they really care about, not only can they push the company on it, but they can organize other like-minded individuals in their network to focus on those issues."[47]

It's not only established companies that need to consider the interests of investors, start-ups—where investment is so crucial—also need to analyze these dynamics. The World Economic Forum provided a detailed case study on Truepic, a start-up that developed a visual verification tool to counter highly edited and curated online content and fight fraud.[48] Although the company's initial focus was not on social impact, its leadership turned its direction toward empowering citizen journalists in remote hard-to-reach or nonpermissive locations around the world.

Perhaps the most immediate benefit of aligning its business with a broader social impact mission was Truepic's ability to attract and retain top talent. Partnerships with social impact organizations expanded the company's horizons in terms of users and use cases for improved beta-testing. The US State Department, TEDx, and many other organizations have picked up on Truepic's social impact work and featured their leadership at major conferences, which has led to new and innovative partnerships with business, government, and NGOs.

Milton Friedman's view on business overlooks one key component: we are all interconnected. Social issues are corporate issues. Employment issues are corporate issues. Discrimination issues are corporate issues.

Compassion is not hiring a "diverse" candidate simply to check a box on a form. Compassion is not mentoring a woman of color as a favor to the community. Hiring and nurturing the talents of people who can bring background, history, and community perspective, along with business expertise, is simply good business. It's smart business. Compassion is about the well-being that all employees deserve, which creates an environment that promotes innovation, creativity, and results in revenue generation.

Mark Cuban has been a leading voice on the issue of employer generosity. As he pointed out in our interview:

> Capitalism has to be compassionate. And if you're a company that is compassionate and understands that the bottom line is built through being nice and through showing compassion, then you're going to get more people supporting you. If you're a company that has a social conscious that has a social mission, you're going to have consumers that are proud to do business with you. And on the flip side, if you're a company that's done something that people don't respect or don't appreciate . . . or you're ignoring your customer . . . your customers are going to leave. They're not going to want to be associated with you.[49]

I'm not a D&I officer, I'm not an HR officer. I'm a leader and I'm simply aware. I'm aware of how a past full of brutality, castigation, income disparities, sexism, racism, classism, and deliberate sabotage affects people's work trajectories, destroys personal economies, and stalls social progress. I'm aware how intentional and unintentional inequality and lack of compassion affects individuals and communities. I'm also aware that systems structured to benefit only certain groups and exploit others cannot survive.

Confronting issues of sustainability, race, gender, and equality in the workplace is a complex task. And yet in another sense it's actually quite simple: put humans at the center of your business model. The movement toward our new structure where corporations, compassion, and culture intersect has been slowly but steadily progressing over the past decades. But as we enter this century's third decade, the rate of change is accelerating daily. Sustainable businesses understand that they work within an ecosystem—by which I mean both the ecosystem of the natural world as well as the metaphorical ecosystem of customers, partners, shareholders, and communities. I'm both optimistic and exhilarated to work with others in removing the old corporate structures and ushering in the new compassionate corporation.

Chapter 10 Takeaways

- Environmental, social, and governance is a lens through which people can screen criteria for how a company uses natural resources, engages with society, and governs their firm.

- Identify how your firm may make a social impact by looking to the UN's SDGs and also look for areas where your firm may have had a negative impact in the past and use social impact to rectify the situation.

- Find practical ways to support employees in challenging times. Social impact and employee compassion can go hand-in-hand.

- Recognize that social issues, business issues, and diversity, equity and inclusion issues are interconnected.

References

1. https://www.sasb.org/standards-overview/materiality-map/
2. https://marketbusinessnews.com/financial-glossary/esg-definition-meaning/
3. https://www.un.org/sustainabledevelopment/sustainable-development-goals/
4. https://www.un.org/sustainabledevelopment/gender-equality/
5. https://www.un.org/sustainabledevelopment/inequality/
6. https://blogs.microsoft.com/blog/2020/09/21/microsoft-will-replenish-more-water-than-it-consumes-by-2030/
7. https://www.prnewswire.com/news-releases/us-plastics-pact-launches-to-ignite-change-toward-circular-economy-for-plastic-301117295.html
8. https://www.prnewswire.com/news-releases/role-of-citizen-consumer-to-tackle-social-issues-rises-as-expectation-of-government-to-lead-declines-106678903.html
9. Interview with the author. Seth Godin, Power customers and large groups of people inside or outside an organization have when they come together to change how businesses operate, August 14, 2020.
10. https://www.sagepeople.com/about-us/news-hub/benefits-volunteer-days-employee-engagement/
11. https://www.streetinsider.com/Globe+Newswire/PayScale+Empowers+Businesses+to+Address+Pay+Equity+in+Partnership+with+the+USC+Race+and+Equity+Center/17382017.html
12. Ibid.
13. Ibid.
14. https://www.nbs.net/articles/partnering-with-ngos-the-4-keys-to-success
15. Ibid.
16. Ibid.
17. https://www.forbes.com/sites/skollworldforum/2015/05/28/corporate-ngo-partnerships-why-they-work-and-why-they-dont/#78a3007015d3
18. https://www.nbs.net/articles/partnering-with-ngos-the-4-keys-to-success
19. Ibid.
20. https://www.msn.com/en-us/money/other/netflix-to-shift-100-million-in-cash-into-black-owned-banks/ar-BB169hVX
21. https://www.greenbiz.com/article/connection-between-diversity-inclusion-and-corporate-responsibility
22. https://www.imf.org/en/Publications/WEO
23. https://www.politico.com/newsletters/the-long-game/2020/05/05/pandemic-companies-rethink-saving-world-489074
24. Interview with author. Leena Nair. CHRO at Unilever, September 2, 2020.
25. https://www.greenbiz.com/article/connection-between-diversity-inclusion-and-corporate-responsibility

26. https://www.greenbiz.com/article/why-diversity-sustainability-matters-and-what-you-can-do?utm_source=linkedin&utm_medium=linkedin%20news letter&utm_campaign=05-24-2018

27. https://www.greenbiz.com/article/connection-between-diversity-inclusion-and-corporate-responsibility

28. https://www.forbes.com/sites/samanthatodd/2020/01/21/who-are-the-100-most-sustainable-companies-of-2020/#3bb4755114a4

29. Ibid.

30. https://www.cisco.com/c/en/us/about/csr/impact/csr-priorities.html#~stickynav=1

31. https://www.cisco.com/c/dam/m/en_us/about/csr/csr-report/2019/_pdf/csr-report-details-2019.pdf

32. https://www.cisco.com/c/dam/m/en_us/about/csr/csr-report/2019/_pdf/csr-report-details-2019.pdf

33. https://apicatalog.mziq.com/filemanager/v2/d/5760dff3-15e1-4962-9e81-322a0b3d0bbd/4f4e2cae-563c-fa5f-7fbe-dec9043ea662?origin=2#page=45

34. https://www.sekisuichemical.com/ir/sekisui_overview/sustainability/index.html

35. https://www.linkedin.com/pulse/its-time-stretch-refinitivs-green-goals-further-luke-manning/

36. https://www.c2es.org/content/business-strategies-to-address-climate-change/

37. https://sciencebasedtargets.org/2017/09/18/more-than-300-to-set-science-based-targets/

38. https://www.themuse.com/advice/companies-making-the-planet-better-2020

39. https://thrivehive.com/benefits-of-going-green-for-business-owners/

40. https://www.businesstimes.com.sg/government-economy/green-practices-gaining-ground-with-companies-in-singapore

41. Interview with the author. Daniel Pink, Electricity is a current, August 18, 2020.

42. Interview with the author. August 24, 2020.

43. https://www.inc.com/anna-meyer/how-small-businesses-support-working-parents-covid.html

44. Ibid.

45. https://www.insperity.com/blog/laying-off-employees/

46. https://www.nytimes.com/1970/09/13/archives/a-friedman-doctrine-the-social-responsibility-of-business-is-to.html

47. Interview with author. Juliette Menga, Chair of ESG/Sustainable Investing Committee at Aetos Alternatives Management, September 16, 2020.

48. https://www.weforum.org/agenda/2019/09/how-one-start-up-made-social-impact-a-business-priority-and-flourished/

49. Interview with author. Mark Cuban, Radical Talent Services Inc, August 24, 2020.

Index

Page numbers followed by *t* refer to tables

AAA (African American Alliance), 255–256
Accenture, 146, 197
Accountability, 128, 257
Accounting for Slavery (Rosenthal), 38, 39
Adidas, 3, 257
Aetna, Inc., 156
Aetos Alternatives Management, 321
Affirmative Action, 132, 152
African American Alliance (AAA), 255–256
African Americans, *see* Black Americans
A.G. Gaston Motel, 45
Agriculture industry:
    Black American working experience in, 39–41
    inclusion in, 152–155
    womens' role in, during the industrial period, 64–65
AI (artificial intelligence), 144–145, 242
AIA, 5–6
AI for Earth program, 304
Åkerström, Carina, 182
Albright, Madeleine, 285
Allen, Terina, 170

All-hands meetings, 215
Ally Financial, 104–105
Allyship, 194–195
Altria, 110
Alumni networks, 230
AMA (American Medical Association), 94
Aman v. Cort Furniture Rental Corp., 223
Amazon, 24, 87–88, 90–92
American Association of University Women, 169, 193
American Medical Association (AMA), 94
American Psychological Association, 98, 118
Angelou, Maya, 229
Anthony, Corey, 270
Anxiety, 103, 114
AppsFlyer, 215
Arbery, Ahmaud, 127–128, 139
Arm, 281
Armstrong, Zion, 257
Artificial intelligence (AI), 144–145, 242
Ash v. Tyson Foods, Inc., 223
Asian Americans, 49, 139. *See also* People of color

Askinosie, Shawn, 158
Askinosie Chocolate, 157–158
The Atlantic, 53
AT&T, 225, 240, 270
Aunt Jemima, 141
Australia, 131, 272
Autocratic leaders, 208–209
Avon, 72, 193
Away, 196

Babcock, Linda, 168–169
Baby boomers, 111, 273, 280
Bailey, Susan R., 94
BAME (Black, Asian, Minority
    Ethnic), 238–239
Bandorf, Stefan, 215
Banking on Freedom
    (Garrett-Scott), 67
Bankruptcies, during COVID-19
    pandemic, 101–102
Barrett, William, 41–42
BBC China, 193
Bed Bath & Beyond, 174
Bedford, CJ, 184
Behaviors:
    threatening, recognizing and
        addressing, 10
    unethical (*see* Unethical
        behavior)
BELFOR Property Restoration, 211
Benchmarks, 184, 213
Bethea, Aiko, 241
Bias:
    and biased language, 195
    gender, 176
    hiring, 144–147
    implicit, 138
    unconscious (*see* Unconscious
        bias)
Biased language, 195
"Birth of a New Nation" (King),
    214

Black, Asian, Minority Ethnic
    (BAME), 238–239
Black Americans:
    ERGs supporting recruitment of,
        241–242
    violence against, 127, 136
    women (*see* Black women)
    working experience of (*see* Black
        American working
        experience)
Black American working
    experience, 31–58
    in agriculture, 39–41
    colorism in, 48–50
    discrimination in, 77–78, 129–132
    and distrust of employers, 36–38,
        57
    and entrepreneurship, 43–47
    history of, 34–36
    in leadership today, 47–48
    unions and, 38–39
    violence and terror in, 41–43
    and workplace racism rooted in
        slavery, 50–57
Blackbirds ERG, 289
Black Codes, 35, 49
Black hairstyles, 81
#BlackLivesMatter movement, 25,
    196
Blackout Tuesday, 139–140
Black women:
    in 20th century workplace, 68
    devaluation of, 65–66
    and #MeToo movement, 191–192
    pay gap of, 173
    plight of, in 19th-century
        workplace, 66
    and post WWII workplace, 71–72
    underrepresentation of, in
        C-suite, 9
Bloom, Nicholas, 109
Blue collar workers, 87–88, 91

328

Index

Board Diversity Census of Women and Minorities on Fortune 500 Boards (2018), 47, 48*t*
Board members, diversifying, 175, 184
Boeing, 186
Boston Consulting Group, 205
Bower, Julie, 79
Brain activity, compassion affecting, 7
Branson, Richard, 206
Brednich, Laurie, 105
Bristol, Douglas, 44, 47
Brookings Institute, 76
Brooks Brothers, 101
Brotherhood of Locomotive Firemen and Enginemen, 38–39
Brown, Danielle, 147
Brown Brothers Harriman, 156
Brown-Philpot, Stacy, 177–178
Brown University, 50
Burke, Tarana, 191
Burnout:
  emotional, 94
  mental, 94
  parental, 98–99
Burns, Ursula, 174, 243–244
Business-owner peer groups, 258
Business Week, 74
Businesswomen, housewives transforming to, 72–75
Business world, current climate of, 21–22

Campbell's Company, 181
Campos, Ariel, 62
CapitaLand Group, 317
Capitalism:
  compassion with, 322
  and profit focus, 14
  racial, 51–52

Carbon footprints, 314
Career-transition companies, 230, 320
Carli, Linda L., 76–77, 170
Carnegie, Andrew, 18–21, 23
Carnegie Steel Company, 20
Carson, Ben, 52
Catalyst, 177, 179–180
Catmull, Ed, 288
CDO (chief diversity officers), 134
Center for Economic and Policy Research (CEPR), 91
Center for Talent Innovation, 254
Centers for Disease Control and Prevention (CDC), 91, 107–108
Centre for Social Investigation (at Nuffield College), 129
CEPR (Center for Economic and Policy Research), 91
Charity, *see* Philanthropy
Chatelain, Marcia, 36, 51
Chevron, 78
Chief diversity officers (CDO), 134
Chief Executive.net, 218
Child care, 166–167, 273–274
Childers, Carolyn, 189
Child-free employees, 277–281
Churches, Kimberly, 193
Cisco's Webex, 110
Cisco Systems, 110, 197, 237, 314
Citigroup, 79
Civil Rights Act (1964), 132
Client surveys, 305
CNBC, 243, 253
CNN, 194
Coates, Ta-Nehisi, 53
The Coca-Cola Company, 148–149, 208
Code words, 222
College & Research Libraries News, 220
Colonial Life, 106

Colorism, 48–50
The Color of Success (Wu), 49
Columbia Business School, 260
Communication. *See also* Language
  and addressing
    microaggressions, 139
  digital, during COVID-19
    pandemic, 108
  with managers, 252–253
  microinvalidation, 221
Communityship, creating, 287–290
Compass, 214
Compassion:
  business impacts from culture of,
    15–16
  decision making with, 16–18
  external philanthropy vs.
    internal, 14–15
  importance of, 7–10
  maintaining, 318–319
  and putting people first, 4–7
  true meaning of, 322
Compassionate corporate culture,
    203–231
  cultivating equitable workplace
    culture, 214–216
  employee resource groups
    contributing to, 216–218
  handling separations in,
    229–230
  internal language for, 219–224
  introspective work for, 205–207
  investing in employees in,
    224–226
  leadership styles for, 207–210
  maintaining focus on, 211–213
  measuring employee
    performance in, 226–229
  picking your team for, 210–211
  role of environmental, social,
    and governance on, 300–302
  sustainable management, 204

transparency and employee
    leadership for, 218–219
  women CEOs building, 180–183
Compassionate leaders:
  benefits of, 195–197
  decision making by, 17–18
  impact of, 7–9
  underrepresented and
    underestimated leaders as,
    24–25
Conscious Capitalism (Mackey), 24
Consumption, and unemployment,
    102
Cooper, Amy, 194–195
Cooper, Christian, 194–195
Cornell University, 186–187
Corning, Inc., 270
Corning Professional Women's
    Forum, 270
Corporate culture:
  colorism in, 48–50
  compassionate (*see*
    Compassionate corporate
    culture)
  cultivating equitable, 214–216
  gender inequity in, 267–269
  inclusion in, 133–136, 138–139
  of the past, 9, 21
  societal norms affecting, 63
  in tough economic times, 17
  workplace racism in, 50–57, 129,
    136–137
Corporate language, 14
Corporate policies, insensitive,
    98–101
Corporate Responsibility Magazine,
    181
Council on Equal Opportunity, 147
COVID-19 pandemic:
  effects of, 320–321
  and environmental protections,
    316

healthcare access during, 6
impact of, 87
increase in protests during, 5
post, workplace (*see* Post
COVID-19 workplace)
and supporting employees,
225–226
and Uber, 21
Cream of Wheat, 141
Create a Respectful and Open
World for Natural Hair Act
(CROWN Act), 81
Creativity, diversity and, 260
Crenshaw, Kimberlé, 172
The Cru, 189
Cruz, Victor, 135
C-suite, 136–137, 137*t*, 171–174. *See
also* Leadership
Cuban, Mark, 209–211, 318–319,
322
Customer relationships, compassion
governing, 7
Customer surveys, 305

Dalits caste, 152
Dallas Mavericks, 209
Dalton, Shamika, 220
David's Tea, 101
Dean & Deluca, 101
Decision making, compassionate,
16–18
Deehan, Bill, 106
DEI (Disability Equality Index), 181
DEI (diversity, equity, and inclusion)
programs, 133–135, 312–314
Deloitte Australia, 182–183
Deloitte Touche Tohmatsu Ltd., 186,
228, 280
Delta Airlines, 150
Democratic leaders, 208
Demographics, of old corporate
culture, 9

Denmark, 181
Denning, Steve, 11
Department of Job and Family
Services (of Ohio), 100
Detroit Police Department, 140
Diamond Offshore, 101
Digital communication, during
COVID-19 pandemic, 108
Dillon, Mary, 181
Direct sales model, 72–73
Disability Equality Index (DEI), 181
Discrimination:
gender, 77–79
racial, among women's corporate
leadership, 77–79
reverse, 184
against women of color in
workplace, 172–173
Discriminatory language, 223
Distrust of employers, 36–38, 57
Diversity:
and creativity, 260
defined, 3
lack of, in C-suite, 136–137, 137*t*
microaggressions and, 138
retaining, in talent (*see* Retaining
diverse talent)
supplier (*see* Supplier diversity)
women of color included in
initiatives for, 175–180
Diversity, equity, and inclusion
(DEI) programs, 133–135,
312–314
Diversity and Inclusion Index,
291–292
Diversity Best Practices, 286
Diversity hire, as term, 250
Diversity Inc., 217
Dixon, Bea, 149
Dobbin, Frank, 150
Dog whistling, 222–223
Doh, Jonathan, 309

Domestic workers, 64, 152–155
Domestic Workers Bill of Rights,
154–155
Donovan, Katie, 169
DoorDash, 97
Douglass, Frederick, 37
DSM North America, 254–255
DuBois, W.E.B., 34
Dufu, Tiffany, 189
Dun and Bradstreet, 246
Dunbar, Paul Lawrence, 55
Dunlap, Al, 12

Eagly, Alice, 76–77, 170–171
EaseCentral, 105–106
Economic exploitation, of women
of color
in 19th century workplace, 66
Edelman, 304
Educational attainment, 168
EEOC (Equal Employment
Opportunity Commission), 75,
132
Ellevest, 247
Elloree Talent Strategies, 176
EMedia, 242
Emotional burnout, 94
Emotional tax, defined, 180
Empathy:
and employee mental health, 104
measuring, 16
and women's corporate
leadership, 81–83
Employee(s):
benefits of happy, 15–16
child-free, 277–281
communication and
collaboration with, 108–113
compassionate separations with,
229–230, 319–320
developing relationships with,
214–215

discrimination of, and inclusion,
129–132
feeling of value in, 16
financial fears of business leaders
and, 101–103
gig workers classified as, 97
importance of valuing, 118
investing in, for compassionate
corporate culture, 224–226
measuring performance of,
226–229
outstanding treatment of, 22–24
prioritizing mental health of,
103–108
retaining diverse, 252–259
safety concerns of, in post
COVID-19 workplace, 89–98
shareholder-first practices
eroding trust of, 13
transparency with, 218–219
trust vs. micromanagement with,
113–116
wellbeing of, 22–24, 116
Employee referral programs,
151–152
Employee resource groups (ERGs):
as culture creators and
advocates, 216–218
female-centered, 269–271,
286–287
as recruitment channels, 240–242
role of, in retaining diverse
talent, 255–256
and social responsibility, 306
ENAR (European Network Against
Racism), 129
EnergyStar, 317
Entrepreneur magazine, 215, 254
Entrepreneurship, 43–47, 281
Environmental, social, and
governance (ESG), 300–302
Environmental protections, 314–317

Equal Employment Opportunity
    Commission (EEOC), 75, 132
Equality:
    flexibility and gender, 82–83
    role of, in compassionate
        culture, 2
    workplace, defined, 4
Equality Act (2010), 129
Equal Pay movement, 193
Equal Pay negotiations, 169
Equity:
    defined, 4
    gender (*see* Gender equity)
ERGs, *see* Employee resource
    groups
Ernst & Young, 209, 217
ESG (environmental, social, and
    governance), 300–302
Eskimo Pie, 141
Estée Lauder, 257
Estonia, 271
Europe, 129, 183
European Network Against Racism
    (ENAR), 129
European Union (EU), 128
European women, 65
European Women on Boards, 172
Executive Order 11246, 147–148
Executive team. *See also* C-suite;
    Leadership
    commitment to inclusion by,
        247–251
    inclusion by race in, 80*t*
    selecting your, 210–211
Exploitation, economic, 66
External organizations, partnering
    with, 306–310
External philanthropy, 14–15
External social impact, 310–312
Exxon Mobil, 145

Facebook, 2, 151–152
Fair Labor Standards Act (1938), 153

Fairness for Farm Workers Act, 153,
    155
Fair Work Ombudsmand (FWO),
    131–132
Family-friendly policies, 271
Family leave benefits, 181,
    271–272
Family Medical Leave Act (FMLA),
    271
FedEx, 92
Feedback, 227
Feimster, Crystal, 192
Fiat Chrysler, 99
Financial Review, 6
Finland, 181
Flexibility:
    for employees during COVID-19
        pandemic, 104
    and gender equality, 82–83
    for parents, 275
    in supporting employees,
        225–226
Floyd, George, 127–128, 139, 150,
    249, 310
FMLA (Family Medical Leave Act),
    271
Fonda, Jane, 192
Forbes, 170, 176, 177, 236
Ford Motor Company, 71, 99
Foster Farms, 93
FounderForward, 206
401(k) plans, 13
Franklin Templeton, 194
Freakanomics, 12
Freebairn-Smith, Laura, 285
Freedman's Savings and Trust
    Company, 36–38
Frick, Henry Clay, 20–21, 23
Friedman, Milton, 10–12, 299,
    320–321
Frontline workers, 87–88
FTSE All World index, 117

Furloughs, 230
FWO (Fair Work Ombudsmand), 131–132

Gallup, 16
Gap Clothing Company, 157
Garrett-Scott, Shennette, 66, 67
Gartner, 249
Gases, greenhouse, 315
Gaston, A.G., 45–46
Gaudiano, Paolo, 236–238
GDP (gross domestic product), 102
GE (General Electric), 12, 133
Gelman, Audrey, 195
Gender-based racism, 79
Gender bias, 176
Gender discrimination, 77–79
Gender equity, 165–198, 265–295
  and benefits of compassionate
    leadership, 195–197
  building community of, 287–290
  in child-free employees, 277–281
  and DEI programs, 313
  as glass ceiling vs. labyrinth,
    169–172
  identifying and addressing,
    266–272
  intersectionality of race and
    gender in, 172–175
  measuring future progress of,
    291–294
  mentorships and sponsorships
    for, 185–189
  and #MeToo and #TimesUp
    movements, 189–194
  and neglecting allyship, 194–195
  and pay gap, 166–169
  pros and cons of quotas, 183–185
  supporting women leadership
    and advancement for, 281–287
  and transitioning back to
    workplace, 272–277

and women CEOs building
  compassionate cultures,
  180–183
women of color included in
  diversity initiatives for,
  175–180
Gender inequity:
  culture of, 267–269
  and family leave benefits,
    271–272
  and female-centered ERGs,
    269–271
  identifying and addressing,
    266–272
General Electric (GE), 12, 133
General Motors (GM), 99, 284
Generation X, 273, 280
Generation Z, 106, 111, 280
George Mason University, 45
Georgia Railroad, 38–39
Georgia Tech, 225
Ghebreyesus, Tedros Adhanom, 93
Gig workers, 88, 96–98
Gilbert, James, 40
Ginger, 103
*Gladiator's Guide to Corporate
  Health & Wealth* (Sahoury),
  108
Glass ceiling metaphor, 76, 169–172
Glassdoor, 291
GlaxoSmithKline (GSK), 255–256
Global 100, 313
Global corporate environments,
  colorism in, 48–50
Global markets, during COVID-19
  pandemic, 117
GM, *see* General Motors
GM WOMEN, 284
Goals:
  setting and maintaining, 211–213
  supplier diversity, 246–247
Godin, Seth, 305–306

Goldman Sachs, 174, 192, 273, 287
Goodyear Tire & Rubber Co., 75
"The Gospel of Wealth" (Carnegie),
    19
Gossip, 282
Gracie, Carrie, 193–194
Graham, Katharine, 171
Grameen America, 193
Grant Thornton UK LLP, 184
Great Depression, 40
Greater Good Science Center (of
    UC Berkeley), 15
Great Recession, 6
Green businesses, 316–317
Greenhouse gases, 315
Gross domestic product (GDP), 102
GSK (GlaxoSmithKline), 255–256
The Guardian, 144
Gucci, 142, 260
Guskiewicz, Kevin, 96

Hairstyles, black, 81
Happy employees, benefits of,
    15–16
Harassment:
    sexual, 78
    of women of color in 19th
        century workplace, 66
Harlem's Fashion Row (HFR), 157
Harper, Shaun, 307–308
Harris, Kamala D., 62, 154
Harvard Business Review, 76, 142,
    241, 247, 268, 287–288
Harvard Business Review Analytic
    Services, 111
Harvard Business School, 144, 267
Harvard Law Review, 170
Harvard Law School, 47
Harvard University, 118, 150
Headspace, 117
Health benefits:
    access to, during COVID-19
        pandemic, 5

auditing, 214
corporations reducing, 13
for gig workers, 97
mental health, during COVID-19
    pandemic, 104–107
Health care workers, 93–94
Heath, Shannon, 224–225
Henderson, Rebecca, 118
Herndon, Alonzo, 47
Herschend Family Entertainment,
    206
Hewlett, Sylvia Ann, 191, 254
HFR (Harlem's Fashion Row), 157
Hilger, Nathaniel, 50
Hill, Napoleon, 19
Hiring:
    diverse panels for, 146–147, 237
    gender biases in, 176–177
    inclusive process for, 236–239
    quantifiable goals for, 150–152
    valuable recruitment channels for
        inclusive, 240–244
Hiring bias, 144–147
H&M, 260
Homestead Steel Works, 20
Homestead Strike, 18–21
Honey Pot, 149
Hook, Cindy, 182
Hospitality industry, 102–103
HP Inc., 249
HR Company Store, 105

IBM, 209
Iceland, 271
IKEA, 145
IMF World Economic Outlook, 310
Implicit bias, 138
Inappropriate language, 220, 282
Inclusion, 127–160, 235–261
    benefits of, 259–261
    in corporate culture, 133–136,
        138–139

Inclusion (*continued*)
   and corporate DNA of slavery, 155–159
   corporate role in, 139–141
   defined, 3–4
   and employee discrimination, 129–132
   executive team commitment to, 247–251
   and external social impact, 310–312
   and fairness in agricultural and domestic workers, 152–155
   and hiring bias, 144–147
   in hiring process, 236–237
   investors affected by, 142–144
   and lack of diversity in C-suite, 136–137
   quantifiable hiring goals for, 150–152
   quantifying true supplier diversity for, 147–149
   by race in executive positions, 80*t*
   regulatory enforcement and legal consequences, 132–133
   retaining diverse talent for, 252–259
   role of, in compassionate culture, 2
   and supply chain diversity, 244–247
   in talent search, 238–239
   valuable recruitment channels for, 240–244
Inclusion Nation, 238
Inclusive language, 289–290
India, 152
Indigenous Australians, 131–132
Inequity, gender, *see* Gender inequity

Insensitive corporate policies, post COVID-19, 98–101
Inspiring Women program, 182
Instacart, 92, 97
Intel, 146–147, 151, 273
Internal language, for compassionate corporate culture, 219–224
International Worker's Day, 92
Intersectionality, 79–81, 172–175, 312–314
"In This Together" campaign, 148
Introspective work, for compassionate corporate culture, 205–207, 302
Investors, 142–144, 300
Ishrak, Omar, 248

Jacobs, Don, 205
James, LeBron, 135
James, Natalie, 131
Jayapal, Pramila, 154
J-Crew, 101
Jim Crow laws, 49
Job loss, during COVID-19 pandemic, 91. *See also* Unemployment, during COVID-19 pandemic
Jobs, Steve, 208
John Jay College of Criminal Justice, 54
Johnson, Gerald, 99
Johnson, Kevin, 23
Johnson, Lyndon, 147
Johnson & Johnson, 141
Journal of American Medical Association, 94
Journal of Applied Psychology, 290
JPMorgan Chase Bank, N.A., 274
Jung, Andrea, 193

Kaepernick, Colin, 135
Kaiser Permanente, 248

Kaniel, Oren, 215
Kaplan, Lindsay, 189
Karbassi, Lila, 315–316
Kennedy, John F., 147
Kent, Muhtar, 208
Khan, Shenaz, 272
Kimbro, Dennis, 19
King, Martin Luther, Jr., 45, 214
Kory, Steph, 196
KPMG, 274
Kraft Foods, 240–241
Krawcheck, Sallie, 247

Labyrinth metaphor, 77, 169–172
Language. *See also* Communication
    biased, 195
    corporate, 14
    discriminatory, 223
    inappropriate, 220, 282
    inclusive, 289–290
    internal, for compassionate
        corporate culture, 219–224
Latinx population. *See also* People
    of color
    in agriculture industry, 153
    in C-suite positions, 137
    women in (*see* Latinx women)
Latinx women. *See also* Women of
    color
    pay gap of, 173
    plight of, in 19th-century
        workplace, 66
Lawsuits, racial bias, 132–133
Layoffs, effects of, 13
Leadership:
    autocratic, 208–209
    communication with, 252–253
    compassionate (*see*
        Compassionate leaders)
    democratic, 208
    financial fears of, in post
        COVID-19 workplace, 101–103

goals set by, 211–213
    importance of representation in,
        56
    introspective work for, 205–207,
        302
    networking with, 258–259
    people of color in, today, 47–48
    providing employee feedback,
        228–229
    role of, in inclusion, 139–141
    role of, in transitioning
        employees back to work,
        274–276
    servant, 207
    styles of, 207–210
    transformational, 82, 208
    women's corporate (*see* Women's
        corporate leadership)
LeanIn.org, 79, 178
Leave:
    for child-free workers, 278–279
    for entrepreneurs, 281
    long-term, 279–281
    maternity, 167–168
    paternity, 181
    and PTO policies, 279
    sick, 90, 98
Leave of Absence for
        Entrepreneurship Program,
        281
Ledbetter, Lilly, 75
Ledesma, Xochitl, 177
Leduc, Bob, 217–218
Legality:
    of discrimination vs.
        microaggressions, 10
    for lack of inclusion, 132–133
Levi Strauss, 249
Lilly Ledbetter Fair Pay Act (2009),
        75–76
Linklaters LLP, 285
Logan, Trevon, 118

337

LogMeIn Inc., 110
London, 130–131
Long-term leave, 279–281
L'Oréal, 304
Lower-income households, 311
Lucas, George, 211
Lyft, 97

Maatz, Lisa, 169
Mackey, John, 24
Malaysia, 152
Male Champions of Change (MCC), 192
Male employees, including, 286–287
Manby, Joel, 206
Manning, Luke, 315
Manpower Group, 145
Marcario, Rose, 274
Mars, 145
Maternity leave, 167–168. *See also* Family leave benefits
MCC (Male Champions of Change), 192
McCarthy, Matthew, 135
McConnell, David, 72
McDermott International, 101–102
McDonald's, 2, 78, 132–133, 145, 146, 280
McDowell, Calvin, 42
McGraw-Hill, 273
McKinsey & Company, 56, 79, 142, 197, 211
McMillon, Doug, 258–259
Meatpacking industry, 92–93
Medical Media, 212
Medtronic, 248–249
Menga, Juliette, 144, 321
Mental burnout, 94
Mental health, of employees, 103–108
Mentorships:
    for gender equity, 185–189
    peer, 185–186

to retain diverse talent, 253–255
    reverse, 187, 256
Merced County Health Department, 93
Mergers, effects of, 13
Merrick, John, 44–45, 47
#MeToo movement, 25, 189–194
Microaggressions:
    addressing, 179
    against Black women, 81
    defined, 54, 220
    effects of, 54–55
    increase in, 10
    and workplace diversity, 138
Microassaults, 220–221
Microinequities, 81
Microinsults, 221
Microinvalidation communications, 221
Micromanagement, 112–115
Microsoft, 304
Microsoft Teams, 108, 110
Middle management, and retaining diverse talent, 257–258
Milano, Alyssa, 191
Millennials, 106, 111, 273, 280
Minority, defined, 238
Mintzberg, Henry, 287
Model minority myth, 49
Moody's Corporation, 276
Morrison, Denise, 181
Moss, Thomas, 42
Motherhood, 166–167, 268
Mozilla, 249
Mu, Damien, 6
Mulgrew, Michael, 95
Murray, Anna, 242
Murray, David, 193
Musa, Nazar, 212
Musk, Elon, 99–100

N7 fund, 136
Nadal, Kevin, 54

Nair, Leena, 311–312
National Alliance of Healthcare
    Purchaser Coalitions, 107
National Black Employees Caucus,
    240
National Center for Health Statistics
    (NCHS), 91
National Labor Relations Act, 40
National Metal Trades Association,
    72
National Minority Supplier
    Development Council
    (NMSDC), 148–149, 246
National Partnership for Women
    and Families, 271
National Urban League, 140
NCHS (National Center for Health
    Statistics), 91
Negotiations, salary, 168–169
Neiman Marcus, 103
Nepotism, 151
Nestle, 140
Netflix, 310
The NETwork, 240
Network for Business Sustainability,
    309
Networking:
    and alumni networks, 230
    leadership, 258–259
    peer, 284
New Deal, 40
New York Life Insurance Company,
    156
New York Times Magazine, 10,
    209–210, 305
New York University, 290
Nike, 135–136
Nineteenth century, working
    women in, 66–67
NMSDC (National Minority Supplier
    Development Council),
    148–149, 246

Nongovernmental organizations
    (NGOs), 304, 307–309
Norman, Jim, 240–241
North Carolina Mutual Insurance
    Company, 43–45
Northrop Grumman, 181–182
North Star, 206, 288
Norway, 271

Obama, Barack, 50, 62
Obama, Michelle, 46
Occupational Safety and Health
    Administration (OSHA), 90, 93
Office for National Statistics on
    COVID-19 Fatalities, 90
Ohio State University, 118
Olsson, Stella, 110
On-demand pay, 319
O'Neil, Cathy, 144–145
Organization for Economic
    Co-operation and
    Development (OECD), 271
Orsted A/S, 313
OSHA (Occupational Safety and
    Health Administration), 90, 93
O'Toole, Matt, 257
Outmatch, 145
Outplacement assistance, 320
Oxfam, 308–309

Pacific Gas and Electric Company
    (PG&E), 105, 174
Pahari, Boe, 192–193
Paid time off (PTO) policies, 279
Pampered Chef, 73
Parental burnout, 98–99
Partnerships, with external
    organizations, 306–310
Patagonia, 273–274
Paternity leave, 181. See also Family
    leave benefits
The Path Forward, 243

Path of Service Program, 280–281
Patterson, Kathie, 105
Pay gap:
    about, 75–77
    gender equity and, 166–169
    and #MeToo and #TimesUp
        movement, 193–194
    in people of color leadership, 47
    by race relative to White men,
        80t
Payscale, Inc., 307–308
Peer groups, business-owner, 258
Peer mentoring, 185–186
Peer networking, 284
People-first focus, 4–7, 118
People of color. *See also* Women of
        color; specific groups
    discrimination against, in
        agriculture industry, 153
    employer distrust in, 36–38
    employment discrimination,
        129–132
    entrepreneurship by, 43–47
    in leadership today, 47–48
People's Grocery, 41–42
PepsiCo Inc, 141
Performance improvement plans
        (PIPs), 226–227
Performance reviews, 226–229
Personal protective gear, 92–93
Pew Research Center, 166
PG&E (Pacific Gas and Electric
        Company), 105, 174
Philadelphia, Jacob, 62
Philanthropy, 14–15, 18, 310
Phillips, Katherine, 260
Pilgrim's Pride, 92
Pink, Dan, 212–213, 318
Pinkerton Detectives, 20
PIPs (performance improvement
        plans), 226–227
Pixar, 288

PLS Learning, 205
Politico, 311
Portugal, 271
Post COVID-19 workplace, 87–120
    about, 87–88
    connecting compassion with
        profitability in, 117–119
    financial fears of business leaders
        and employees in, 101–103
    for gig workers, 96–98
    for health care workers, 93–94
    and insensitive corporate and
        government policies, 98–101
    keeping employees physically
        safe and healthy in, 89–98
    and prioritizing employee mental
        health, 103–108
    redefining employee
        communication and
        collaboration, 108–113
    for teachers and students, 94–96
    trust vs. micromanagement in,
        113–116
Post traumatic stress disorder
        (PTSD), 94
Pour Your Heart into It (Schultz), 23
Prada, 142, 260
Pratt & Whitney, 217
Procurement management, 245. *See
        also* Supplier diversity
Productivity:
    and flexibility, 226
    and gender discrimination, 193
    stress affecting, 103–104
    while working from home,
        109–112
Profitability, 12, 117–119
Profit-driven leaders, 12–14
Progress, measuring, 213, 291–294
Progressive Farmers and Household
        Union, 40–41
Protests, increase in, 4–5

Prudential Financial Inc., 273
Psychology Today, 138
PTO (paid time off) policies, 279
PTSD (posttraumatic stress
    disorder), 94
Public accountability, 257
Purchasing power, stagnation of, 13
Pymetrics, 145–146

QBE Insurance Group Ltd., 193
Quota programs:
    gender, 183–185
    racial, 150–152

Racial bias lawsuits, 132–133
Racial capitalism, 51–52
Racial discrimination, 77–79
Racial sexual violence, 66
Racism:
    gender-based, 79
    workplace, 50–57, 129
Rainford, Valerie Irick, 176
Ralph Lauren, 150
Rape, 66
Reagan, Ronald, 132
Reconstruction era, 35
Recruitment channels, 240–244
Reebok, 257
Reffkin, Robert, 214
Refinitiv, 291–293, 315
Refinitiv Sustainability Perspectives
    Podcast, 302
Regan, Patrick, 193
Regulatory enforcement, for
    inclusion, 132–133
Reid, David, 106
Reid, Maryann, 175–176
RE-IGNITE program, 276
Remote work initiatives, 89, 226. *See
    also* Working from home
Re-onboarding programs, 273,
    276–277

Reparations, 54
Responsibility, social, 15, 302–306
Retail jobs, 102–103
Retaining diverse talent, 252–259
    communication with managers
        for, 252–253
    employee resource groups role
        in, 255–256
    leader networking for, 258–259
    middle management influence
        on, 257–258
    public accountability for, 257
    sponsors and mentors for,
        253–255
Return on investment (ROI), 107,
    274
Reverse discrimination, 184
Reverse mentorships, 187, 256
Richemont, 129–130
Richter, Marty, 225
Rising Tides, 286
Robbins, Chuck, 237
Roberts, Bari-Ellen, 77–78
Rocket Companies Inc., 140
ROI (return on investment), 107,
    274
Role model effect, 62–63
Rosenthal, Caitlin, 38, 39
Rothery, Simon, 192

Sabbaticals, 279–281
Saboteurs, 31–32, 281–283
Safety, during COVID-19 pandemic,
    89–93
Sahoury, Roger, 108
St. Luke Insurance Association,
    67–69
St. Luke Penny Savings Bank, 67–69
Salary negotiations, 168–169
Sandberg, Sheryl, 82
SAS, 224–225
Schooling, virtual, 95

341

Index

Schroders, 79
Schultz, Howard, 23, 207–208
SDGs (Sustainable Development
    Goals), 302–303
Second Great Migration, 71
Segregation, in US agriculture
    industry, 153
Sekisui Chemical Co. Ltd., 314
Separations, 229–230
Servant leaders, 207
Service jobs, during COVID-19
    pandemic, 102–103
Severance packages, 320
Sexual harassment, 78
Sexual violence, racial, 66
Shareholders:
    compassionate engagement with,
    8
    leadership focusing on, 11–14
Shine theory, 285
Shipstation, 319
Shipt, 5, 92
SHRM (Society for Human Resource
    Management), 106, 280
Sick leave, 90, 98
Silverglate, Paul, 280
Silverthorn, Michelle, 238
6888 Central Postal Directory
    Battalion, 70–71
Skin lightening creams, 141
Skype, 110
Slack, 286
Slavery:
    corporate DNA of, 155–159
    history of, 34
    and workplace racism, 50–57
    workplace racism rooted in,
    50–57
SmallBusinessPrices.co.uk, 280
Smith, Suzanne, 45
Smithfield Foods, 92
Snyder, Dan, 141

Social accountability, 128
Social distancing, 89
Social impact, external, 310–312
Social media, 21, 223
Social responsibility, 15, 302–306
"The Social Responsibility of
    Business Is to Increase Its
    Profits" (Friedman), 10–11
Social Security Act, 40
Society for Human Resource
    Management (SHRM), 106, 280
Solid8, 196
Solomon, David, 174
Sotomayor, Sonia, 62
S&P 100, 117
S&P 500, 13
S&P 1200, 117
Splunk, 109
Sponsorships:
    for gender equity, 185–189
    to retain diverse talent, 253–255
    for women leadership
    advancement, 285–286
    for women of color, 179
Stakeholders, commitment to
    inclusion by, 247
Stanford University, 109
Starbucks, 5, 23–24, 107, 135, 207
Stewart, Martha, 209
Stewart, Will, 42
Stoxx 600 index, 172
Street Insider, 307
Stress, 103–104
Strikes, 20–21
Stryker, 197
Students, 94–96
Sunbeam, 12
Supplier diversity:
    achieving, 244–247
    auditing, 214
    quantifying true, 147–149
    through history, 45

342

Index

Surman, Mark, 249
Survey Monkey, 103
Surveys:
    customer, 305
    for employee feedback,
        292–293
Sustainability, and DEI, 312–314
Sustainable Development Goals
    (SDGs), 302–303
Sustainable management, 204
Svenska Handelsbanken AB, 182
Sweden, 271, 281
Swiss Re, 308–309
Systemic racism, 41

Talent search, *see* Hiring
Tan Seng Chai, 317
Target Corporation, 5, 149, 304, 317
Task Rabbit, 177–178
Tax, emotional, 180
Taylor, Breonna, 127, 139
Teachers, 94–96
Team, picking your, 210–211
Technology Community Women's
    Network (TCWN), 270
Technology sector, lack of women
    leadership in, 62
TED Talk, 82
TEDx, 321
Teletherapy, 106
Terror, in Black American working
    experience, 41–43
Tesla, 99–100
Texaco, 77, 133
Think and Grow Rich (Hill), 19
*Think and Grow Rich: A Black
    Choice* (Kimbro), 19
This Way Ahead program, 157
Thomas, Clarence, 132
Thompson, Ken, 156
Threatening behaviors, recognizing
    and addressing, 10

Timberland, 280
TIME magazine, 193
#TimesUp movement, 189–194
TNS Social Research, 131
Tokenism, 184
Torrey, Scott, 307
TransferWise, 117
Transformational leadership,
    82, 208
Transitioning back to work,
    272–277
Transparency, for compassionate
    corporate culture, 218–219
Traveling Vineyard, 73
Truepic, 321
Trump, Donald and administration,
    92–93
Trust:
    lack of employer, in Black
        American working experience,
        36–38, 57
    while working from home,
        113–116
Tulsa Massacre of 1921, 42
Tupper, Earl, 73, 75
Tupperware, 73–74
Tweeps, 289
24-Hour Fitness, 101
2020 Women on Boards, 174
Twitter, 289
Twitter Parents, 289
Twitter Women, 289
Tyson, Bernard J., 248
Tyson Foods, 5, 92

UAW (United Auto Workers), 71–72
Uber, 2, 21, 97
UberEats, 21
UBS (Union Bank of Switzerland),
    78
UC Berkeley, 15, 38, 39
Udacity, Inc., 225

UFCW (United Food and Commercial Workers International), 89, 93
Ulta Beauty, 181
Uncle Ben's, 141
Unconscious bias, 139, 146–147, 175, 239
Underrepresentation, 9, 50, 62
Unemployment, during COVID-19 pandemic, 100–102
Unethical behavior, 5, 43, 57, 220–222
UN Global Compact, 315
UNICEF, 271
Unilever, 146, 311
Union Bank of Switzerland (UBS), 78
Unions, 20, 38–39
United Auto Workers (UAW), 71–72
United Federation of Teachers, 95
United Food and Commercial Workers International (UFCW), 89, 93
United Kingdom, 271
United Nations, 302
United Negro College Fund, 140–141
University of Mississippi, 66
University of North Carolina, 96
University of Oxford, 129
University of Rome, 94
University of Southern Mississippi, 44, 47
University of Tennessee, 245
US Bureau of Labor Statistics, 102
US Census Bureau, 267
US Chamber of Commerce, 103
US Congress, 36
US Constitution, 34
USC Race and Equity Center, 307

US Department of Labor, 71, 100
US Government Accountability Office, 184
US Homestead Act (1862), 153
US Plastics Pact, 304
US State Department, 321
US Supreme Court, 151, 223

Verizon, 6
Villagran, Michele, 220
Violence:
    against Black Americans, 127, 136
    in Black American working experience, 41–43
    racial sexual, in 19th century workplace, 66
Virgin Group, 206
Virtual schooling, 95
Von Hayek, Friedrich, 14

Wachovia Corporation, 156
Wage disparities, see Pay gap
Wagner Electric Corporation, 72
Walker, Madame C. J., 43
Walker, Maggie Lena, 67–70
Wallaert, Matt, 250–251
Wall Street Journal, 171
Walmart, 82, 92, 259, 317
Walton, Debra, 291–293
Ward, Robyn, 206
Warden, Kathy, 181–182
WarnerMedia, 134
The Washington Post, 171
Washington Redskins, 141
Weapons of Math Destruction (O'Neil), 144–145
Weinstein, Harvey, 191–192, 250
Welch, Jack "Neutron," 12
Wellness programs, 108, 117–118
Wells, Ida B., 42

Wells Fargo & Co., 22, 150
Welsh, Hugh, 254–255
WePow app, 145
Westfall, Mark, 148
Westpac Bank, 272
We Wear the Mask (Dunbar), 55
White collar workers, 87, 89
White Men's Leadership Study,
    286
White-run businesses, 41–42
Whiting Petroleum, 101
WHO (World Health Organization),
    107
Whole Foods Market, 24, 90
Williams, Geisha, 174
Williams, Serena, 135
Wilson, Joseph, 240
Winfrey, Oprah, 61
Wing, 195–196
Wise, Brownie, 73–75
W@M (Women at Microsoft),
    217
WOA (Women of AT&T), 270
Women:
    of color (*see* Women of color)
    European, in agriculture sector,
        65
    in leadership (*see* Women's
        corporate leadership)
    mentorships for, 187
Women at Microsoft (W@M),
    217
Women Don't Ask (Babcock),
    168–169
Women of AT&T (WOA), 270
Women of color:
    in corporate America, 178–179
    in corporate leadership, 79–81
    devaluation of, 65–66
    diversity initiatives including,
        175–180

and gender equality, 172–173
gender inclusion for, 292
supporting the advancement of,
    283–284
treatment of, in work
    environments, 80
Women@Pixar, 288
Women @Refinitiv, 269–270
Women's corporate leadership,
    61–84
compassion and empathy to
    improve workplace for,
    81–83
historical context of, 67–75
and the housewife as a
    businesswoman, 72–75
Maggie Lena Walker, 67–70
racial and gender discrimination
    among, 77–79
supporting, and advancement,
    281–287
and valuing the work of women,
    64–67
and wage disparities,
    75–77
women of color in, 79–81
WWII and transformation of
    work culture, 70–72
Women @ Thomson Reuters,
    269–270
Work-family balance, 269, 278
Work from Home IT Impact study
    (2020), 110
Working from home, 87,
    109–112. *See also* Remote
    work initiatives
Working Mother, 147
Working Mothers, 276
"Working-while-Black," 34–35
Workplace equality, defined, 4
Workplace racism, 50–57, 129

World Bank, 11
World Economic Forum and
  Business Roundtable, 3, 62,
  258, 321
World Health Organization (WHO),
  107
World War II (WWII), 70–72
Wu, Ellen, 49

Xerox, 240, 243
XOR, 145

Yale University, 192
Yellen, Janet, 76
Yellen, Sheldon, 211–212

Zoom, 108, 110, 242–243
Zubulake, Laura, 78